REIMAGINING AMERICA'S DREAM

Making It Attainable for All

BERNIE J. MULLIN

THE ASPIRE DIFFERENCE FOUNDATION | DENVER, COLORADO

Published by
The Aspire Difference Foundation | Denver, Colorado

Publisher's Cataloging-in-Publication Data
Mullin, Bernard J.

Reimagining America's dream : making it attainable for all / Bernard J. Mullin. – Denver, CO : The Aspire Difference Foundation, 2024.

p. ; cm.

ISBN13: 978-0-9601241-0-7

1. Mullin, Bernard J. 2. Sports executives--United States--Biography. 3. American Dream. I. Title.

GV697.M855 A3 2024
796.092--dc23

Project coordination by Jenkins Group, Inc. | www.jenkinsgroupinc.com

Interior design by Brooke Camfield

Printed in the United States of America
28 27 26 25 24 • 5 4 3 2 1

Contents

Part 2

Acknowledgments

It is rare for anything of value to be created by one person alone. Equally, anyone who has achieved something in their life will have many people to thank for their contributions. This book and my own life story are no exceptions. I would first like to thank Dr. Paul Scade, the cocreator of this work, for brilliantly taking my own writings as a starting point and turning them into this book. Through our twice-weekly interviews over the course of a year, the many deep discussions that arose from them, and his detailed research work, Paul has completed the mission I set him in fine style.

That mission was to tell the story of a reimagined American dream through my own encounter with this country, first as a visitor more than fifty years ago, and then as an immigrant, resident, and finally, a citizen. To begin with, I assumed that the trajectory of my life in America reflected the shared dream that holds this nation together. But as my career soared, I increasingly became aware of a disconnect between my imagined dream and the reality of the many imbalances in our society, imbalances that seem to me to have intensified dramatically over the last twenty-five years. My evolving social conscience bubbled up into a need to help redress the tensions that appear now to be on the brink of pulling this wonderful country apart. Initially, I contented myself with serving on local community boards and contributing to good causes. But as the systemic problems we face have become increasingly apparent to me, it has become clearer and clearer that more direct and concerted action is required.

One strand of action I have taken has been the creation of the Aspire Difference Foundation, which seeks to make an immediate difference in the lives of young Americans who might otherwise be left behind by our system. This book is a second contribution toward that end (all net proceeds from the sale of the volume will be used to support the foundation). While *Reimagining America's Dream* begins with my own journey through America, it ends with a series of essays encouraging the moderates of this nation to rally together to reclaim it from the forces pulling it toward the extremes. I suggest that by coalescing around a small number of simple, practical, and cost-effective policies that have majority support, we can lay the foundations that are needed to make the American dream accessible to all. The book ends with an ambitious prescription for changing America, in the medium and long term, into a more cohesive and happier society.

My personal story has intersected at many points with those of others who have had an important impact on my life, values, and thinking. Perhaps most decisively, I owe a debt of deep gratitude to my parents. My father, Bernard Francis "Ben" Mullin, taught me the two greatest lessons in life: the importance of unswerving honesty and integrity and the value of hard work. My mother, Mary "May" Mullin, was always at home to greet me when I arrived from school to listen and to teach me how to be a better person in all the little interactions that sum up to the totality of life. Two other relatives helped set me on the path toward my American dream: Great Uncle Pat and Uncle Percy. Who could have known that their inspiration at such a young age would so dramatically change my life?

To my primary-school best friend, Mike Dickinson, and my two best friends from high school, Mike and Joe, thank you for your friendship and support across so many years. My thanks also to Elizabeth Ivans from Eastern Michigan, who sent me the book on *Summer Camp Jobs in America* that led to my first visit. And to Morty Goldman, who took me under his wing at Camp Takajo in Maine and became one of the most influential allies in my young life, I cannot thank you enough for that first incredible summer, for the invitation to return year after year, for the scholarship to attend graduate school in Kansas, and for the emergency loan that enabled me to complete the purchase of my home in Massachusetts. There are three

Mullin kids and six grandkids who are proud Americans today because of your kindness and support. The values of Camp Takajo remain deeply embedded in my heart half a century after we first met, and I hope they are reflected throughout the pages of this book.

To Hank Fortin, one of my first friends in America, an amazing man, a wonderful teacher, and a good friend, thank you for supporting Chris and me in so many ways early on. I will never forget your kindness in lending me money during the hardest of times and being there as godfather to my eldest daughter, Julie.

My gratitude also goes to the individuals and families who welcomed us when we arrived in Kansas, including Ron Schneider, whose encouragement and slides of Kansas University (KU) and Lawrence drove me to apply to the university; Pat and Suzie Lawler, who welcomed us into their home for so many Middle American dinners; and Larry and Joyce Moreland, who became such close friends and taught us how to be Midwesterners; Roger Ebert, my closest buddy on the KU soccer team, and still a good friend today; and Eugene Johannes, who managed to be our landlord in Kansas, an amazing friend, and the source of my fascination with American sports. All of you made us fall in love with America and become determined to build our lives here. I can never repay you for the seeds you sowed and for the love of country you demonstrated to me over and over again.

I must thank Dr. Bob Swinth for his faith in me and his mentoring through the KU Business School PhD program. Bob has one of the purest spirits of any human I know. From the University of Massachusetts, Amherst, one individual stands out above everyone else: Dr. Guy Lewis, my friend, colleague, mentor, and an inspirational force in the discipline of sport business. Guy was the visionary who laid the foundations for the program, and he is the reason why UMass Sport Business is now considered the number-one sport business program in the world.

During my time at the Pittsburgh Pirates, I was blessed to be mentored by a brilliant businessman and strong leader, Malcolm "Mac" Prine. Mac empowered me to reject easy short-term fixes for the challenges we faced at the Pirates and, instead, to take decisions based on the long-term interests of the team. My right hand at the Buccos was VP Marketing Steve Greenburg. Greenie began his career in ticket sales and had more practical knowledge of sport marketing than anyone else I know. He taught me so much and was always loyal and supportive to me. Long underappreciated by many in the industry, Steve got the recognition he deserved when, as president of PNC Park Development, he headed the design and construction of the club's new home, rightfully acknowledged as one of the finest new ballparks in Major League Baseball.

I am so grateful to Steve Ehrhart, who, as CEO of the Colorado Rockies Baseball Club, gave me the opportunity to put together the All-Time Record Attendance Plan and then staff the club and execute our plan to perfection. I was also blessed during my time at the Denver Grizzlies to get to know top Minor League operator David Elmore, who provided me with a fantastic opportunity to head up the team side of a sport business for the first time. Together we hired Head Coach Butch Goring and Assistant Coach Kevin Cheveldayoff, who were an incredible pair to work with as we took the team to a record of 72–20 and 6 in its inaugural season.

At the University of Denver (DU), I had the privilege of working with one of the most amazing individuals I have ever met. Daniel L Ritchie had been a C-suite executive in the investment banking, movie, and communications industries before taking over as chancellor at DU. Dan is not just a brilliant businessman but also a great humanitarian who saw in his work at DU a chance to increase leadership opportunities across all disciplines for members of groups who had often been frozen out. It was a true honor to work with him.

When I moved to New York to work for the National Basketball Association (NBA), I had the opportunity to learn from the mighty (some called him "the almighty") Commissioner David "DJS" Stern. DJS was truly a force of nature: incredibly smart, always working, very well read, and data driven. He was also all-powerful in his field, verbally coarse when he chose to be (which was often), and extremely effective at his job. David did not tolerate fools at all and expected the highest levels of performance at all times. This created an uncompromising work environment that managed to be both terrifying and exhilarating at the same time. Working directly under DJS was not only personally rewarding but helped move my career onto a new level, for which I will always be grateful. In my humble opinion, David was by far the best Major League sports commissioner anywhere in the world, and it will be a long time before anyone supplants him. I would be remiss if I did not thank, here, Dr. Bill Sutton, my brother from another mother. Dr. Bill was my coauthor, along with Dr. Steve Hardy, of the standard textbook *Sport Marketing*, and it was he who connected me with DJS and set me on my way to a job at the NBA.

My time at the Atlanta Spirit group, running the NBA's Atlanta Hawks and the NHL's Atlanta Thrashers, was extremely challenging and unfortunately marred by disagreements among the nine-person ownership group. A clear highlight of this difficult time was working with my EVP/CFO Bill Duffy, who later became my partner at the Aspire Group. Bill is an individual of the highest integrity and an enormously competent executive. We significantly improved the team performance of the Hawks and the Thrashers during my time in Atlanta, but it was in no small part thanks to Bill that we were able to leave the clubs in much better financial shape than we found them.

The first person Duff and I hired at the Aspire Group was Bill Fagan, who came on board to run our operation at Georgia Tech. This was the smartest move we ever made. Bill, who now serves as CEO of Playfly/Aspire, exemplifies the strengths of the very best C-suite executives I have ever known. He is a first-class human being who runs an authentic, very successful, highly profitable, and community-conscious organization. I am proud of how we built Aspire together and of where Duff, Bill, our senior team of Tony, Chad, Val, Boz, and Jack, and I have taken it as an industry-leading company.

I would like to acknowledge my three amazing children—Julie Ann, Lara Jane, and Steven Paul—and my stepson, Chad. They are all good

Americans who make the world a better place for others to live in, through their work and in their family lives, as caring, conscientious individuals. Val and I are proud to have such a wonderful family, now extended to include our six grandchildren, Ian, Niame, Roran, Grace, James, and Sadie, all of whom fill our lives with so many blessings. In this respect, thanking my incredible wife, Val, is one of the easiest and, as every married man knows, smartest things I can do. For over thirty years now, Val has shown me a kind of love I had never experienced before. She has supported me in every career move I have made, rarely ever missing a game, whatever the season. And she has done this first while building her own very successful marketing and PR business and, more recently, while taking on responsibility for all the administration, business, and financial operations at Aspire. Her diligence and attention to detail has been vital for the company's stability and financial success. To say that we are life partners cannot do justice to what Val means to me.

Finally, I would like to thank everyone on the *RAD* production, marketing, sales, and PR crew for their work toward making this book a success. It has been a long and fascinating road, and I appreciate the contributions of every last member of the team.

This book emerges from and reflects my deep appreciation of the country that has given me the opportunity to succeed in a way I could barely have dreamed of when I first arrived on these shores. I am grateful to all the Americans who embraced me, adopted me, and made me one of their own. My most fervent hope now is that I can contribute to passing on this same incredible gift to future generations, including both those born in this land and those who are following the same immigrant path that I took. I hope I will soon look upon a day when we come together again as a united people to create a better America, an America in which all our children can achieve everything that their hard work and talent deserves.

Introduction

More than 40 percent of Americans think that civil war is likely in the next decade.[1] Twenty percent believe violence can be justified in support of political objectives.[2] And as many as 37 percent say they would support their state or region seceding from the United States.[3] To top it all, the majority of Americans are no longer confident that the electoral system reflects the will of the people,[4] and nearly half believe that one party or the other will overturn the legitimate transfer of power in the near future.[5]

America is more divided today than it has been at any time in the last fifty years. The divisions in public life run so deep that they can often seem insurmountable. Language that was once considered beyond the bounds of reasonable discourse is now common. Those on the other side are "traitors," "fascists," or "deplorables." They are "sick," "dangerous," and "deranged." They can be labeled as purveyors of a "mind virus," aiming at "the destruction of our republic," or perhaps simply as "enemies of the state."

What makes this lack of national unity so dangerous is not that it is rooted in radically divergent ideologies and policy positions. After all, the deeply held political differences we see today are nothing new in America. What *has* changed is the way these views are understood and advanced. Disagreements about policy have become battlegrounds on which the forces of good and evil take to the field; legislative decision making is now treated by many as a war for the soul of America. The intensity of disagreement we see reflected back at us from our TV screens, talk shows, and social media has reached a level not seen since the civil rights era. And for an alarming number of activists and commentators on both the left and the right, victory is more important than unity. If winning means pulling the country apart, then that is a price that a significant proportion of Americans are now seemingly willing to pay.

The groundwork for this crisis was laid more than a generation ago, with a series of small legislative and cultural steps that have led us to this breaking point. But the process has accelerated dramatically in the last decade and a half. Every year now, the divisions widen. Every year, more trust in our shared union slips away. Every year, the wounds in our national fabric become harder to heal.

But it doesn't have to be like this. There is a clear path back from the brink, a path away from the growing extremism and dissatisfaction that is endangering our country. And that path is grounded on a shared and attainable vision of what this country can be.

* * *

When I immigrated to America fifty years ago, I was following in the footsteps of generations of wanderers who saw the United States as a beacon of hope for a better life. I did not arrive with any kind of theoretical view of what it was to be an American. All I saw was a land of opportunity, a place where things were possible that I couldn't even dream of in my country of birth.

In the five decades since, I have been fortunate to experience much of what this exceptional country has to offer. I have lived in three time zones and have worked extensively in the fourth. I moved from the midwestern heartland to New England and back again; from Pennsylvania to Colorado; and from the frantic bustle of New York to the refined southern hospitality of Georgia. I have experienced the liberal idealism of the college campus and the hardheaded fiscal conservatism of the American business community. I have been a university professor, an author, a senior executive in one of the most competitive business environments—the sports and entertainment industry—and a consultant to government and businesses across many sectors. I have climbed the greasy career ladder as a corporate executive and have built and managed my own successful businesses. In a very real sense, I have lived out much of what the American dream has to offer, and I will always be grateful to this country for the challenges and opportunities it has given me.

That dream—a vision of being able to build a better life for myself and my family through hard work and enterprise—has sustained me through the toughest times and has inspired me to push further and reach higher than I once thought was possible. I only became aware of what the American dream meant to me in stages, gaining an insight here and there as I immersed myself in my American life. And while I appreciated what that dream offered me as an individual, I came to understand that it was also what connected me to others. The feeling of being one part of the many, of joining a community devoted to life, liberty, and the pursuit of happiness, bound me together with the other Americans I met on my journey. We were united by a shared ideal, held together and marked out from the rest of the world by the dream we had in common.

Yet as I watched my adopted home become increasingly divided against itself, I was forced to confront an uncomfortable truth. While the American dream had worked for me, for many others it was little more than a fantasy. The United States is the wealthiest and most technologically advanced nation on earth, with the best universities, the best hospitals, and the best business start-up environment in the world. But for many Americans, this shining city on a hill might as well be another country. Poor educational opportunities in the most disadvantaged communities mean that large numbers of children are never given the tools to even think of living out the dream themselves, to say nothing about real opportunities to succeed. For many Americans, a serious illness in the family can wipe out years of savings, or even create a financial hole from which the only escape is bankruptcy. Social mobility is becoming increasingly limited, middle-class workers watch as their jobs and aspirations disappear abroad, and many rural and rustbelt communities have become economic ghost towns.

For millions of citizens, the opportunity to earn and then live the American dream is not the birthright it should be. Instead, it is a hostage to fortune, with access determined by accidents of birth and circumstance.

The American dream should be the glue that holds us all together, a unifying vision that connects the many into one and forges a whole that is greater than its parts. But when that unifying dream becomes unattainable, the glue that holds our society together starts to fail. The sense of disillusionment that follows, the feeling of being detached, ignored, and excluded from the possibility of a better life, is a key force driving the anger in our political discourse.

Making the best of America accessible to all Americans is a necessary step for bringing this country back together. As long as some are excluded from our shared national vision, we will never be a truly unified nation. But my experiences in different regions, sectors, and roles around the country have also convinced me that access to opportunity is not enough. The version of the dream that sustained America through its first 250 years no longer meets the needs of the modern world.

This shouldn't be surprising. The world has changed dramatically since America's Founding Fathers drew up the Declaration of Independence and created the first enduring modern democracy. The traditional version of the American dream emphasizes the kind of rugged individualism that suited life as a homesteader or frontiersman. In more recent times, this ethos has helped Americans to push back the boundaries of the possible to a remarkable extent. From the construction of the first aircraft to the development of nuclear power, from landing men on the moon to the creation of the information technologies that power the digital revolution, American men and women have been at the forefront of global innovation. But while this kind of striving self-belief will never cease to be of the utmost value, it needs to be tempered by a parallel focus on the needs of the hyperconnected communities in which we currently live.

More than 80 percent of Americans now live in urban areas, compared to just a few percent at the time of independence.[6] Ninety-seven percent of

Americans carry a cell phone and 93 percent use the Internet,[7] connecting them into an unparalleled communication network with global reach. We live closer to one another and are more connected to each other now than we have ever been at any point in history. And if the American dream is to serve its purpose of holding us together in the modern era, we need to reimagine it to reflect this evolving interdependence. If we do not, the vision that once connected us will increasingly seem like a relic of the past.

As both an academic and a businessman, the question at the heart of my life's work has been how we can build and sustain flourishing and unified communities. In my early career, as a university professor, I helped found the disciplines of sport business and sport marketing. In fact, alongside a pair of esteemed coauthors, I literally wrote the book on the subject. (*Sport Marketing* is now in its fifth edition and is published in eleven languages.). I applied these insights into the ways communities work when I moved into the business world, first as a senior executive and later as a CEO, at top-flight baseball, basketball, and hockey teams around the country, as well as when heading up the NBA's Team Marketing and Business Operations (TMBO) group. In all these roles, the teams I worked with achieved great success on the field, court, or ice. But more importantly, in every case, my teams experienced dramatic increases in revenue and fan support because we prioritized deeper and more meaningful engagement with the communities we served.

Sports and politics are very different worlds in many respects, but they both reflect the societies from which they emerge. I strongly believe that the underlying principles that connect humans together as cohesive groups can be transferred from one type of community to another. To give just one example, a proven principle for building communities of sports fans is "Ask them what they want and then give it to them." That sounds obvious. And it should be. People simply will not commit their time, money, and effort to communities that ignore their basic wants and needs. But when it comes to politics, I do not believe that either of the major political parties is listening to, or delivering, what the majority want. And that detachment from the priorities of the public is one of the most corrosive factors undermining the cohesion of our national community.

For the last fifteen years, the proportion of Americans who are satisfied with the country's trajectory has rarely broken out of the 20–30 percent range.[8] No president this millennium has sustained an average approval rating across his term of more than 50 percent. Meanwhile, public approval of the job Congress is doing hovers around a dismal 20 percent.[9] These shocking figures reflect the fact that, whichever party is in power, the diehard supporters of the other "team" will oppose them. But more importantly, they also show that mainstream politics has come adrift from the politics of the moderate majority of Americans.

While a little more than a third of Americans explicitly identify as moderates,[10] rather than as liberals or conservatives, a substantial majority hold opinions that consistently fall between center-left and center-right.[11] And yet, as far as I can see, there is no political grouping that offers the policies this majority wants, and there are very few politicians who choose to speak to this moderate center. Both parties are now held hostage by their increasingly extreme activist bases, and both parties consistently support views that are far to the left and far to the right of the majority. Most people want a government that delivers policies somewhere between those of the Democratic and Republican party lines on questions of the economy, minimum wage, education, immigration, healthcare, defense spending, civil rights, and most other major bones of political contention. But these options are just not on offer. The consequence is that whichever party pushes their agenda through, the result fails to reflect the views of the opposition *or* of the moderates. It would be hard to design a system more certain to alienate the majority of voters if we tried.

In fact, so polarized has the political debate become that it can be hard to even measure the opinions of the majority. Because so many polls use simplistic methodologies with yes/no answers to questions framed in terms of the positions of the two major parties, they often fail to capture the nuanced views of moderates.[12] More sophisticated data analytics tools are thus needed to identify which policy positions can attract real majority support.

So how can we overcome the divisions and dissatisfactions that have led to talk of secession, violence, and civil war? The answer seems obvious to me: As moderates, we must take back our national politics from those who would push Americans further apart. We are the majority. We have the loudest voice and the greatest say—if we choose to use it. Yet breaking cover and reclaiming the town square can be a terrifying prospect for individuals. To make such a shift viable, we need to move together toward a common goal.

In this book, I will argue that, without a shared vision, without a unifying banner for the majority to march behind, the United States will remain in the grip of the extremists and their enablers, including those many bad actors abroad who wish to undermine the stability of this country.[13,14,15] The first, essential step to bringing our nation together is reimagining an American dream for our current times that meet the needs of all Americans. Once we have that clear and crisp touchpoint to rally around, we must refresh, renew, and rebuild our national ethos around an aspirational vision that can be attained by anyone who is willing to work hard in pursuit of it, no matter their family background or financial standing.

Part 1

CHAPTER 1

Coming to America

Like so many others, my first sight of the United States was the view from a plane arriving at JFK International in New York. As the Pan Am jet dropped through the clouds and into its final approach, I leant across my neighbor to catch a glimpse of the country that would be my home for the summer of 1970. The view that greeted me was certainly not the most beautiful America had to offer, but the impression it left has remained with me ever since. The Van Wyck Expressway unrolled below me, a broad slash of asphalt cutting through the close-packed housing of Queens. The scene would have been thoroughly trivial to any resident of New York, but as a newcomer, I was shocked by the sheer scale of what I saw.

It wasn't that I was some country rube. I was only twenty-one, but I had seen London's sprawl from the air, not to mention the more refined environs of several major European cities. But here, there was just . . . more. More buildings, hunched in on each other, everything densely packed with hardly a patch of green garden growing between. More cars spread across a broader canvas of road than I had ever seen in an urban environment. Even the vehicles themselves were bigger than those we had back home. Wider, taller cars built to match the expanses of America's open roads. And vast trucks (lorries, as they are called in British English), their cabs twice the size of those I was used to.

As I sat back in my seat and waited for the plane's wheels to touch down, I couldn't help but grin. It was just like the movies . . . but even more so. The sense of America as a big country where more is always possible would become a cornerstone of my personal American dream when I moved permanently to the United States a few years later. Yet it wasn't completely new to me, even on that first trip.

I grew up in Liverpool, England, in the 1950s and '60s. Once one of the most important industrial cities in the world, the Liverpool of my youth was adjusting to the decline of British heavy industry in the face of post-war economic realities. Like the city itself, my family found itself teetering on the fence between a blue-collar history and white-collar aspirations for the future. My father was the son of a dock worker and, as the seventh of eight children, he had experienced true poverty in his childhood. His first job, working as an assistant to the butcher in a local grocery store, set him on the path to a classic blue-collar life. But he rejected the well-worn tracks that stretched out ahead of him, instead applying to work as an insurance salesman for the Prudential. His rapid sales success moved our family up a rung on the ladder of Britain's complex class system, so his children never experienced the kind of hunger and deprivation he had during his youth. Still, we were far from wealthy, and the household budget did not always stretch to meat for dinner. While the financial pressures eased after Dad was promoted twice, as a youngster it was rare for a week to pass without a dinner of sardines on toast or blind scouse, a meatless version of the Irish beef stew for which the city's inhabitants were named. We were never on the verge of starvation, but as an energetic and sporty lad, I often spent my days feeling hungry.

As England's great Atlantic port, Liverpool was the point of departure for nearly ten million emigrants over the years, including many of the Irish Catholics who found their way to America's shores. My own family, my mother resolutely insisted, were *English*, despite my having three grandparents born to first-generation immigrants from Ireland (my maternal grandfather was a Scot). Nevertheless, the connection to Irish culture and the Irish diaspora was everywhere in our community. I was educated by Irish nuns at primary school and then by the Irish Christian Brothers at St. Mary's High School, alongside many Flanagans, Murphys, and O'Tooles, at least one Paddy O'Hagan, and unforgettably, the uniquely Hibernian Ciaran Finbar O'Gallagher.

With more people of Irish extraction living on the east coast of the United States than in Ireland itself, the sense that new lives, better lives, could be built in America was ever present in our community. But while the idea remained in the realm of unspoken possibilities for most, my own family had two very vocal cheerleaders for the North American continent in the form of Great Uncle Pat and Uncle Percy.

Pat, my mother's uncle, had moved to Montreal as a young man to take a job in a cork factory that made the stoppers for Seagram's Seven Crown whiskey. While there, the factory owner had taken him under his wing, and he had risen to a senior position, eventually buying the business when his benefactor retired. This made Pat, from my eight-year-old point of view at least, enormously wealthy. He did little to disabuse me of the idea. For several years, he came to spend the summer in Liverpool, bringing his daughter and her three children. One weekend per trip, he would throw a huge party in his large, rented house, gathering Murrays, Dolans, and, of course, the Mullins from across the city for a blowout. While I remember the parties fondly, what stuck with me even more was hearing Pat wax lyrical about North America. It was, he insisted, the land of milk and honey, a place where anyone could grow from nothing to something and where the only limit to success was how hard you were willing to work. This was heady stuff to me. Since my geography wasn't up to fine distinctions at that age, Pat's Canadian dream became the first North American dream I would drift off thinking about at night.

I met Uncle Percy, my dad's cousin, a few years later when I was ten. Percy's story was different, yet in many ways, very familiar. By this time, I could tell Canada and the US apart, and I loved to hear Uncle Percy hold forth on the real deal. He didn't just live and work in America. His job was in New York City—Manhattan, no less!—where his desk was in the Chrysler Building, the second tallest skyscraper in the world. While Pat was a business owner, Percy represented the other side of economic success, having climbed the corporate ladder to become vice president of operations at Richardson-Merrell, the company that owned the Vick's pharmaceuticals brand.

Percy was born and bred in the Bronx and considered himself a spokesman for all things American. His eyes would light up as he described the towering buildings that made the Manhattan landscape unlike any other place on earth. (In 1960, twenty-five of the world's thirty tallest buildings were in New York.) He loved to talk about baseball, and his beloved New York Yankees in particular, to his slightly baffled British audience. But he was at his most passionate when holding forth about the incredible opportunities his land had to offer, speaking with a zeal I had only seen before in the nuns and Christian Brothers at school when they tried to recruit us into religious orders. If Percy was to be believed, a wonderful life awaited every new arrival in America, where there was more land, more wealth, more freedom, and more opportunities than could be found in any other country.

I noticed that some of the other adults frowned when he spoke like this, disliking the unflattering comparison to their own country suggested by his words. There was also something deep in the English soul, particularly among those with blue-collar backgrounds, that found the idea of bettering oneself distasteful. On the one hand, it implied that there was something wrong with who you were right now. And on the other hand, it sounded suspiciously like a complaint about the current situation. Complaints of this sort were the arch British sin, a failure of the stiff upper lip that many saw as essential for getting by in life. The stoic determination to carry on no matter how bad things got was fundamentally at odds with Uncle Percy's proclamations that we shouldn't put up with where we were now, and that we should always strive for more.

Despite the suspicions of some of my extended family, Uncle Percy's words were like nectar to me. The possibilities of this other world he spoke about added new depth to my picture of life in America, constructed primarily from the few American shows on TV and the occasional Hollywood movie we saw as a treat. The gaps in what I knew were vast, but this only created a space for my youthful imagination to go to work. The America in my head became an aspirational dream, but it also remained a fantasy. Throughout my teens, I rarely thought about the United States as holding a *real* possible life for me. Liverpool was enough to fill my horizons.

My memories of Liverpool in the 1950s are of a resolutely gray environment, defined by Atlantic rain, drab clothing, heavy unemployment, high crime, and industrial smog. Yet while the physical environment was dull, the people of Liverpool were warm, and if we needed color in our lives, the great division between blue and red was more than we could ask for.

Liverpool was then, and still is, a city devoted to soccer, or football, as any right-thinking Brit calls it. Soccer is a virtual religion in the city, which is home to not one but two of the most famous top-flight clubs in England. Liverpool Football Club (F.C.), the Reds, are now one of the best-known soccer teams in the world. But in advance payment for future sins, I grew up in a household where the Blues, Everton F.C., reigned supreme. While Liverpool have won eleven league titles and have had forty top-five finishes in the past fifty years, Everton has only won twice, with no additions to the trophy case in more than three decades. Sadly, "The Toffees" now spend more time in the bottom half of the league than in the top tier of teams.

In the 1950s, however, things were very different. When I was two years old, Everton suffered the ignominious fate of falling out of English soccer's top competitive league, after finishing last in the First Division. The only thing that made the pain of relegation bearable for my father was that Liverpool F.C. followed his team down two years later, briefly leaving the city without any top-flight clubs. But while Liverpool didn't claw their way back until the early '60s, the Blues returned to the First Division in 1954.

I attended my first Everton game that same year, at the age of five, joining my father in the stands at Goodison Park as part of the roaring, swaying crowd urging the team on to victory. The feeling of being part of something greater, a living mass focused together on a single shared experience, marked me for life. Understanding that feeling of community, of strangers coming together to form a one-from-many, would eventually become my lifetime's work.

When you take on the mantle of a fan of a sports team, there is a commitment there. You bind yourself to the institution, the players, and your fellow supporters through thick and thin. In exchange for your place in the community, for your right to share in the triumphs, you take on the responsibility of sticking with each other through the tough times. It is a lot like patriotism: a voluntary sacrifice in which you give yourself over to something bigger, something beyond the individual. I found it inspiring, that sense of becoming something more than myself by giving something away. It was a feeling I experienced again a few years later, only in a more profound way, when I took my first communion as a member of the Catholic Church.

The gray Liverpool of my early childhood memories took on a more colorful hue as I moved into my teens. Where the cityscape had once seemed old and tired, now it was bright and exciting. The epicenter of Britain's swinging sixties was undoubtedly London, but the greater Liverpool area more than held its own on the cultural front. Liverpool was home to a vibrant arts community, radical political firebrands, and hundreds of bands. The Merseybeat sound that emerged as the standard bearer for the local scene went on to conquer the world, carried first across the country, and then later into the US, led, of course, by the Beatles.

The decade was an exciting time for soccer fans as well. The '60s saw Liverpool F.C.'s return to form, with the club climbing back into the First Division in 1962 and then going on to win the league title in '64 and '66. My Blues covered themselves in glory as well, with league title wins in '63 and '70 and a cupboard full of trophies in the '70s and '80s.

I loved being together with other Everton supporters on match day, and I loved the shared smiles and boundless good will that passed between the fans. But much as I enjoyed watching soccer, I loved playing it even more. The American dreams I had inherited from my uncles were incredible, mesmerizing, but ultimately, it felt to me, unrealizable. The dream of becoming a professional soccer player, on the other hand, and of eventually wearing the blue of my club, may have been even more fantastic, but I at least understood the steps I would have to take to try to turn it into a reality. And I went after that dream as hard as I could. I arrived early at school each day to play before classes started, and then spent every moment of morning recess, lunch time and afternoon recess practicing. When the days were long enough, I would continue playing after school in the sunlight. Then, as winter drew in, my friends and I would take our ball onto a patch of playing field where we would continue our game under the dim glow of the streetlights that spilt over onto our improvised pitch.

Ironically, it was my activities off the pitch that laid the foundations for my future in sports. My high school did not consider soccer to be a respectable game. Reflecting a broader class-based split in English sports, the Christian Brothers held that soccer was a gentleman's game played by hooligans, while rugby was a hooligan's game played by gentlemen. And since their goal was to turn young gentlemen out into the world, the school's sports facilities focused solely on rugby. So, to get my soccer fix, I played competitively at the weekend. On Saturdays, I organized a community league, with eight teams put together by my fellow students, each representing one of the suburbs around the city. Then, on Sundays, I played for a well-established team in a regular league.

There was no doubting that I was pretty good. I could play well enough that the idea of a professional career was more than just an idle daydream. When I landed a try-out at the age of fifteen with Blackpool F.C., a top-flight First Division team, I was so excited my feet barely touched the ground for a week. The day of the trial brought me back down to earth hard. For the first time in my life, I was no more than average compared to the other would-be pros on the field. I think I already knew the truth before my dad passed on the verdict at the end of the day, but it still hit me with the force of a sledgehammer: I was never going to be good enough to play as a full professional. The technical gap was big enough that no amount of training would bridge it.

I was, naturally, crushed. A dream of almost a decade had been wiped away in a single day. But I bounced back quickly, as many other teenage boys have under similar circumstances. I still loved soccer, I could still play the game, and I could still be part of the chorus in the stands on match day. But it wouldn't be my profession.

So, what would stand in its place? Despite being a bright kid, I wasn't very forward-thinking at that stage of my life. I had neglected my studies at school for several years, spending most of each class daydreaming about soccer. After all, I reasoned, since I was going pro, I wouldn't need any academic qualifications. I had to quickly reassess my life choices at the age of sixteen, when the school told me that I would have to repeat a year if I wanted to progress to the Sixth Form (eleventh and twelfth grades in America). With no football career and little in the way of an academic record, I needed to rebuild from the ground up. I decided that I was still going to be a success, but I would make my fortune in business instead of soccer. I knew I had done myself no favors with my work ethic so far, so I would just have to be patient and work my butt off to make up the lost ground. After talking it over with my parents, I left high school to pursue a vocational course instead.

That January, I signed on for the student development program with the gas board in Liverpool, the local branch of the government's nationalized energy monopoly. That position let me gain some much-needed work qualifications while spending a day each week studying to earn the equivalent of my high school diploma. After two years of hard work, I passed the exams I needed to secure a place on a business degree program at Lanchester Polytechnic (now Coventry University Business School).

The course I took suited me perfectly. Each year, roughly 20 percent of my time was spent studying economics and business, while the other 80 percent was devoted to working in an energy industry job placement. There was also plenty of time for a four-week vacation in the summer, so at the end of my first year, I set off on a hitchhiking tour of Europe with my closest friends Joe and Mike. Unlikely as it might sound, that journey around Europe was what eventually propelled me toward a life in the United States.

My first trip to America had its start in a Dutch brewery. While in Amsterdam, my friends and I took the tour of the Heineken facility there, having been tipped off that it was a great opportunity to acquire some free food and, more importantly, free beer. (This giveaway was a great marketing success; I am still a loyal Heineken drinker some fifty years later). While we were waiting across the street for the English-language tour to start, we got talking to three American girls who had also heard about the opportunity for a free lunch. They seemed excited to hear that we came from Liverpool, so we put on our thickest accents and started spinning tales in the hope that they might be impressed enough to share their beer allocation with us. Fortunately, they had the good sense not to take our stories about our "close friendship with the Beatles" too seriously, but one of the girls, Elizabeth, enjoyed my company enough to share her address back in Michigan with me. Over the next year, we became pen pals.

With our occasional letters flying back and forth across the Atlantic, I now had a more tangible connection to the United States. Those brief pages of flimsy airmail paper pulled America out of my childhood dreams and into reality. Suddenly, the US didn't seem so far away at all. The thought of moving away from England didn't cross my mind, but my European journey had whetted my appetite for travel. I was soon planning a great American adventure for the following summer.

Looking for ways to fund the trip, I came across an organization called the British Universities North America Club. One of the opportunities they offered was the chance to work as a soccer counselor at a kid's sleep-away summer camp on the East Coast. In exchange for coaching the campers, I would get a summer work visa, free food, and accommodation for the length of the camp, as well as enough spending money to take me on a tour of the states afterward. The plan quickly fell into place. I would spend nine weeks living and working at Camp Takajo on Long Lake in Maine, and then I would have five weeks to experience everything the United States had to offer. And for a young English student in 1970, that was a lot.

My goal was to tour across the country, taking buses or trains until I reached San Francisco. Stories about the Summer of Love, the US counterculture and the civil rights movement were all big news in Britain, and I had listened with interest as Liverpool's most famous musicians underwent their own psychedelic transformation in the late '60s. As a business student and an athlete—not to mention a literal choirboy and boy scout in my earlier years—I didn't feel much of a personal connection with the flower power ideology. But the chance to check out the hippies of Haight Ashbury on their home turf was irresistible. Who knew, I thought, I might even experience my own personal enlightenment. I wasn't holding my breath, though.

I flew into New York that June ready to be dazzled, and my experience at the airport did not disappoint. As soon as we were off the plane, I was blown away by the mosaic of people crowding the halls. As a child in Liverpool, I had not encountered a single nonwhite face at either of the schools I attended, and there were few enough on the streets of the suburbs I grew up in. While Liverpool has the oldest Chinatown in Europe, dating back to the early 1800s, that side of the city was not something I had experienced beyond a meal or two in the area's restaurants. The only nonwhite person I knew personally before arriving in the United States was our family physician, Dr. Yousef "Joe" Mansour. But here, in my first moments in America, I was shoulder to shoulder with faces and voices that carried dozens, if not hundreds, of different histories. Some were clearly tourists like me, checking in from distant lands, but I was struck by the number of African Americans and Latinos I saw, many of the latter switching back and forth between English and what seemed to me to be a rapidly spoken Spanish, depending on whom they were talking to. America's racial politics were by no means easy at that time. In the UK, we had seen the footage of marches, counter protests, angry politicians, and even angrier cops, but to a naïve newcomer in 1970, watching everyone going about their business in peace, it was easy to think those were problems of the past.

The image I had built up of America over the years was a silver screen projection of the country, so I will always be grateful for the rapid reality check I received in my first few days. I laughed off my encounter with the customs and immigration officer who had asked me to take all of the "removable studs" (cleats) out of my four pairs of "football boots" (soccer shoes), apparently because he thought I might be hiding drugs in the tiny holes. But watching the police winch the body of a dead homeless person out of the Hudson on my first night in NYC was harder to turn into humor. Getting caught in the middle of a drugs bust the next day as armed police arrested dealers on the west side of Times Square was about as much fun as it sounds. And when, no more than thirty-six hours later, we heard gunshots ringing out from a bank near the New York Stock exchange while an armed robbery took place inside, we quickly decided to cut short our stay in the Big Apple and head for safer climes.

It took just three days in New York to move me from thinking I had landed in a utopia to asking, "What the hell is wrong with this country?" A couple of nights spent out on Long Island with Uncle Percy and his family gave me the chance to process the disconcerting experience. Percy reassured me that we had just been unlucky. But anyway, NYC was its own little world, he said. And that was something we would see all over the country: hundreds of communities—states, counties, cities, towns—each with their own histories and cultures, each with their own way of life. America was a country of contrasts, he insisted, and if I didn't find much to like in one place, I only had to travel down the road a short way to find something entirely different.

As we drove up to Maine a few days later, I saw that there was something to my uncle's words. The journey through the soft-scented pine trees under a clear summer sky washed away the craziness of the city and reminded me that America was more than New York—almost a whole continent more.

Camp Takajo itself turned out to be another of the small communities my uncle had spoken of, albeit a temporary village that came together for two months each summer before shutting its gates and sending its citizens back out into the world. The product of Morty Goldman's powerful imagination, Camp Takajo had become a summer institution for many wealthy Jewish families. The kids came to Maine for eight weeks to play sports, build their independence, make friends, and develop the old-fashioned values of integrity, community, and peaceful coexistence as they lived together in the fresh air of the woods. Morty's grand idea was that these magical summer experiences would help the children become better people, and help their home communities, and even the nation as a whole, become better in turn. As I watched the kids change and grow over the weeks I spent with them, I became convinced that Morty's plan was sound, even if it was only accessible to families with considerable means.

The weeks I spent at Camp Takajo that summer were idyllic. Long days in the sun, surrounded by lakes and forests; cool evenings sweetened with breezes that seemed to blow down straight off the distant mountains. Mentoring the campers and teaching them soccer was an endless source of fun, and they in turn took great pleasure in initiating me into the mysteries of American English ("cookies," "candy," "cooties," as the kids taught me, rather than "biscuits," "sweets," and, well, I'll leave the last one for the reader to decode). My fellow counselors, meanwhile, provided my first real insight into the wildly divergent lives young Americans might experience as they grew up.

While some of the Takajo counselors had been born and raised in the kind of picture-book American lives familiar from TV and the movies, others were able to offer me a different perspective. I remember once making plans to go drinking in the nearby town with Charles, a student from the University of Illinois and the first black American I became friends with. When the ride I was expecting turned up, I was surprised to hear from the two white counselors in the front seats that there was no room for Charles, despite the back seats being completely empty. I shrugged it off and said we would get another ride, completely oblivious to what had just happened. I didn't realize what was going on until Charles mentioned that there was no way in hell he would have got into that car anyway, not with its Alabama plates and two white guys riding up front. Yet, despite facing a level of prejudice that put him in fear of his life in some circumstances, Charles still viewed America as "the best place in the world." He saw the American dream as his birthright, just as it was for every other American. As far as he was concerned, the fact that there were some who would try to deny it to him was an aberration, a problem to be fixed, not a flaw in America as a whole.

As my two months at Camp Takajo drew to a close, I already knew that I would be returning to America. There was something here in the warmth of the people and in the beauty of the landscape that resonated in my soul, nourishing the seeds that were planted in my childhood by my uncles. So, when Morty pulled me aside to tell me he would like me to return to Takajo in future years as head soccer coach, I was elated. Brimming with happiness, I went to sleep that night thinking of the road trip that would soon introduce me to even more of this fascinating, promising, perplexing country.

It was not to be. A few days later, Morty pulled me aside again, this time with sadness in his eyes and a telegram in his hand. It read,

Regret Dad died. Call home soonest. Love Mum.

Within eight hours I was on a plane back to London. It would be nearly two years before I set foot in the United States again.

CHAPTER 2

Two Countries Separated by the Same Language

My father's death marked a watershed in my life. Before that moment, I had a safety net. I knew I could always turn to Dad for help or advice (so long as I complied with his rules that the questions I asked him were logical and there was nothing emotional involved). While Mom survived and thrived for another forty years, with Dad's passing I felt that I had to become fully responsible for my future. I was an adult now. It was time to step up to the plate and prove myself.

Within a little more than eighteen months, I was a homeowner and engaged to be married, a rapid evolution from the beer-swilling hitchhiker of just a few years before. Shortly after returning to Coventry, I met a beautiful and smart young woman named Chris, who was studying to become a teacher. We began dating, and it wasn't long before the relationship became serious. A brilliant athlete, Chris excelled as a diver, a field hockey player and on the netball court (netball is the British version of women's basketball, played with a hoop but no backboard). Within a year, we decided we wanted to spend our lives together. Despite the apparently perfect match, things were not always easy between us. Chris was often quiet and withdrawn, leaving me feeling uncertain of myself and how we stood with each other. Nevertheless, we had more than enough in common that we could paper over the cracks, and we remained together for over seventeen years. Sticking it out in the face of adversity was, I felt, part of being a responsible adult, especially as a Catholic who had been raised to take the marriage vows very seriously indeed.

The more straightforward step into the grown-up world was the purchasing of a house. One of the reasons for Dad's success as an insurance salesman was that he believed wholeheartedly in the products he sold. Not long after the funeral, Mom took me aside and explained that Dad's life insurance policy had paid out, and she wanted to divide the money equally between me and my two sisters. I was *not*, she emphasized with a piercing look, to blow it on a sports car. (She knew me well and had a good grasp of the direction my mind would be turning.) This was for bricks and mortar, nothing else. It wasn't a fortune—£4,000, which would equate to about $40,000 in today's money—but it was more money than I had ever seen in my life and sufficient to buy a three-bedroom starter home in a blue-collar neighborhood in Coventry, where my studies continued.

While I have had to work hard for what I have achieved in my studies and my career, that massive leg up on the financial ladder made many things easier for the rest of my life than they would otherwise have been. I have come to believe very strongly that the ability to pass a start in life down from one generation to the next is one of the most important factors for holding a society together. That intergenerational connection gives us a stake in the future and a reason to strive for more than we need right now, a reason to build something that will outlast us. The chance to pass something on to the next generation ties families and communities together across the ages and makes us value stability and unity. Yet at the same time, if we fail to ensure that *everyone* has access to a secure foundation for launching their lives and careers, we set our communities up to fail. If society is divided between those who are given a head start by their parents, and those who begin with nothing and have little hope of getting much more, then it should be no surprise that a significant proportion of the population will not be invested in the shared national endeavor. Generational wealth is one of the keys to living the American dream. As such, it requires significant attention when thinking about how to make that dream conceivable and then accessible to everyone, including the least wealthy families.

While I later came to see that solving this problem was critical for healing the rifts that now divide our nation, in my early years it was not division but unity that defined America for me. Sure, it was a country struggling with the legacy of many dreadful past injustices, but I believed—perhaps too easily, as a white male—that it was struggling successfully to bring people together. However, while the arc of the moral universe felt as if it was bending in the right direction across the United States, I was much less certain about how things stood in my homeland.

Not long after I returned to England from my first trip to the States, I received a very kind and thoughtfully worded letter from Morty Goldman reflecting on how my world must be changing. Toward the end, he included a paragraph repeating his invitation for me to return to Camp Takajo in the summer of 1971 to take up the role of head soccer coach. Reluctantly, I let him know that would not be possible. I had been fortunate to win a highly competitive scholarship that offered me full-time employment while I completed my studies as well as a job after graduation. The scholarship was awarded by one of the giants of British industry: the British Leyland Motor Corporation (BLMC). The initial work placement stretched from January to September 1971, meaning it would be impossible to spend the summer in Maine that year. So great had been the impact of my first trip to America that I briefly considered pulling out of the BLMC placement, but my newly responsible self shut down that idea almost as soon as it arose. Morty being Morty, it wasn't long before another letter came flying across the Atlantic to tell me not to worry; he would expect me the following summer instead.

In 1971, British Leyland was one of the largest industrial concerns in Europe. With nearly a quarter of a million employees and control over a vast slice of the automobile market in the UK. and many western European countries, BLMC was the fifth largest car manufacturer in the world. Its portfolio included world-class brands such as Austin, Morris, Jaguar, MG,

Rover, and Triumph, and it also made the bodies for Rolls-Royce's cars. During my internship, I was given the chance to experience work at almost every level of the company, from the production line to sitting in on senior management meetings. I got an inside look at the marketing strategies for coveted auto brands such as Jaguar and Mini, and an introduction to the arcane technicalities of local, regional, and global distribution. It was, without doubt, one of the best starts a young person could ask for if planning a career in heavy industry. But I soon learned that no matter how impressive the brands and how far-sighted the leadership team, a house divided against itself simply could not stand. And BLMC was a community in the throes of ripping itself apart at the seams.

The problems at BLMC were a reflection of broader fault lines in British society at the time. I already understood that there were issues; both my studies and the nightly news made it clear that we were living in a tumultuous time. Labor relations were strained almost to breaking point as British industry struggled to adapt to the free-market forces that were reshaping the world's economy. Where Britain had once been the engine room of the industrial revolution, it was faring poorly in this newly globalized competitive environment. Closed markets were being flung wide open as a result of the post-war settlement, and the need for efficiency was paramount. But industrial efficiency meant smaller workforces generating larger outputs, and there was, understandably, deep resistance among the workers themselves to the idea of redundancies and changes in employment practices in Britain.

Still, there was nothing here that could not be solved with a spirit of goodwill and cooperation on all sides. Unfortunately, that spirit was in short supply, with increasingly confrontational attitudes eventually driving much of British manufacturing to the wall. While the economy has since recovered, pivoting to become a world leader in the service industries, the manufacturing sector is a shadow of its former self, and it is unlikely that the lost global market share will ever return.

There is a great deal for historians and economists to learn from this story of decline. But what stands out to me when considering the political landscape in the United States right now is the disastrous consequences that follow when moderates cede control to extremists. A key part of the problem was that, while most blue-collar manufacturing workers at the time leaned left on the political map, those who represented them in the negotiations held such radical views that they might as well have been from another planet. Nowhere was this clearer than at BLMC, where many of the key union leaders were communists. And I don't use the term in the loose way it is thrown around today by some media commentators in America. I mean that the BLMC union leaders were actually proud and public members of the Communist Party of Great Britain. At a time when the Communist Party polled around 0.1 percent of the popular vote in general elections, its members controlled most of the key union posts at BLMC. And because they had taken control of the levers of power in the unions, the voice of the much more moderate workforce was lost behind the aggressive grandstanding of people with a divisive and destructive agenda.

I remember once being invited to listen in at a critical meeting between the union reps and the senior management of the company. I had never been present for anything this important before. I entered the meeting room at the MG plant in Abingdon, Oxford, excited to hear the cut and thrust of the debate and to see the kinds of power plays that would settle the long-standing disputes. The room was vast and the table at its center had space for more than sixty negotiators. The sheer scale of the surroundings gave the proceedings a certain dignity in my mind. Sadly, it didn't have the same effect on everyone else present.

Of course, I didn't have a seat at the enormous table. Like the other assistants and junior functionaries, I sat out of the way on a chair pushed up against the wall of the very large banquet hall. On one side of the table sat Lord Stokes, formerly plain old Donald Stokes. Stokes had worked his way up from the rank of apprentice engineer to eventually lead the Leyland Motor Corporation. He had then been appointed Chairman of BLMC when it was formed in 1968 from the merger of his company and British Motor Holdings, the other major player in British motor manufacturing at the time. Despite his recently acquired title, Stokes was not the kind of establishment businessman from whom British industry needed rescuing. He was a modernizer who was interested in making the company fit for purpose in the newly globalized economy.

The dominant figure on the other side was Derek Robinson, or Red Robbo as he was known to the British media. Robinson was a dyed-in-the-wool communist who led the workers at his Birmingham plant to down tools and walk out on more than 500 occasions in just two and a half years, averaging one walkout every two days for thirty months. As a communist, Robinson rejected the whole principle that there should be owners and managers of a company like BLMC. As such, there simply could not be any common interests between the two sides at the table. The only way for either party to succeed, in his view, was by taking something from the other side. There could be no cooperation, no collaboration in search of a mutually beneficial solution. As far as Robinson was concerned, he was fighting an existential enemy, and the only way forward was to bring that enemy to its knees.

Robinson made his attitude abundantly clear in the way he acted toward the BLMC management representatives at the meeting. When it came to his turn to speak, instead of offering any kind of analysis of the pros and cons of the innovative "measured work rate" deal that had been offered, he simply stood up, dropped the offer document on the floor, and then graphically mimed undoing his fly and urinating all over the report.

I had to fight back my astonishment at this display. I knew that there were no easy fixes for the conflict between workers and management, but I had no idea just how bad things had become. It was obvious that there could be no happy ending here. Without the ability to have civil discussions about proposals, attempts to negotiate would only become further tools for the extremists. There could be no negotiated compromise here because one of the parties to the discussion simply did not recognize that the other deserved to exist. Robinson was the kind of firebrand who would be happy to burn the whole system to the ground, even if that meant the union members he represented would ultimately be worse off, or even unemployed. In the end, this ideology brought BLMC, the pride of the British motor industry, to its knees.

In my experience, it is an unfortunate truth about voluntary associations like unions and political parties that often it is those who speak the loudest and those who speak with the greatest contempt for the so-called enemy who will rise to the top. The reason is simple: Those with more extreme views are often more energetic and passionate in expressing and supporting their views. It is easy to feel that radicalism is more important than moderation, so the radicals invariably take on the unpaid jobs, volunteer, speak more frequently and, in turn, energize their own base. It doesn't matter if the moderate majority vastly outnumbers the radicals. If the moderates in an organization or community do not engage actively and energetically, they will invariably be dragged along by extremists. We see this happening now in America with both main political parties, neither of which speaks effectively for the majority of Americans. If this is to change, moderates will have to match the commitment of the extremists and put in the time and effort needed to bring our communities back from the brink. The moderate voice needs to be dialed all the way up to ten if we want it to be heard over the yelling of those on the far right and left.

While the views pushed by the union negotiators at BLMC were extreme, the more I began to look at the business environment in the UK, the more disillusioned I became. In my short time in America, I had felt that almost everyone I met was interested in adding value to what they did. People, it seemed to me, were almost universally focused on making the American pie bigger so that their own share would grow in turn. In the UK, on the other hand, the main debate seemed to be about how to divide the shrinking pie that was already on the table.

During my time living and working in Oxford, I tried out for and was signed by the semiprofessional Oxford City F.C., who now play in the National League, immediately below the fully professional English Football League. Although we were mostly mid-table during my time with the team,

I enjoyed three seasons of fun and healthy competition that kept me in tip-top shape, playing twice each week in addition to two intense weekly practice sessions. The money I received for each game was a nice bonus.

When I thought back to my summer in Maine, I often found myself sucked into the memories, preferring to spend my time American dreaming in the green forests, golden light, and optimistic spirit of my mental Camp Takajo rather than return to the grey skies and discontents of England. But I was sufficiently tethered to reality to recognize that these daydreams might not tell the whole story. Was I just idealizing America because I had enjoyed a few pleasant months there. Was I turning a familiar but different society into something more in my head because I wanted an escape?

There was only one way to find out. In 1972, I returned to Maine for a second summer, this time traveling with my fiancé Chris, who took a waterfront counselor job at a girl's camp directly across Long Lake. I was prepared for disappointment, for my doubts to be realized and for reality to bring my illusions crashing to the ground. Instead, I came back to England more convinced than ever that there was something calling to me in the new world, something that spoke directly to who I was in a way that my home country did not. Chris felt exactly the same way, I suspect in part at least, because she saw in America an opportunity to escape the shadow of her well-meaning but domineering father.

I returned home with my mind laser-focused on taking the first steps on my post-college business career. But my heart remained in America. With Dad's passing, Morty had become something of a surrogate father to me, and I had confided in him that I was interested in studying for an MBA degree in the States. America was the economic capital of the world, with almost a third of global GDP created between sea and shining sea. The most innovative business practices and technologies, as well as the most enlightened world views, were all to be found in the United States, so it seemed obvious that this was where I should come for advanced studies in management. The problem was money, or rather a lack thereof. I couldn't sell my house to fund the course—Mom would have been heartbroken—and I had nothing in the way of savings. So, I would have to earn a scholarship of some sort, and those were few and far between. Morty promised to think on it and to look into different opportunities on my behalf.

As soon as I landed back in London in 1972, the idea of an MBA in America seemed ridiculous. While I loved everything about life on the other side of the Atlantic, I knew I couldn't afford to be romantic about it. Chris and I were due to be married the following April, and I would no doubt soon have a family to support. That meant I needed a job, not fantasies of extending my education in an expensive foreign environment. And the only place I could realistically find ongoing employment was at home in the UK. So, with my degree complete, I took up the guaranteed position at BLMC. With the additional cash I was earning at the weekends as a semipro soccer player, I had more than enough to create a nice home and put food on the table. But the labor problems that were crippling the firm made it a dispiriting place to work. Just as bad, promotion to a managerial position with any authority would mean clambering one step at a time up a vast and inefficient bureaucratic pyramid. This was not an attractive future, so I decided to cast my net more widely and apply for executive jobs that offered the chance to move my career forward more rapidly.

A couple of months into the process, I was surprised to receive an offer letter from the marketing director at Serck Tubes. Serck was a medium-sized enterprise that produced specialized high-tolerance metals for industrial uses. With big ambitions for expanding into Europe, they were hiring a marketing manager to assist with the push. My application was an ultralong shot, as the position was not an entry-level role, and I couldn't imagine landing a manager's job almost straight out of college. It took a while for the words, "We would like to offer you the position . . ." to sink in. I later learned that I had been picked ahead of 250 other applicants, apparently impressing the managing director with my argument that you couldn't sell products unless you could sell yourself to the client first. This relationship-based approach to doing business struck a chord with Serck's management and has remained central to my thinking and operational planning ever since.

It soon became clear that my new bosses saw me as someone with long-term potential. Instead of getting me started on the bottom rung accounts, they sent me to the factory floor to learn how the various products we carried were made. Once they were satisfied that I understood what we were selling, they sent me over to work with the team responsible for landing European customers. Our top target was a DuPont chemical plant in Belgium that was sourcing several types of anticorrosive copper and brass tubing from one of our competitors. DuPont preferred our product but were wary about signing a contract with a British company because of the constant labor disputes plaguing the UK at the time. DuPont couldn't afford to have their supply lines disrupted if our workers downed tools or if the British ports went on strike, so I suggested a workaround to eliminate their risk. I asked the Dupont contact if they would commit to signing with Serck if we agreed to build a warehouse near their factory in Belgium and stock it with a year's worth of their most needed products in advance. It would mean we would have to bear significant upfront costs, but it was more than worth it to lock in a very large long-term client.

I wasn't surprised when DuPont decided to give us their business. It seemed pretty obvious to me that if you want to win someone's support, first you find out what they want and then you find a way to give it to them. My bosses, on the other hand, were startled. I was just nine months out of college and had been with the company for only twelve weeks before helping to land the largest deal they had ever closed. All of a sudden, I was the golden boy. I knew Dad would have been proud, and I was only sorry that I couldn't share the achievement with him.

Just as my business career was getting off to a flying start, Morty tossed a hand grenade into the mix. He knew I had returned to England to join the workforce, and that nine-week-long summer breaks to teach soccer in Maine would now be impossible. Creative thinker that he was, he put a scholarship package on the table. If I agreed to come back in '73 and '74 as head counselor for the youngest group of children (those aged six through ten), he would cover the tuition and living costs for me to study for a master's degree in the US in the intervening year. If I accepted the offer, I would be able to continue my summers at the camp, finally see some more of America, and at the same time take up a valuable professional development opportunity.

The options in front of me were hard to weigh. I was frustrated by the direction Britain was taking, and I increasingly felt held back by the attitude that you shouldn't get "too far above yourself." Yet, at the same time, I had a great job for my age with bosses who encouraged me to keep pushing forward rather than settle for mediocrity. My family was in the UK, my house was in the UK, and I had only spent about thirty or so weeks outside the country in my whole life. Could I really give all that up for a roll of the dice in America?

I decided to push for the best of both worlds. I approached the firm's marketing director to see if they would be willing to grant me a fifteen-month leave of absence to study in the United States. My stock was high at Serck, and I was naïve enough not to realize just how big an ask that was. I felt this path would be a win for me and a win for the company. I would take up Morty's scholarship offer and earn a master's degree in marketing from a US business school. Then, at the end of my leave, I would come back to Serck brimming with newfound North American knowledge that would help propel us toward the twenty-first century. It was a pretty good pitch, if I say so myself. My boss weighed it up, talked to Fred, the managing director, and then, to my surprise and great relief, gave his approval.

Chris was 100 percent on board with the decision. We married in April 1973, and two months later we flew out to the US for what felt like the beginning of a great adventure. I never did make it back to Serck Tubes in Birmingham. Instead, I began my life as an American, settling in the great country that has been my home now for fifty years.

CHAPTER 3

Toto, We *Are* in Kansas!

We flew into Kansas City in late August 1973. Other than reading the brochures for Kansas University's business school when I first applied to their post-grad program, I knew next to nothing about my destination. There had been no time for a familiarization visit and, without the wonders of the Internet, no way to get any first-hand information about what Chris and I were letting ourselves in for.

While Camp Takajo recruited counselors from all around the country, most had their homes either in the densely populated area running from Boston to Washington that holds nearly 20 percent of the country's population or in one of the other great American cities. As such, there was more than a little teasing about my destination. It was, as one friend put it, mimicking my English accent, "In the middle of bloody nowhere."

Staring at a road atlas in my accommodation at the camp, I began to see what they meant. Geographically, Kansas was in the dead center of America, both north to south and east to west. Going north from Kansas City, the next real urban center was Des Moines, 200 miles away. It was 250 miles east to St. Louis and 220 miles south to Tulsa (although you could make it to bustling Wichita in just 180 miles by veering a little to the south west). And if you were heading west, well, then you had some 550 miles to cover before hitting Denver, Colorado. Trying to make some sense of the numbers, I calculated that you could lay the whole of Great Britain down lengthways between Kansas City and Denver and still have a few miles clearance at each end. Scattered across that whole-nation-sized space, a traveler would find only a few hundred thousand farmers and residents of small towns.

The scale was breathtaking, even on paper. I ran my fingers along the roads, picking out the tiny specks of places with odd, evocative names: Medicine Lodge, Eureka, El Dorado, and then the towns with a familiar Anglo-Saxon sound—Caldwell, Fowler, Garfield, Smith—that felt linked to, if not quite part of, England's history. And as I rested my finger on Mullinville, I wondered if any of my Irish ancestors had joined the wagon trains of humanity moving inexorably from east to west, settling the plains as they went.

I couldn't help but think about how they had lived, the frontiersmen and pioneers who had founded the hundreds of settlements dotted around this "middle of bloody nowhere." My mind conjured up images of hardy folk, pushing back the wilderness and establishing new outposts of civilization. (I am embarrassed to say that it wasn't until years later that I thought seriously about the tragedy of the Native Americans, who had not considered their homes to be in any need of "civilizing.") That rugged individualism seemed to me to be a key part of the American identity. To live out the American dream, I firmly believed, you had to be able to look after yourself, outrun the plodding step of government-mandated progress, and build your own worlds as you went. I was excited to see how much of that frontier spirit remained in Kansas as I built my family's future in the state.

Chris and I were picked up at the airport by Ron Schneider, a friend from Camp Takajo, and his girlfriend, each of them driving a tiny convertible MGB sports car with just two front seats and little room for baggage. As we struggled in the late evening light to strap cases and bags into piles that would survive the journey, I could feel the heat closing in around us, the humidity sticking my shirt to my back as I finally clambered into the front passenger seat. That mild discomfort was blasted away by a man-made breeze as we roared out of Kansas City, Missouri, and into Kansas proper, heading west on K-10.

Ron was chattering away happily next to me, three-quarters of every sentence lost to the wind. I grinned and nodded at what little I heard, but my attention was focused on catching glimpses of the new world around me. Field after field of shoulder-high corn whipped past, the golden-brown color barely visible in the car's headlights. Then, suddenly, it hit me: A low thundering sound swarmed up on us from all directions, drowning out the noise of the car's small engine. "What the hell is that?" I hollered at Ron. It was his turn to grin. "Crickets!" he shouted back at me.

The sensory overload of the trip to Lawrence was capped by the sight of one of the prettiest towns I have ever been fortunate enough to visit. Despite the late hour, our tour took me past a courthouse that looked like a Disney reimagining of a European castle, an enormous belltower that I later learned was known as the campanile, and the looming, fortress like outline of Fraser Hall on the top of Mount Oread. The derogatory comments made by the other camp counselors, together with the drive through miles of farmland, had prepared me for a rundown, rustic, backwoods kind of place, possibly with a hitching post in front of a central tavern. (My expectations may have been swayed by the sight of the famed Dodge City on my roadmap of Kansas.) The last thing I expected was a balance of modern and period buildings nestling among beautifully kept greenery. Everywhere I looked there were gorgeous buildings, manicured open spaces and cozy-looking restaurants and bars. I had no idea at the time that the United States was dotted with college towns like this, each one a physical reflection of the pride Americans took in their home state and their alma mater.

The next day, I enrolled, registering in the historic Allen Fieldhouse, and then quickly settled into my studies. The marketing course was fascinating but rather easy. With my practical experience in industry to hang the concepts on, everything seemed to click almost immediately, and with the born-again work ethic that had emerged after my father's death, I was now a straight-A student for the first time in my life. Sometime around the middle of my second semester, one of my professors, Dr. Bob Swinth, pulled me aside to ask if I would like to stay on to study for a PhD. I had a knack for asking the right questions, he said, and my results so far suggested that research work would suit me well.

The idea seemed incredible to me at first. I was only two generations away from a line of almost destitute dockworkers and had left high school at the age of seventeen with no qualifications. Getting accepted to study for a bachelor's degree had once seemed like a far-off peak of intellectual achievement. Now, I was being told I could earn a doctorate and carry out research of my own.

I discussed the opportunity with Chris, who was more than enthusiastic. While we had both assumed that I would return to the UK to resume my job with Serck Tubes, a whole new world of possibilities had now opened up. If I entered the PhD program, we could remain in America for at least three more years, and Chris and I were both desperate to stay. Since the doctoral program would come with a job as a graduate teaching assistant, we would have a basic income and, if I sold the house in Coventry, we would also have the deposit for a new home in Lawrence. With the savings on rent that would give us, there would be just enough spare in our monthly budget to start a family. As Chris and I worked through the possibilities, it quickly became clear that the opportunity was too good to turn down. Toward the end of March 1974, I sent a letter to my former boss at Serck Tubes thanking him for holding the job open for me and apologizing that I would not be returning to work there. My future, I was now sure, lay in America. While I have never regretted staying in the US, to this day I still feel bad about asking Serck to hold my job open for me for so long and then not returning. It does not sit well with me that I let down a group of wonderful executives who put their faith in me.

The switch from seeing myself as a promising young businessman to an academic-in-waiting was almost seamless. While the MBA I earned in the first two years of my postgrad work was a useful backstop, as soon as I began thinking about framing and testing research hypotheses, it felt clear that this new world was a natural home for me. It wasn't that I wanted to move away from business, but rather, that *studying* businesses, organizations, and the ways that individuals interact opened up a new realm of thought. In business, the task at hand tells you what ideas are worth exploring in more detail. But as an academic, I could range across whatever subjects interested me. The prospect of that intellectual freedom excited me, so I reached out and grabbed it with both hands. I was convinced then, and I still believe now, that this change from one career to another in almost the blink of an eye could only have happened to me in America. It wasn't just that the United States happened to be the place that gave me the opportunity. Much more than that, it was the sense of freedom and flexibility that came with living here that made the incredible seem plausible and let me make a decision that I would almost certainly have shrugged off as crazy back in England.

A big part of the attraction was the chance to spend three more years in Kansas. For a sports fanatic like me, the buzz of KU's major varsity sports teams succeeding on the national stage was something I could really throw myself into. When the basketball team reached the National Collegiate Athletic Association (NCAA) Final Four in 1974 and the football team made it to Bowl games in 1973 and 1975, the atmosphere on campus was electric. Of course, not everything was on quite the same scale. It was true that the options for theater and concerts locally were more limited than they would have been in New York or Los Angeles. But still, everything I wanted was here in some form or another, and I was surprised to find that the smaller scale didn't make the experiences any less meaningful. In fact, if anything, the closer bonds with friends, and the more tight-knit Midwest community made a victory by my Jayhawks or a good performance by a local band ring all the louder.

In Kansas, and later in my travels throughout the American heartland, I found a warmth, an openness, and a generosity of spirit that I had not experienced before. From the smallest town up to the state level, these communities had been shaped by geography and history to become complete little worlds, physical reflections of the independent-minded individuals who had first opened up the land to settlers from the east. It is true that there can be a certain inward-looking tendency or parochialism in places like this, a naturally insular mindset that comes from being hemmed in by the ocean of human absence on all sides. But the very same forces act as a spur to the creation of human connections.

I remembered my uncle Percy telling me on my first trip to the US that America was a patchwork of communities. At the time, I thought his message was, "Don't worry! It's not all as bad as New York!" And that was a message I needed to hear just then. But now I was coming to see that there was a deeper point, and one that increasingly fascinated me. Each town I visited as I traveled around the state had a unique culture, a self-image that was shared by most, if not all, of its citizens. It was as if each town was its own little republic, confident in its views and values and with a deep understanding of the subtleties that distinguished it from the next town over. Yet at the same time, lying over this variety like a comfortable blanket was another culture, a common Kansan identity that tied people together no matter where they were born or where they lived now. This complex layering of local and state identities, mirrored again in the relationship between the states and the nation as a whole, came to define, for me, what it is to be an American.

I was more than happy to embrace most of the key touchpoints of the Kansan identity: steak, beer, and sports came naturally to me. However, I struggled a little with the almost obsessive focus on the weather. Back in England, we talked about the weather a lot, but it was a subject for small talk. Get your predictions wrong and you might be caught in a rainstorm or end up carrying an umbrella on a fine summer day. In Kansas, it could be a matter of life and death. Flat as a pancake and with little in the way of barriers to the north, Kansas has no natural protection from the cold fronts that sweep rapidly down across the plains from the arctic circle. The changes in temperature I experienced in Lawrence were faster and more dramatic than anything I have known before or since. I remember heading out of the house one unseasonably warm February morning in my shorts in balmy seventy-five-degree weather only to switch into jeans and a sweatshirt at lunchtime after the mercury dropped all the way down to fifty. By the time I returned home after sunset from classes that evening, my teeth were chattering as the temperature had plummeted to just a few degrees above freezing. Chris was six months pregnant at the time and had a hankering for ice cream later that night. I dutifully drove to the local grocery store to pick up a bucket of chocolate chip to satisfy the cravings. As I returned, the snow that was now falling blanketed the cars parked along the roadside. It felt as if I had lived through summer, fall, and winter in a single day.

Tornado season was another new experience for me. Many KU students, me included, took a tornado warning as an excuse to gather together, grill, and drink: a dumb gesture of youthful defiance in the face of nature's ferocity. Still, regardless of how heroic we were feeling, we kept a constant watch on the skies to the southwest, always aware that the forces we were challenging could be fatal if we became too nonchalant. It wasn't until my third year in Lawrence that I finally saw one of the great monsters appear. The storm clouds were zipping by when suddenly, about five miles distant, the racing sky began to bulge downward. For a moment, it was not clear whether the narrowing gray V-shaped cloud would reach the ground. Then, as if a switch had been flicked, the color of the spout changed to black as it made contact and dragged the fertile Kansas soil upward, spinning together wind and dirt to darken the sky above. The tornado was now moving directly toward us, tearing up the ground as it advanced on southwest Lawrence where our house stood exposed on a ridge. I had never seen anything like it before and had to fight back the urge to run. When the twisting mass of wind suddenly turned at a right angle to head east, my sigh of relief was nearly as loud as the storm itself. Later, seeing the devastation the tornado had caused when it ran through the western suburbs of Kansas City, I felt terrible about that moment of happiness. When one person's wellbeing comes at the cost of another's, there is no real joy to be found.

The vast scale of the Kansas landscape and the wild swings in the weather were an important reminder that Americans, like the rest of the human race, are products of their environments. In America's metropolises, and in the heavily suburban areas that surround them, community is, of course, vital to life. But parts of that community can easily fade into the background. When so many people are gathered together in such a small place, it is rare to know who grows your food or provides many of the other services you rely on to live. The social structures that support us can easily turn into background noise: ever present but inaudible unless we make a specific effort to pay attention to them. My experience in Kansas, and later living in some of the small towns and heartland states of America more generally, was that community identity is more immediate, more sharply defined and more essential to day-to-day life. People wear their identities on their sleeves, and I suspect are quicker to welcome newcomers into the fold because knowing and relying on your neighbor can make the difference between surviving and not making it through the week.

Of course, sometimes a close-knit community spirit can have less fortunate effects. A strong sense of identity can also quickly become a wedge that sets groups apart from one another, encouraging like to flock with like and to look darkly on those who do not quite fit. My first encounter with this problem in America came when I went looking for a sports team to join at KU.

I had played rugby at high school, so when I found out that Kansas had a club devoted to a sport that I thought had no presence in the US, I immediately signed up. But while the games were fun, the players at the KU Men's Rugby Club appeared to view their matches as a social activity first and a competitive event second. There were enough players across the university that we could field two varsity rugby teams, but matches against other colleges were played in a way that was new to me. The KU first fifteen would play the first half of their match and then cede the field to the second team. While the second team played a half of its own, the members of the first team gathered around a keg on the sidelines, loudly encouraging their clubmates while consuming two or three cups of beer. They would then stagger back onto the field to complete their match while the second team took a turn at the keg. Fun as these afternoons were, I had a more competitive itch that needed scratching.

Soccer was taken a little more seriously at KU. While the school's focus was naturally on the classic American sports of baseball, basketball, and football, the sizeable body of European, Middle Eastern, and South American students studying petroleum engineering and English as a foreign language threw up plenty of soccer fanatics. There were also quite a few American players, as Kansas City and St. Louis each had several high schools that treated soccer as a major sport. While this variety of backgrounds sounded promising, I was surprised to learn that there was not just one soccer club at the university but two. It turned out that all the American players congregated together under one banner, the KU Soccer Club, while the South American and British players, together with a few Africans, Europeans, and students from the Middle East, had their own KU International Soccer Club. Shortly after I first arrived in Lawrence, I went to practice with both teams to see which one I liked the most and came away having enjoyed my time with both. So, for purely selfish reasons, I decided to engineer a merger between the two clubs.

Whenever I asked someone from one side or the other why the Americans and the international students didn't practice together, the answer was always something like, "We just don't like each other and we don't like the way they play." These sentiments did little to enlighten me about the real cause of the problem, so I used the small amount of status I had as a semipro player to arrange a friendly match. I offered to act as the referee and, to sweeten the deal, I arranged a trunkful of beer and set up a grill to barbecue some food for afterward.

Watching the warmup, the different attitudes on each side came through loud and clear. While the Brits and Latinos did some individual work with the ball, took shots at the goal, and chatted casually, the Americans were . . . well . . . American. They huddled together, stretched profusely, and psyched each other up with loud chants and high fives to get ready for the coming battle. There was a lot of backslapping, grunting, and the occasional disparaging remark about the rather bemused opposition. When the game began, the difference in playing style was just as obvious. The internationals clearly had more technical soccer skills—unsurprisingly since most of them had played the game since grade school—but they were also much more individualistic players. The Americans, by contrast, were more athletic and physical and played as a close-knit team, but they lacked finesse. Both styles of play were viable, but I could see that the players on each side quickly became frustrated by those on the other. When Juan, the diminutive Venezuelan striker on the international team skipped the ball round an American player, the defender's response wasn't to be impressed by the neat little move. Instead, I could see a flush of anger rising in his face, as if he had been embarrassed. Later, when a hard tackle from an American dropped Juan to the ground, I had to rush over to split up the fight and put a stop to the angry death threats from the livid Venezuelan.

The game ended without any more fireworks, but it was pretty clear why the two teams didn't like playing each other. Their recruiting policies created a self-reinforcing feedback loop that had solidified each club around a particular mindset and playing style. Players were encouraged to join the team that matched their own approach to the game, so the clubs became more tightly focused with each new cohort. Players who might shake up the status quo at one club never got the chance because they would soon realize that the other club was where most of their compatriots were playing, leading them to switch.

The frustration on the pitch was a different matter. In fact, it was almost coincidental: it just happened to follow from the typical backgrounds of the two clubs that, when put together as monolithic teams, they each had a playing style that the other side found uncomfortable. But that wasn't a good reason to divide them up. On the contrary, it was a consequence of the division. I quickly realized that if we could bring the two clubs together, we could field two practice teams that each had a good mix of playing styles, and perhaps even build a much more competitive team to send to the Big 8 (nowadays the Big 12) conference games. Not only would that get rid of the frustrations that came from pitting one style against the other, it would also make the teams we fielded better! Balancing skill and physicality, teamwork, and independence, would mean a greater depth of play and, I believed, a much more enjoyable experience all round.

In short, the two clubs were only a bad fit because they had created a situation that emphasized their differences. It didn't take long to bring them together around their shared love of the game. A bellyful of food and a skinful of beer was enough to melt away most of the antagonism. Once Roger, the leader of the American club, became friendly with the Santos cousins from Colombia and began to find some common threads to build around, uniting the two teams was relatively easy. After we had practiced together and played a few games with mixed teams, the self-fulfilling prophecy that "We're incompatible" quickly became history.

It would be trite to claim that the answer to modern America's divisions can be found in the merging of two college soccer clubs. Ultimately, the guys on each side discovered that they liked each other a lot. And we were helped along when two of the holdouts bonded over shared hobbies: as I found out much later, one of them smoked a lot of pot and the other supplied it. But for me, at least, this experience marked the moment when I started thinking more deeply about how social groups come together and fall apart, often for no inherently good reason. There was an important lesson here for me that I carried over into all my future work: Division cements distrust, while connection overcomes it. The only way to stop groups drifting away from each other into self-reinforcing echo chambers is through a radical commitment to forging new bonds. It isn't enough to stand on the sidelines once the forces of division are in play. If you do, things will only ever get worse over time. We must make a conscious attempt to bridge the gaps between disconnected groups, and that means making a choice to put unity ahead of difference. It means talking to people who are different from you or who have different points of view. But that communication can only begin when there is a shared forum in which the two groups can come together.

CHAPTER 4

What's a Jayhawk and What's a Minuteman?

My studies at KU were as engaging as I had hoped. The first year of graduate school earned me an MS degree in marketing and then the next two years covered what was essentially the MBA curriculum, introducing me to the fundamental concepts required for administering a large organization, or at least, to the version of those concepts that was current in the United States in the 1970s. While MBA degrees had become available in other countries, and certainly in England, America was still seen as the homeland of the qualification at that time, with a superior curriculum and a higher standard of teaching. Committed to the idea that companies could be run on scientific principles, the course provided a systematic baseline of knowledge that could, so the theory went, be applied in any sector of the business world.

To achieve good grades, all I had to do was listen diligently, read what I was told to, and study hard: the knowledge we needed was already out there in the world and our job was simply to learn it. The step up to doctoral research in the third year was a whole different ball game. Instead of just absorbing information that already existed, PhD students were required to make their own new contributions to the knowledge base. We had to identify a novel research question and then find a way to answer it. Hard work by itself was no longer enough. Now we needed inspiration and creativity as well.

The transition from being a skilled and experienced learner to becoming a novice knowledge creator took time. Identifying gaps in what we knew about business management and organizational theory wasn't too hard: these were still relatively young disciplines in a rapidly evolving world, so there were plenty of blind spots. But finding a question that needed to be answered, that *could* be answered, and that interested me enough to spend nearly two years of my life on was not an easy task. This shift in the difficulty of my studies coincided with the birth of my first child, Julie Ann, and all the attendant stresses and strains that young couples face as they find their way into parenthood. A few months into the research part of the program, I reported to the campus medical center with a severe case of stomach ulcers.

As the doctor took my family medical history, I was confronted by a distinctly uncomfortable pattern. My grandfather had ulcers in his forties, diabetes in his fifties, and died from a heart attack at sixty-one. My dad had ulcers in his thirties, diabetes in his forties, and died of a heart attack in his fifties. I now had ulcers in my twenties . . . The doctor did not need to do much more than raise his eyebrow as he noted the pattern to make me realize that some big changes were needed. I was drinking five, maybe six, large coffees a day. Those needed to go. And the three to four cans of Coca-Cola that I had embraced as part of my American lifestyle? Sure, I was burning off the calories as an active soccer player and coach, but my stomach and the family history of diabetes had a different story to tell. Reluctantly, I said goodbye to the two quintessential American beverages.

Those were easy steps. What was much harder was getting to the root cause of the stress I was experiencing. I started reading anything I could lay my hands on about stress management. The literature at the time was small, but two books in particular made a huge impact on me. The first was *Type A Behavior and Your Heart* by Meyer Friedman and Ray Rosenman. Here I found for the first time a personality categorization that seemed to encapsulate many of the key features I recognized in my own character. Prior to reading the book, I had thought that driving myself hard, being competitive, and an impatience with failure were purely positive qualities, traits that helped me to work hard and get ahead. But now I began to see they could also have a significant negative impact on both my physical and my mental health.

The second book complemented the first by offering solutions to my personality type diagnosis. Dr. Kenneth Pelletier's message in his *Mind as Healer, Mind as Slayer* was pretty straightforward: Stress is something we create for ourselves, and it is therefore something we have the power to control. It is up to us to change our attitudes, our behavior, and our environments to reduce the amount of stress we experience. I didn't have a problem with my environment, but looking at my own attitudes and behavior, I saw that I was holding myself to unrealistically high standards in many areas. The competitive drive that had helped me become a good soccer player and, more recently, a promising student, was also leading me to think I should aim to be the best at everything I did. If I dropped a mark on a test, I would give myself hell for days afterward. If I played tennis like an enthusiastic amateur, I would get angry at myself for not having the skills of a pro, even though I only got out onto the court once or twice a month. The more I thought about it, the clearer it became: The cause of my stress was the way I talked to myself inside my head.

In my personal life, this realization led me to become more forgiving of myself and more realistic in my expectations. I still had high standards, but I forced myself now to calibrate my expectations against reality. As I thought these issues through, I had a sudden spark of inspiration. It was as if the driving force of the universe had given me the clarity I needed to define my doctoral research program. I decided to focus on executive stress in organizational contexts, examining how different personality types responded to stress stimuli when engaged in business decision making. The experimental research went exceptionally well, with the test results producing strong correlations between the participants physiological responses to executive tasks and their "stress personalities," as defined by their answers to Friedman and Rosenman's stress personality type questionnaire.

With my supervisor's encouragement, I started to apply for academic teaching jobs during my final year at KU. I received invitations to join the faculty at business schools in Iowa and at Montana State, as well as the offer of a plum post at the University of Texas, Austin, which had one of the best business programs in the country. I turned them all down, betting everything on an application to the University of Massachusetts. UMass had a great business school, but the post that caught my eye was, curiously, being advertised in the Department of Physical Education, as part of the Sports Studies program.

Sports has long been big business in America, but there was not a single academic program anywhere in the country before the 1970s dedicated to studying and teaching management or marketing in the industry. The first program opened at Ohio University in the early '70s, but its impact was limited, and it was not until the middle of the decade that a second university followed suit. UMass had started its famed Sport Studies program contemporaneously with Ohio, but the Massachusetts quadrangle—sports history, sports psychology, sports sociology, and sports philosophy—focused almost entirely on the academic study of sports. When it turned out that the majority of students really wanted to learn about sports administration, they farmed the classes out to the business school. When UMass finally decided to take a systematic approach to the business side of sports, there was no established sport business discipline in the country and a vanishingly small number of academics with any research or teaching history in the field. So, rather than asking for sport business qualifications, the advertisement for the UMass post instead invited applications from people who had both a PhD in business management and direct experience in the world of sports, either playing or coaching at the professional or collegiate level. As I read the ad, I couldn't imagine a better fit for myself. I later learned that I was the only applicant to meet the full set of criteria.

At the interview, I leant heavily on my experience as a semipro soccer player and my track record in managing and coaching soccer at the collegiate level. In my first year in Lawrence, I had persuaded KU's two small and competing soccer clubs to join forces. I had then set about expanding the presence of soccer on the campus. In the second year, we ran a KU Soccer World Cup to tie in with the 1974 International Association Football Federation (FIFA) tournament, which ballooned our club membership from thirty-five up to three hundred. The next year, the Jayhawks' newly expanded soccer club won the Big 8 Tournament Championship with me as both coach and player. In my final year at KU, I was responsible for organizing the Big 8 soccer tournament we hosted in Lawrence as the previous year's victors. This was a hobby for me, a second string to my research work, but I took it very seriously. Together with my qualifications in business management, I thought it made a compelling case for giving me the very first sport business job at UMass. In truth it was a very thin set of qualifications, but of the many who applied for the post, I was the only candidate to meet the minimum requirements. And so, I traded in my identity as a Jayhawk for a new affiliation as a Minuteman.

The day I arrived in Amherst to take up my new position, life felt as full of promise as it had ever been. The sun was shining, the summer heat had not yet faded, and as I strolled across the campus, I felt as if I had arrived at a turning point in my life. After four years of postgraduate studies, I would be a professor now. I had an academic job at a prestigious university, and I was working in a field for which I felt uniquely suited. I was a person on the move, perhaps not yet a noted author or a beloved teacher, but at least on the path to academic success. None of that changed during my first brief meeting with my head of department, but I still left his office feeling like my legs had been kicked out from under me.

The contract I had signed with UMass in spring 1977 specified a salary of $17,500 a year, not a fortune by any means, but a princely sum to someone who had spent most of their twenties as a graduate student without a proper income. Unfortunately, as my new boss explained, the university could not give me the position that had been advertised. Because my doctoral thesis had not yet been examined, UMass policy would not allow me to be appointed at the rank of assistant professor. Instead, I would be an instructor, with the upgrade in title coming only when I had my PhD certificate in hand. The slight loss of formal status didn't bother me much. I was, of course, eager to be Dr. Mullin at last, but my job title was of little interest. The words that followed were another matter entirely: "And I'm afraid that means you'll be paid on the instructor's pay scale."

I was furious. The post had been advertised as open to those who had completed their thesis but were still waiting for the final confirmation, those who were ABD ("all but dissertation," in the academic lingo). My own status was clear throughout the interview process, so this could not have come as a surprise to the committee. I later learned that the department head had not fully understood the university's own rules when offering me the job and that the contract we had signed had been issued in error. Although the difference in pay was not huge—only $2500 per annum—I needed every nickel and dime of the assistant professor salary. Chris and I had already signed the purchase contract and paid a 10-percent cash deposit to buy a house in nearby South Deerfield, but our old home back in Lawrence, Kansas, had not yet sold. Until it did, we were on the hook for mortgages on two houses (including a second mortgage we had taken out to remodel the basement in Kansas). We also had to make the payments on the new station wagon we had purchased to meet the needs of our growing family. Chris was pregnant with our second daughter, Lara Jane, with a due date of mid-January. With the promised salary in mind, the extra expense had seemed reasonable. Now, it felt like an extravagance that I couldn't escape from. The salary cut was only 14 percent of my total pay, but it meant that the $100 we had budgeted each week for food and utilities would be impossible to sustain.

Matters soon got worse. When we went to the bank to complete the closing on the house, the bank manager informed me that they could no longer offer us a 90 percent mortgage. Their loan-to-value decisions were based on the salary of the borrower. Seeing my new employment contract with a $2500 pay cut, and two mortgages on the house back in Kansas, they now wanted a 20 percent down payment. Not knowing where to turn, I called Morty at Camp Takajo. Morty showed me that day what having a big heart really means. Despite the fact that I had stopped working at Takajo the summer before, he wired the money directly to the bank in Amherst that afternoon. I will never forget Morty's kind and simple words, "You can pay me back when you have it." I will be forever grateful for that peerless act of generosity.

Thanks to Morty's loan, we were able to pick up the keys and move into our new home that same night. The house was situated on the north-facing side of Sugarloaf Mountain in South Deerfield, on four acres of our own wooded land. It was a beautiful chalet-style home constructed with chocolate brown vertical siding, California yellow pine ceilings and huge windows that gave us an incredible view of the forest all around. It wasn't quite a rustic cabin in the middle of nowhere—to the northwest, we could look out over I-95 as it threaded through the forests up to Vermont—but the hewn wood and the isolation made me feel as if I was carving out a piece of the world for my family, as if we were settling our own personal frontier. I couldn't imagine anywhere better to raise the kids. Julie was now nearly two years old and Chris was five months pregnant with our second child. We both wanted at least one more child, ideally adding a boy to the mix, and the idea of watching my little clan grow in this idyllic setting made my heart swell. But I found it hard to focus on the pleasures of our new home for more than a few seconds at a time. Whenever my mind wasn't busy with work or family matters, it turned immediately to the bills that were piling up on the kitchen table.

The truth was, the bank's assessment of what we could afford to pay on the mortgage had been generous, even allowing for Morty's kindness. I had gambled on being able to sell the house in Kansas quickly, but things were moving at a glacial pace. Every time I called our realtor in Lawrence, I became more frustrated. As a born-again Christian with some unfortunate beliefs about relying solely on God's plans for the world, he was happy to leave the sale in the lap of providence. I believed in God as well, but my own view was that we were put here to exercise our free will through hard work and determination, not to leave all the work to the man upstairs.

Unfortunately, my repeated attempts at theological persuasion had little effect, and his efforts to find a buyer remained minimal. In the meantime, I was slipping deeper and deeper into debt.

As the summer sun gave way to the chill of fall, I found myself facing a new problem. Beautiful as our home was, it was also an icebox. The large windows were single panes of thin glass that seemed to be designed to radiate heat out into the surrounding forest instead of keeping it in. Meanwhile, our magnificent A-framed roof had only three inches of foam insulation under the asphalt tile. Our dream home was almost always cold. Worst of all, the house relied on an inefficient baseboard electric heating system that generated far less heat than we needed while burning through far too much expensive electricity. When I got the heating bill for January 1978, in the middle of a blizzard that dropped more than thirty inches of snow in a single day, it drove me close to despair. We owed $250 for just one month's electric bill, and we had still shivered our way through those bitterly cold nights, huddled together under blankets and comforters. February that year was expected to be even worse, and we would have a newborn baby in the house.

Within days, we were surrounded by high drifts of snow on all four sides of the house, with more than three feet of snow and ice on our roof, draining ever more heat from the house and ever more money from my wallet. The situation was unsustainable, but there was no obvious route out. Even without taking the cost of energy into account, I was spending far more than I was earning with no scope to cut back further. I had to have a car to get to work as there was no bus service up on the mountain. We were economizing on food already, but with Chris pregnant there was only so much we could do without endangering the baby. The only thing I could think of was to take advantage of the forested land around the house as a source of fuel. But that would mean installing a woodburning stove, and the last of my savings had evaporated a few weeks earlier. For the second time in just a few months, I was forced to turn to others for help.

My mother, God bless her, loaned me the $500 I needed for the stove and a cheap metal chimney. As she was soon coming to visit us to support

Chris through the birth, she joked that it was really for her, so it was only fair that she should contribute. I felt embarrassed to be asking for money from my mom in my late twenties, ashamed that I had failed to provide my family with everything they needed, and enormously thankful for the grace and good humor with which she responded to my request.

Purchasing the stove was one thing, setting it up was another. I leaned on every bit of ingenuity I had to build a tiled fireproof hearth and to maneuver the heavy metal object into place with the assistance of my still-pregnant wife. But even as I worked on these tasks, I knew something more daunting waited for me outside. If we were to have a fire without smoking ourselves out of our house, we would need to attach the thin metal chimney to the outside wall of the house and run it up clear of the roof. That would mean cutting a hole through the roof overhang for the pipe to pass through, which in turn would mean finding a way through the three feet of compacted snow and ice that covered the roof.

I had no way of getting up to the overhang except a rickety ladder that felt as if it might collapse under me at any minute. I couldn't ask my pregnant wife to hold it in place while I sent chunks of ice falling two stories to the ground around her, so I rigged up some concrete blocks to stabilize the base of the ladder. Once that was done, I shuffled upward, one hand on the icy rungs and the other holding a pickaxe over my shoulder. Perching precariously near the top, I began to clear the roof, letting the pick hang over my back with one hand and then jerking my shoulder awkwardly forward to send it arcing up, past the overhang and into the snow and ice. On the third or fourth swing, the pickaxe wedged itself tight into the ice. As I shifted my weight to try to wrench it loose, I lost my balance, toppling backward off the ladder and into the darkness twenty feet below.

The landing was messy and painful, but I was lucky not to hit anything on the way down and luckier still that I fell into a deep drift of soft, fresh snow. Looking back, I can only consider myself blessed that the pickaxe that fell with me landed a few inches away from my body instead of piercing me through. I was unable to appreciate my good fortune at the time, however.

Instead, I lay in the snow and, for the first time as an adult, I began cursing and weeping uncontrollably.

That moment was undoubtedly the lowest point of my life. As far as I was concerned, I was a total failure of a human being. I had let down my wife, my baby, and my unborn child. I was a leech who had to beg for money from friends and family. Our finances were a disaster, and I couldn't see any way of fixing them. I hurt all over, and worst of all, I knew I had to stand up, get back on the ladder again, and get back to work. I felt it would be easier to just lie there until the cold took me. After several minutes of feeling very sorry for myself, I pulled myself together. I believe that my dad spoke to me that night, or at least, I heard the tough but loving words I needed to hear in his voice: "Stop feeling sorry for yourself Bernard, and get your arse back up on that ladder!" I immediately got to my feet, praying hard to God for the strength to finish the job.

Somehow, despite the heavy bruising, I managed to clear the roof. In what I can only describe as a minor miracle, I also managed to cut a hole through the overhang, wielding a chainsaw while swaying from side to side at the top of the ladder. The next morning, I called in sick to work and hoisted the tin pipe into place, stabilizing it with three feet of clearance above the roof line. By the afternoon, the stove was roaring, and the house was finally beginning to feel warm for the first time in months.

I should have taken some joy in this small victory, but the relief was minimal. The stove would save us a lot of money, but not nearly enough. We were still falling deeper into debt every day. All I had done was slow the speed of the descent. My situation still felt hopeless, and I went to bed that night wondering how I could possibly carry on.

As winter descended in full force in February that year, I settled into a new way of life. To staunch the financial bleeding, we came to rely on the stove for almost all our heat. That meant my job at the university was now supplemented by a new role as amateur lumberjack at home. As the air became more frigid, so the stove's appetite for wood grew. To begin with, I spent an hour a day, and more at the weekends, collecting the wood that had fallen to the ground across our land. I sawed the wood into manageable pieces where it lay, and then hauled the logs down the hill to the house on my daughter Julie's plastic sled.

As the snow continued to fall, the part of my day devoted to physical labor grew. Just as the lower temperatures demanded greater amounts of fuel to keep us warm, so the effort involved in bringing each load to the stove increased. The ready supply of deadfall in my patch of woodland soon ran out, forcing me to cut down and break up whole trees. Once the work with my chainsaw was done, I would then carry the wood down on my back, wading through snowdrifts that got deeper and deeper by the day (a typical winter in the Pioneer Valley at the time saw up to 250 inches of snowfall).

I tried to keep our supply of wood at least a week ahead of our needs. The newly cut timber was completely unseasoned, so we had to plan ahead if we wanted it to burn. I started by stacking it on our side porch under the overhang of the roof. Then I would bring a batch into the house three or four days before I intended to use it, to give the ice a chance to melt and to let the wood dry out a little. Even with these efforts, the amount of creosote the logs sent up the chimney was alarming. Less than a month after I installed the stove, the wood tar in the chimney pipe caught light, setting fire to the side of the house. We were fortunate to catch the blaze in time to put it out, but it was another low point. Asking my mom for a second loan to buy a properly insulated chimney pipe rather than the cheap tin tube we had been using only reinforced my sense of failure. Between the hard manual labor, my full teaching load at the university, and the anxiety of unpaid bills, I spent much of January and February 1978 feeling as if I was about to snap. The experience was even worse for Chris, who carried our baby to term without any of the financial or environmental security she deserved, in a home that sometimes felt as if it would be the death of us both. The birth of our beautiful new daughter Lara Jane and Julie Ann's development into a smart, big-hearted toddler were our only sources of joy in those months, although having a newborn to care for added its own share of challenges, with Chris bearing the brunt of them.

I was fortunate to have an escape at work. Every morning, I would drive into Amherst in collar and tie to work in my overheated office and to attend meetings and classes around campus. Apart from the faint whiff of woodsmoke that hung to my clothes, I was just like any other junior professor. Then, when classes were done, I would head home, change into work clothes, and start cutting and moving wood until it became too dark to work safely. It sometimes felt as if I was driving back and forth between two lives, one in the modern world and the other fixed firmly in the eighteenth century.

Of course, unlike the European settlers who carved their homes out of the landscape, I could escape at any time. The option was always there to hand the house back to the bank, take a big haircut on the property in Kansas for a quick sale, clear my debt by declaring bankruptcy and move into rented accommodation. The long-term financial cost would have been large, wiping out all the home equity we had built up, but still, however bad things seemed, there was ultimately no real chance of us freezing or starving to death. But Chris and I were determined to keep our home and live out the American dream. We both felt that we had worked too hard and delayed laying the foundations of our economic lives for too long to start with a failure in the very first year of my professorial career. We were determined to tough things out for the sake of our futures.

Little by little, things improved. Chris recovered from Lara's birth with almost superhuman speed and took over responsibility for much of the logging work. As the weather eased at the end of February, we began to see green shoots on the horizon. With the days becoming warmer and with winter turning to spring, we would need less fuel, reducing the physical burden on both of us. Even if the house in Lawrence failed to sell, I would be defending my thesis in March and would formally become a doctor soon after, opening the way to the pay rise I so desperately needed. Chris and I had both arranged to work at a camp over the summer, which would bring in enough extra to clear our most pressing debts. And I was also beginning to earn an additional income from part-time consulting work outside the university. The journey would not be easy, but it began to feel at least manageable again.

The year I spent on my personal frontier taught me just how precarious life can be. A few events beyond my control along with a few mistakes of my own had moved my family from a careful but comfortable position to the precipice of financial disaster. Every day for months, I woke up with a feeling of crushing pressure bearing down on me, a sense that just one more thing going wrong could ruin us. The experience of being caught in this trap with no way out and being forced to plead on an almost daily basis with debt collectors to be patient, sucked all the pleasure out of life.

Things turned around for us. After six months of purgatory, I could see the light at the end of the tunnel. Within a year we had stabilized our situation and after another twelve months we had climbed out of debt. When I was finally able to put these problems behind me, I looked back, and I was proud of Chris and myself. We hadn't given up; we had shown grit and determination, pulling ourselves out of the hole with long hours and hard labor. Chris and I hadn't driven across the plains in a covered wagon, but we had suffered hardships and overcome them. Although the experience left some scars on our relationship that I believe never truly healed, we had fought like hell to keep our home equity and avoid bankruptcy. And that, to me, seemed the essence of the American dream, the will to never, ever give up. It was a dream forged on the frontier, tempered in hardship, and seized by those who had the drive to reach out and take it. That is the story we tell about our country, about the settlers who first dreamed this dream, wrenching a life from an unforgiving environment. Anyone with the will and determination can thrive, even on the hardest ground.

As the years passed, I came to see that there is another story. Yes, it is true that Chris and I overcame some great difficulties when we first arrived in Amherst. And I believe we deserve fair credit for digging in and working through the tough times. But it would have been harder, perhaps even impossible, without the help of friends and family. That support is not something that is earned by diligent action or clever planning. It comes from good fortune and the grace of others. It was my very great luck to have people in my support network who were both willing and able to help. My ability to succeed at that time depended on them as much as it did on me. I was nearly brought down by events beyond my control, and by some poor choices for which I was fully responsible, but I was raised up again by others. Any story about success in this country, any account of the American dream, that focuses solely on the part we play ourselves and that ignores the role of others and the unearned blessings that help the lucky along, tells only part of the story.

Perhaps there were some early frontiersmen who were solely responsible for their own success, owing nothing to their upbringing or to anyone else in their life. But as soon as the first community began to grow, these early Americans began to rely upon each other for their well-being and survival. As I learned about South Deerfield's history during the decade I spent there, I could not help but see that interdependence and mutual reliance are also a key part of America's founding story. Bloody Brook, the creek that runs through the town, is named for a battle in 1675 that saw the early settlers assailed with great loss of life by Native Americans who objected to the presence of the interlopers. Here, as elsewhere in the Pioneer Valley, the conditions for settled life depended entirely on banding together for mutual defense and aid. This dimension of life was just as important as the hardy individualism that enabled settlers to move across the continent in the first place.

When we reimagine the American dream, it is not enough to look at those who have succeeded and to ask what they had in common. Of course, these common traits have something important to tell us, but survivorship bias means an important part of the story is missing. What we don't see are all the exceptional individuals who did not succeed, despite having the same qualities. We don't see those who were struck down by chance or held back by a lack of support. If we want the American dream to be accessible to all, we need to think seriously about what is missing from the story of the rugged individual pioneers. And we need to tell ourselves a new story that brings together the critical importance of individual effort with the societal context that makes it possible for that effort to bear fruit.

CHAPTER 5

Meet Me in the Middle

Psychologically and financially, my first year at UMass was the hardest year of my life. But on the intellectual level, it was an exciting time. When I was on campus, distracted from my worries at home, I immersed myself in a highly challenging yet rewarding pursuit that few academics have the good fortune to experience: laying the foundations for a new discipline. Since there were no pre-existing course materials or textbooks on the subjects I would be teaching, and very little in the way of published research, I had to create everything from scratch. I was determined from the beginning that anything we taught in our sport business courses should be anchored to the practical needs of the industry. So, to help determine what those needs were, I took a tour of the northeastern United States before the start of my first semester, speaking to people in senior leadership roles at any major or minor league sports team that would let me through the door.

I wanted to discover what skills team owners and senior executives were looking for in the next generation of industry leaders. I had hoped to transcribe this wisdom so I could pass it on directly to my students. Instead, I learned an important lesson of my own: Unless you first create a common language and a shared conceptual vocabulary to communicate in, asking questions won't get you very far. My initial goal was to gather lists of traits and abilities that sports industry leaders thought would assist young managers working in various roles. What I actually heard were the kinds of insights I could have picked up from the owner of a small-town gas station.

Time and again I was told that a good employee was someone who showed up early and did what they were told. Period. Beyond these basic requirements, many of those I spoke to found it hard to put the leadership needs of their business into words.

On reflection, this should not have been surprising. For the most part, these were smart people and good businessmen (at the time, these roles were filled exclusively by men). But none of them had studied their industry systematically and many of them had spent most of their career working for a single team. As a result, there was no industry-wide framework or language for communicating the skills and attitudes that were particularly valuable. And without a shared conceptual language, words and ideas simply fly past as meaningless noise. While I did not get much useful material from the leaders I spoke to, I did fix on a central principle that came to guide all my future work: What really matters is how people connect and communicate. Everything else follows from this.

My core business DNA, and the DNA that formed the basis for sport marketing and sport management as academic disciplines, is based on the concept that relationships are fundamental to everything we do. Watching and enjoying sports is an essentially social experience, made meaningful by relationships. We normally watch in the company of others, whether as part of a crowd at a stadium or sports bar, or in our living room with friends and family. We talk about our teams to other fans and, even when we watch or listen alone, we connect by social media or feel as if we are part of a conversation with the commentators, often complaining loudly about referee decisions even if there is no one around to hear. Even the most antisocial curmudgeon who despises the company of others feels a meaningful connection of some sort with their team and the community around it. If they did not, they would have no reason to support the team in the first place.

Just as the sports experience is about relationships, so too is sport business.[16] My goal as a teacher was to help my students see that relationships are at the heart of everything we do in this industry and to show them how to build communities in which these relationships can flourish. When the semester started, I couldn't wait to introduce these ideas to some of the first students ever to study the topic.

The success of the sport business program at UMass was, and continues to be, remarkable. Starting with fewer than forty undergraduates and twenty or so grad students in our first year, by 1983 we had well over three hundred students in the program across the bachelors, masters, and PhD levels. Many of the undergraduate and graduate students who passed through the program during my time at UMass went on to have highly successful careers, with some rising to the very top of their profession. Dennis Mannion, for instance, went on to become president of the L. A. Dodgers and later the Detroit Pistons. Brian McNamara became a professor and then Dean at Cal State, Bakersfield, before being appointed a superior court judge by the governor of California. Peter Luukko served on the board of governors of the National Hockey League (NHL) and National Basketball Association (NBA) as president of the Philadelphia Flyers and the Philadelphia 76ers, in addition to running Wells Fargo Arena. One of my students, Jeff Clowes, even helped carry the discipline back across the Atlantic to England, becoming a professor at my alma mater in Coventry and then dean of the business school there. The program he helped create is now the leading sport business program in Europe, while UMass still holds the crown as the number-one sport management program globally. It is a legacy of which I am extremely proud, and I hope the many other students who went on to become CEOs or CMOs in many different sport properties and organizations will forgive me for not mentioning them as well.

The other lasting impact of my academic work at UMass was a textbook on my area of specialization, the marketing side of the industry. Working with Steve Hardy and Bill Sutton, two incredible collaborators from other universities, *Sport Marketing* emerged from a manuscript I first wrote for my students, which was then honed over a period of more than ten years. The book was finally published in 1993 and remains the best-selling and standard text on the subject today. It is now in its fifth edition, with over 125,000 copies sold in eleven different languages. While Steve, Bill, and I discussed the ins and outs of sport marketing in laborious detail across 500 pages in the book, the basic thesis can be boiled down to a few simple principles. These are, I believe, relevant not just for people running businesses in the world of sports, but for anyone trying to build a community or a social or political movement.

The first principle is straightforward: start with market research. You begin by asking people what they want and then you give it to them. This sounds simple and easy to deliver, but it is such a common point of failure that its importance needs to be stressed again and again. It is very easy for businesses to be distracted from what really matters. Executives get wrapped up in their new products, senior management spends months rolling out new strategies, and, as those working on these projects invest increasing amounts of energy and effort in the nuts and bolts of innovation and administration, they frequently forget about the core goal: delivering goods and experiences that meet the needs of their customers.

The same problem exists in an even more extreme form in the political sphere. Politicians are there to serve the public. And that means finding out what the public wants and finding ways to deliver it. Yes, at times we expect our political leaders to make unpopular choices when they have special insights into situations that might not be apparent to the general public. But in a functioning, representative democracy, these should only be exceptional instances. When politicians consistently fail to represent the views of the people, democracy is stifled. Unfortunately, at the time of writing, I believe that far too many members of the political class in this country are so detached from the expressed wishes of the majority that they can barely be thought of as representing our national community at all. Most politicians today have chosen to represent small fractions of the population, serving the interests of activists, political action committees, interest groups, lobbyists, donors, and corporate big spenders, within and beyond their own parties. There are very few figures on the national stage who even pretend to represent the people as a whole, rather than the narrow slice of the population that provides their power base.

The primary system bears much of the responsibility for this drift. To be elected, a politician must first pass through an internal selection process run by their own party. Politicians are thus forced to listen to and prioritize the views of those with the greatest power within their party's machinery, and the public at large are then presented with a simple choice between the candidate who was most convincing to Democratic Party activists and the candidate who was most convincing to activists in the Republican Party. This tendency has helped to drag the representatives of both parties away from the center, and toward the extremes. Politicians are listening, then, but they are listening to the wrong people. And because the moderate majority is frozen out in this way, it has become more and more disengaged from the two main parties. It has also, as opinion polls repeatedly show, become more and more dissatisfied with the state of the nation as a whole. To re-energize the majority and unite the country behind a working political system, we need to find a way to give the people their voices back. Only then will we hear what the majority really wants, and only then will we be able to act accordingly.

The second key principle I advanced in the book was the attendance frequency escalator. This principle was based on the idea that growing communities is more about increasing the avidity of fans and the frequency of attendance or involvement than it is about increasing their raw number. Changing how many games a fan attends is a much more effective way of growing crowd size and overall season attendance than simply attracting new fans whose level of engagement is very low. From a sport business perspective, if a fan never watches the team live, never buys merchandise, and only catches a couple of games on TV a year, then that fan barely exists. The book thus argues that the successful marketing plan for an established team should emphasize existing fan retention first, growing the avidity of casual fans second, and new fan acquisition only third. For new sport properties, the order of the marketing plan and its emphasis is obviously reversed.

While the name I gave to the escalator is industry specific, the underlying principle applies to all communities. The labels and affiliations people choose are much less important than their level of engagement and the actions they take. Small communities can be more impactful than large communities if they are more active and avid in their support of the cause they have rallied around. With a large but disengaged community, the critical task is not to add more members but to deepen the connections that tie the community together and convert affiliation into action that can make a difference. But this will only be possible if you listen to what the people want and then offer a compelling vision of what it is to be a member of that community. In our current political moment, we lack both that compelling, shared vision for a united America *and* political parties that are willing to listen and then build a unifying platform around what they hear. As a result, it should not be surprising that our political community is fracturing, and that people are increasingly looking for their group identity in factions rather than as part of the whole.

The core tools you use to build community always remain the same: listening first and then delivering a compelling vision. I firmly believe that this kind of approach is what is needed to unite our country once again, whether that is through the creation of a new political movement or by moving the current parties back toward a reasonable, moderate, or centrist perspective. As a died-in-the-wool marketer, I cannot help but look for symbolism and taglines in the world around me. It was not long after settling on the title of the current volume that I began to think of RAD as standing not only for reimagining America's dream, but also for the Republicans and Democrats at the extremes, hemming in the moderate Americans in the middle. For these parties to remain relevant as we move into the future, they will need to hear what Americans are saying and move toward them. If they fail to do so, we will need to find alternatives that are capable of bringing the country back together.

Most movements start from ideological presuppositions and try to convert members of the public to their view. This is, of course, valuable in the right time and place. But right now, at this moment in American history, the critical step we need to take is to re-enfranchise the moderate majority who have been frozen out of politics. If we want a community that works for as many people as possible, if we take *that* as our ideological starting point, then we need to listen to what those people want and deliver on it. We can apply this approach in one direction to support the growth of a new, or renewed, political movement while applying it in the other direction to repair the fractures in our national community and re-entrench our shared identity and vision for America as our national unifying principle.

Of course, when I wrote the sport marketing book with Steve and Bill in the early 1980s, politics and the broad sociology of community interactions could not have been further from our minds. The text we put together was the result of years of thought and study on the *business* of sports, and I understood business to be first, last, and always about making money. I had always been a fan of money, but when I switched my goals from a career in industry to a career in academia in my mid-twenties, I also recalibrated my expectations on this front. An academic salary could secure a comfortable life—even the lower pay I received as an instructor put me in the top 50 percent of earners at a time when the US median income was just $13,500—but I knew that it was never going to make me wealthy. That was fine, I decided, because the payoff was great job security in tenured posts and a fascinating life of the mind. My attitude changed as I went through my personal winter from hell in 1977–78. I promised myself that I would never . . . *never* . . . allow my family to be this financially vulnerable again. To prevent that from happening, I would, of course, have to avoid repeating the mistakes of taking on too much debt and making unrealistic household budgets. But the most direct and powerful way of making sure I didn't run out of money again would be to acquire a whole load of it. And if that meant looking beyond the walls of my ivory tower, then that was something I was happy to do.

The first step I took toward boosting my income straddled the academic and the nonacademic worlds. Michael Dukakis, governor of Massachusetts at the time and later the Democratic presidential candidate, had decided that the state's bureaucracy was in need of professionalization. One of the sources he turned to was the Institute for Governmental Services (IGS) at UMass, which had been founded to provide academic support and training for local government officials throughout the state. When I was invited to participate as a trainer, I seized the opportunity with both hands. The pay was $300 a day, which seemed an incredible sum to me at the time. Just one day a week would be equal to the whole weekly salary I was getting in my primary job. Naturally, I asked for two.

My request met with some skepticism at first. The work would have to be carried out alongside my full-time teaching and research job, and the training gig itself was far from an easy ride. For each training day, I would have to get up at 4.30 a.m. to drive to a government office, normally in Boston, where the training would commence at 8.30 a.m. I would then be in the classroom until four in the afternoon and would typically not make it home until seven thirty in the evening. The fifteen-hour day was a challenge, but the prospect of a financial lifeline made it more than worthwhile, and I quickly showed that I could be trusted to teach every Tuesday and Thursday throughout the academic year. Of course, that meant I had to squeeze the work of my regular job into three days instead of five, but that didn't bother me in the slightest. In fact, I rather regretted the long academic holidays, although these breaks did allow me to catch up on my research and writing.

When Chris and I returned from our summer vacation in 1978, I added another income stream, becoming a trainer for the American Management Association (AMA). This job combined my experience at the IGS with my doctoral research, which provided a great foundation for offering a three-day stress-management course every quarter. The AMA went beyond even what the IGS was offering, paying me $500 a day. By the time 1978 drew to a close, Chris and I had moved from the brink of penury to an extremely comfortable living, with my earnings from external sources amounting to more than double what the university was paying me for my job as a professor.

My first experience with the US private sector was a valuable reminder that someone willing to work hard could earn far more money in business than in academia. As I thought about the next steps I needed to take to increase my financial security, it was only natural that private business was where my mind turned. Over the next eight years, I built a series of small businesses that leveraged my theoretical, analytical, and communications skills to create new money-making ventures.

Much of my work continued to be in the training and consultancy areas, where I set up a company to market both my skills and those of others. My partner in this venture, Glenn Wong, came to UMass in 1978 to teach sports law and quickly became a firm friend. He is now perhaps the most respected legal mind in sports law in the country. In addition to the consultancy work, I also deepened my understanding of sport business by dipping my toes directly into these waters as well. One venture with Glenn involved setting ourselves up as player agents for players in the North American Soccer League (NASL). NASL players were the top tier of soccer players in the United States at the time, but it was still very much a niche sport and there was little money to go around. While agents for top basketball players were negotiating million-dollar contracts and pocketing 5 percent of the deal, we were taking away 5 percent of a $24,000 annual base pay packet, which didn't provide much compensation for the time and effort involved. Still, the work was a great education in the reality of some of the darker corners of sport business, and I learned lessons here that later helped me steer through the ethical shoals involved in running major sports franchises.

The sideline as an agent was fun, if exhausting. But the business venture that fascinated me most was an attempt—in fact, one of the very first attempts—to apply data analytics to the field of sports. The importance of collecting data and applying tools to extract value from it is a commonplace now. We all interact with data aggregation and analysis tools on a daily basis, from the apps on our phones to Internet search engines and workplace digital environments. Even the world of sports has caught on, as seen most famously in the movie *Moneyball*, with Brad Pitt's portrayal of Billy Beane's successful application of statistics to baseball.

Back in the late '70s and early '80s, by contrast, anything involving computers was a novelty outside a few hi-tech businesses. When I took up my post at UMass, my research and course materials were still laboriously hammered out on a typewriter (albeit an electric model with changeable fonts and a tiny memory that let me correct typos if I caught them quickly enough). However, the statistical work for my PhD research had given me some insight into the power of computers when it came to crunching numbers, and I was keen to see how this could be applied in my new field. Several years down the line, this interest led my consultancy business to create a database solution for tennis clubs, racquetball clubs, and health clubs, which we called Court SPIN (Sport Information Network). The goal of Court SPIN was to retain members by both improving quality of life and using data patterns to identify likely needs. We did this by installing a computer terminal at the front desk of each club, where members could check in using a membership card carrying a barcode (we were, I believe, the first company in America to use barcodes in the health and fitness niche). The computer would then verify that the member's club dues were up to date. This represented a huge advance for the industry, as the inconvenience of paper files meant that members typically continued to use a club's facilities for two months without paying once their membership expired. Similarly, simply getting up-to-date figures on club membership was a significant administrative task for owners and managers that meant spending time combing the files to look at each member's status individually. A membership database meant they could now access this information with the touch of a button.

In addition to easing the administrative burden on the club, we could also use the check-in data gathered through the cards to look for patterns in member behavior, with the goal of improving retention. Our methods were extremely crude compared to the sophisticated algorithms in use today, but they provided a fantastic foundation for developing a meaningful relationship between the club and the member. We could, for instance, see that a member had not come to play for two weeks, prompting someone at the club to reach out to ask if everything was okay. If, say, the member had developed an injury that prevented them from playing, the club could then offer the services of a resident doctor or physiotherapist with specialist training. Alternatively, if the person had broken a bone or sustained another injury that made play impossible, the club could offer to pause their membership charges for a month or two, creating valuable goodwill and giving the individual a reason not to cancel the membership instead. The program could also use data to match players with each other based on their preferred time slots and skill levels, guaranteeing that members could get a competitive and enjoyable game at any time while building connections across the membership base. While the technology was pretty rudimentary, the racquet and health clubs loved what they could do with Court SPIN and the positive impact on member retention and club income was significant.

I have continued to be fascinated throughout my professional life with the way data empowers us to reach people and connect them to each other. Of course, the digital frontier has shot ahead since my brief time as a tech pioneer in the '80s, and in the years since we have seen how data mining, data analysis, and digital connectivity can be turned toward dark ends. But I remain excited by the potential of technology, especially when I see a gap in how a social system operates. I strongly believe that we need to harness sophisticated data analysis tools if we are to bring America back together again.

Perhaps the most important role these tools can play is to help us understand the political identities of the American public with more precision and nuance. We have a blind spot in our politics at the moment: the dominance of the two main parties not only determines the policy trajectories we follow but also distorts the way we think and talk about politics by forcing individuals into misleading boxes. At the moment, all political allegiances are defined in terms of proximity to one or the other of the two-party identities. Those who do not identify with either party are not assigned any positive category of their own. Instead, they are labeled as independents or moderates, with group membership determined by the person's distance from the red and blue political poles rather than by any positive characteristics. One of the first steps we need to take if we want to re-enfranchise what researchers have identified as the majority of Americans is to adjust our data collection and analysis approach. We need to ask what unites the moderate majority rather than just what stops those with moderate views falling under the Democratic or Republican flag. Some important steps have been taken in this direction recently, but we are still far short of the kind of rich aggregated data that will really allow us to understand the needs and desires of this majority in their own terms, rather than in relation to the current two-party paradigm. It is only once we begin to grasp the common defining features of the two thirds of Americans who sit in the political center ground that we can begin to build a movement around this majority. But once we have a deeper understanding of who wants what and where their priorities lie, we can start weaving together the disparate threads to build a shared identity, a brand, that can unite these groups into a single coherent force.

CHAPTER 6

Yo Ho, Yo Ho! A Pirate's Life for Me!

When I first landed in America in 1970, it was at the beginning of a decade that would be defined by upheavals in all areas of American life. The clash between counterculture and establishment took on an increasingly dark hue as the decade progressed. Radicals turned to domestic terrorism, racial tensions exploded into violence, and the powers that be deployed highly questionable tactics in support of the status quo. The '70s also saw the end of the post-war economic boom, with the US economy suffering from a combination of low growth, high inflation and rising unemployment. Events beyond America's borders played a significant role in these changes, with US heavy industry beginning its long decline in the face of global competition while a succession of energy crises undermined consumer confidence. The national self-image of the United States as a military superpower and bastion of good governance was also dealt a heavy blow by defeat in Vietnam and the resignation of Richard Nixon, which exposed corruption and deceit at the highest levels of power.

Yet to a newcomer like me, these events were just background noise. They did nothing to take the shine off the gleaming promise of an America that offered a way of life unavailable anywhere else in the world. My experience of the country took place at the grassroots, conditioned by contact with the people and communities that formed the individual tiles in the American mosaic. And at this level, the social tensions and macroeconomic trends that dominated political discussion felt as if they were a world away. The America I was busy falling in love with was the nation composed of the many wonderful individuals I met. It was defined by the warmth and energy of its people, a core that remained untouched by the increasingly rancorous disputes the newscasts loved to spotlight.

As the 1980s began, my relationship with my adopted home began to change. I had been a resident of the United States for ten years now. America had been the site of personal triumphs and great struggles for me. My two beautiful daughters had come into this world as US citizens, and they were soon to be joined by a brother, Steven Paul. A whole generation of the Mullin family would be Americans from birth. My academic work had contributed to the body of knowledge produced by American universities. I had coached and led more than a thousand American children at summer camps and several thousand students at the college level. I was now training government officials in Massachusetts, as well as at the Federal Reserve Bank of New York, the US Navy War College, and the New York Stock Exchange. In short, I no longer felt like a migrant. I was embedded in America. I was invested in America. And, as a result, I was now far more attuned to the shifts in the public discourse than I had been when I first arrived. I still avoided political discussions as much as I could, but I was increasingly aware of the impact of policies on American society, my community, my family, and my own quality of life.

Looking back, the timing of my American journey could not have been better. I had escaped much of the doom and gloom of the '70s because my attention was focused on my studies and on building my family. Now, as I began to tune in more fully to the nation's political life, it was during a much more content and forward-looking decade. My own goals aligned with the direction of travel across the nation: instead of scrambling to survive, my target now was to achieve financial stability for my family and to lay the foundations for my children's futures.

The general consensus among Americans was and continues to be that America in the 1980s enjoyed something of a golden era, a time when the country was unequivocally moving in the right direction. With the charismatic figure of President Reagan setting an optimistic tone from the Oval Office, America was rediscovering its cultural confidence. The scars of Vietnam and the Nixon years were fading into the past, while the Soviet Union's disastrous invasion of Afghanistan cast America's positive qualities into sharp relief. The increased threat of war with the Eastern Bloc, or at least the perception of such a threat, served as a powerful unifying force, rallying the country together in the face of danger while crystallizing a new, intensified vision of what it meant to be American. The political slogan used in Reagan's re-election campaign in 1984 rang true. For tens of millions of citizens, it really felt as if it was "morning in America."

This sense of optimism was helped along by an increasingly healthy economy, but the ideology behind it was shifting away from the post-war consensus. To an extent not seen since the Roaring Twenties, Americans now backed the idea of a low-tax society with a small government at its center. The engine for economic growth was to be the individual, with the state playing an increasingly peripheral role. To support this vision, regulations were slashed across a broad range of industries, with the goal of creating a more open and more free economy in which the government would stand out of the way of the forces of economic progress.

In the course of the decade, unemployment was cut in half, inflation was brought under control, GDP soared, and the Federal Reserve interest rate fell to little more than a quarter of its 1980 peak. America, in short, was back in business. It was a time of prosperity and financial exuberance such as I had never seen before. When Oliver Stone had Gordon Gecko pronounce that "greed is good," it was intended as a criticism of the excess of the period. But for many moviegoers, the line brought an approving half smile. The idea that we should be free to pursue monetary gain without any hangups about personal enrichment was empowering for many. For me, a positive attitude toward building wealth did not mean abandoning a social conscience, it just meant accepting that individuals were best placed to choose how to help one another. That role, I and many others felt, should not be ceded to an inefficient and ineffective bureaucracy.

While I was too busy building my own businesses to become politically active, I was broadly supportive of the government's economic goals: A booming economy, I was certain, would be good for all Americans. My Catholic upbringing caused me to shy away from the notion that greed itself could be good, but I was a committed supporter of the view that growing my family's income and financial security was my primary responsibility as our principal breadwinner. As far as I was concerned, hard work was the only route to ensuring that the Mullin family could have a comfortable life, and the more fruits of my labor the taxman left in my own hands, the better.

By the mid-1980s, I had managed to build a consistent annual income in excess of $100,000. That seemed a phenomenal amount of money to me, almost absurd in its scale when I thought back to my ambitions in England fifteen years earlier. My father had represented a great economic success story for our family, taking us out of government-subsidized housing and into a comfortable middle-class life. Yet his peak earnings had never exceeded the equivalent of $20,000 per annum. As a child, I could barely imagine overshooting that amount so early in my life, let alone by such an order of magnitude. And I believe now, as I did then, that it was only possible because I had moved to America. I was proud of the accomplishment, especially when set against the financial woe of my first year at UMass. Yet I still wanted to achieve much more. The bequest my father had left to me had been relatively small, but it made an enormous difference in my life, and I wanted to give my own children the same kind of advantages. But I also saw my future in business as a challenge: I wanted to see how far I could push myself and my ideas, and in that respect the money was just a way of keeping score.

Perhaps unsurprisingly, my career as a consultant and entrepreneur was increasingly pushing my academic work to the sidelines. This shift in focus was accelerated by the difficulty of moving up in the academic world. My book on sport marketing was still in manuscript form, in part because there was not yet an established market to make it appealing to a publisher. While it was exciting getting in on the ground floor of a new discipline, an important consequence was that there were no specialist journals to publish in, no body of tens of thousands of students across the country, no field-specific career ladder to climb and few opportunities to secure research funding. With the publish-or-perish mantra becoming increasingly embedded in academia, my path to tenure, and perhaps one day a chair, seemed increasingly fraught. The business world, on the other hand, offered so many opportunities that my biggest problem was choosing which one to grasp.

Academia had been my anchor, my primary identity, ever since I began my PhD research in 1975. But I now often found myself wondering if it was time to move on entirely rather than limiting my business career to what I could fit around my teaching. So, when a speaking engagement at a meeting of Major League Baseball (MLB) owners led to an invitation to interview for a job as a senior executive at a team, the potential to take my career in a new direction was hard to resist. The position I was invited to apply for was senior vice president of business at the Pittsburgh Pirates. The role would give me responsibility for everything that took place at the franchise outside the white lines. I would be in charge of every last thing related to the business side of the team, from overall strategy and revenue generation to ticket marketing and sales, sponsorships and promotions, TV and radio broadcasting, and stadium operations, game presentation, and the fan experience. Most importantly, it would be my job to rebuild and re-engage the once-thriving Pirates fan community.

The Pirates were in an unenviable position going into the 1986 season. The 1970s had seen the team become one of the leading MLB franchises in the nation, winning seven division titles and two World Series. Then, in the early '80s, everything came crashing down. By the time I was interviewed, the Pirates were the worst team in baseball, losing a record-breaking 104 games for just fifty-seven wins in the 1985 season. Team morale and the support of the fan base had also been turned upside down by the Pittsburgh drug trials, a scandal that saw seven current and former Pirates implicated in the widespread culture of drug use on the team. The result was that the Three Rivers Stadium, the home the Pirates shared with the Pittsburgh Steelers, was hosting just 7000 fans a game on average, in a venue with a capacity of just under 60,000. The dire state of the accounts—the Pirates were losing $10,000,000 a year by this point—made it clear that the operation needed to be turned around, and fast.

The fact that the situation was so terrible gave me an opening. It was obvious to the owners that business as usual was not an option, so they were looking for someone with fresh ideas. And I had a textbook full of them. During my first interview, I pitched a data-driven approach rooted in meeting the needs of the community no matter how the team itself was doing. The board seemed keen and invited me back for further talks. But after the second round of interviews, reality set in. As part of the attempt to save the Pirates and stop the franchise moving elsewhere, a local consortium had purchased the team from its former owners. The new partnership, Pittsburgh Associates, consisted of the city itself, which put up $14 million, and the fourteen largest Pittsburgh-based companies, which put up a million each. As a result, the board was dominated by highly incisive and successful businesspeople, such as Doug Danforth, chairman of Westinghouse, and Paul O'Neil, CEO and chairman of ALCOA, (who later became secretary of the treasury under George W. Bush). With decades of business leadership to draw on, it was unsurprising that the question of my own leadership experience became a central sticking point.

After the interviews, the Pirate's president, Malcolm "Mac" Prine, took me aside and explained that the board loved my vision for the team and were convinced that my ideas were the right ones to take the business forward. But there was no way they could take the risk of hiring me. After all, I was a college professor who had run a small business with six employees. The scale at the Pirates was a whole different world. If they gave me the job, I would have nearly a hundred staff reporting to me and would be responsible for tens of millions of dollars of income and expenditure. Eager not to let this amazing opportunity slip through my hands, I suggested that they give me a trial project to test my ability to take on the full role. That way, they could see if I would mesh well with the business team and whether I could do more than just talk a good game. The board agreed, and so I began work on the highest-stakes project of my life so far.

The trial task sounded simple—look at the Pirates' season ticketing strategy and work out how we could sell more tickets—but I knew we were going to need sophisticated tools to achieve the goal. When I arrived, the Pirates only had 2,500 full season equivalents (FSEs), the industry metric for season ticket sales (two half season tickets, for example, would count as one FSE). This was a truly miserable number compared to the average of almost 10,000 across MLB at the time, and only 10 percent of what the industry leaders, the Los Angeles Dodgers, were achieving. The first thing I did was look at exactly what was on offer to Pirates fans and then assess that offering against what the fans really wanted. When I started the project, supporters of the Buccos could only buy three types of season ticket: a full season plan covering all eighty-one home games; a weekday ticket plan that covered all Monday through Friday games (roughly fifty-five games); and a weekend ticket covering all the games played from Friday through Sunday (roughly forty games). These unimaginative plans offer little flexibility for the fans, and this fact—alongside the team's dreadful on-field performance, of course—was the key reason our FSE figures were so lamentable.

What the fans wanted was a wider range of smaller mini-plans and a high degree of flexibility. For a fan to get good value from a Friday to Sunday ticket, they had to be truly dedicated in terms of the number of games they watched, and ultra-committed fans who wanted to spend every day of the weekend at the ballpark were hard to find in Pittsburgh at the time. So, the first change I recommended was to stop the senseless overlap on Friday night games between the weekday and weekend plans and to significantly broaden the offering: We would sell a Monday to Thursday ticket for the business crowd and the same full weekend ticket for the superfans.

But having listened to the market research, we then offered a range of single day plans that made it much easier for more people to come to more games. As a second step, we created something we called the flex book to give fans another way of getting discounted tickets without having to stick to a fixed schedule. If you bought a flex book, you got eleven coupons for the price of ten tickets. Each coupon could be exchanged for a ticket on any day and the book came with a voucher for a free hot dog, a free coke, and 25 percent off any merchandise purchased in the stadium. These kinds of partial plans sound obvious now, but they were innovations at the time. The Dodgers, for instance, offered only one type of season ticket, and that was the full plan, take it or leave it.

The next step was to start looking at pricing. Just like the types of season tickets on offer, there wasn't much variation in the way the Pirates had been pricing the different seats in the venue. In the course of the four months that I worked on the project, I collected the season ticket plans and prices for every other MLB team and studied them to see who was charging what for which seats. Based on this data, and the input of focus groups drawn from the Pirates' fan base, I recommended a variety of changes to *rescale the house* (redefine the pricing tiers for the different areas of seating). I then used the Buccos' financial department to run some data analysis around the strategies I developed. I was pleased to see that the modeling results showed a significant projected increase in revenue even if we only maintained the current attendance levels.

Finally, I drew on the retain-grow-acquire strategy I was teaching at UMass to argue that it was much more important for the Pirates to secure and deepen the engagement of their current fan base by getting existing fans to attend more games than it was to add new fans. Ironically, my own views on this principle of sport business had been shaped by a study I had read years earlier about attendance at Pirates matches in the 1970s. The study authors, from the Department of Economics at the University of Pittsburgh, had shown that between 1978 and the 1979 season that saw the Pirates win the World Series, the overall number of unique fans attending the games had stayed roughly the same. But because the fans had been more deeply engaged in the team's championship winning performance in 1979, each fan attended more games that year, adding 200,000 extra ticket sales to the coffers (with an even larger increase in the 1980 season after the World Series victory).

My goal was to achieve the same kind of result for the smaller number of fans still coming to see the less impressive performances of the mid-1980s Pirates. That meant building a database of supporters and marketing directly to them to try to increase attendance and to persuade people to extend their season tickets to cover more days. However, instead of sending out blanket communications to everyone on the list, I advocated taking a smarter, and more targeted approach. For instance, we knew that Friday was a big night for single guys who liked to have a few drinks with the game. Saturday night, on the other hand, was a couple's night while Sunday was largely family with kids, possibly with the grandparents in tow as well. So, instead of wasting time trying to talk family or business groups into buying packages of at least forty games, I recommended targeting the most promising groups for the games that suited them best. By taking this approach to every match day, we could reach specific groups with specific messages that were directly tailored to their specific needs and desires.

Of course, simply pushing a product will never be enough to really engage a community and build loyalty to their team. What matters is making the fans feel they are important and part of a shared endeavor. And the only way to ensure that outcome is to build meaningful relationships with them. That meant listening to what the fans wanted, being responsive to their needs and being flexible in accommodating them. For instance, if a season ticket holder had friends coming in from out of town and wanted an extra pair of tickets, but there weren't any seats available near the season ticket spots, then we needed to find a way to seat all four together even if that meant expending a lot of effort on moving things around. We needed to bend over backward to do whatever we reasonably could to improve the experience for our loyal season ticket holders.

At the end of the four months, I pulled all these elements together and presented them to the board, arguing that we needed to overhaul our business and marketing operations from top to bottom if we wanted to achieve our strategic goals. By this time, I had shown that I could work at the head of a large team and that my personality was a good fit with the existing workforce at the Pirates. From the feedback I received from Pirates executives during the project, I was confident that I had put the leadership experience worries to bed. Now it was my ideas that had to be sold. A lot of the elements I argued for, such as targeted marketing or efforts at fan retention and growth, are standard parts of the sport business playbook today. But at the time, they were so novel and so theory driven that I worried the board would see them as too much of a break from tradition. Sure, four months ago they had been keen on someone with new ideas who could come in and shake things up, but after so much time, I was concerned attitudes might have changed. I expected to take questions at the end of my board presentation, so when Mac Prine asked me to leave the room instead, I was concerned I was going to be shot down in flames. Instead, to my immense gratification, he came out fifteen minutes later with a smile on his face to offer me the job.

Excitement at having the chance to put my theories into practice had carried me through the four-month trial, but when I parked my car in the Three Rivers Stadium parking lot a few weeks later, on my first day as SVP, I had something close to a panic attack. The board had decided that they trusted me to run a major league team with dozens of staff members. I had convinced them to believe in my leadership capabilities. The problem was, I hadn't quite convinced myself. The transition from college professor to the senior executive role proved to be a real shock to my system. For the first few months in my new post, I had to talk myself into walking through the office door each morning rather than fleeing for the Pennsylvania hills.

A key part of what got me through was my own version of the American dream. To me, America was the land of possibilities, the one place in the world where anybody could become the person they wanted to be if they just showed enough grit and determination. I was being held back by my own beliefs about my limitations. But in America, more than any other country, I felt I had permission to grow beyond those limits. Like a whole generation of American executives and business owners, I found a way past the barriers I had erected with the assistance of Zig Ziglar. I often listened to his cassette tapes in the car on the way to work to help get myself into the right frame of mind, and one of his stories in particular became very meaningful for me.

Zig talked about how easy it is to train a flea for a flea circus. All you have to do is put it in a glass jar of a certain height and screw the lid on. After an hour or two of trying to jump out and hitting itself again and again against the lid, the flea will learn that it can't jump higher than the lid allows. But the important thing is, once the lid is taken off again, the flea will continue to restrict its jumps to the height it has learned is its maximum limit. The point of the story is that sometimes there are very real obstacles that prevent us from taking certain actions, yet many of us act as if we still can't achieve more even when the obstacles are removed. We have been trained to believe the myth of "thus far and no further," and this training prevents us from achieving all we can achieve. When the lid comes off our jar, we have to make a conscious effort to retrain ourselves, to align our beliefs about what we can achieve with what is now possible for us.

By the end of my first year at the Pirates, the lid was well and truly off my jar. Of course, it helped a great deal that there were measurable results I could assess my success against. Self-belief is vital for taking the first steps in a new endeavor, but sustaining that belief normally requires evidence. And watching ticket sales and revenue tick upward month by month was exactly the evidence I needed. Working in tandem with my superb VP of Marketing, Steve Greenberg, we also grew our sponsorship and broadcasting revenues significantly. In fact, as my most loyal lieutenant, much of the business success we had as a team was thanks to Steve's coaching, expertise and dogged commitment to expanding the Pirates' community.

The broadcast side of the job was entirely new to me. As part of my role, I found myself acting as executive producer for the radio broadcast of our home games. A key question I had to answer early on was whether the presenters were going to be neutral observers or slanted toward the Pirates in their descriptions of the games. With my focus on retaining and engaging our current fan base, my natural inclination was to let the presenters be full-throated partisans, so long as they didn't rip into the umpires so much that we got fined. On reflection, however, we decided to take a more moderate approach. Keeping the fans happy was one thing, but we also had to remember that going too heavy on the players—on either side—could have very real human consequences. The wives and girlfriends of players often listened in to the games, and bashing their loved ones to get a laugh from the audience could be extremely hurtful.

My views were conditioned in part by my strong support for the Fairness Doctrine, the Federal Communications Commission policy which mandated that mainstream broadcasters should deal with political topics in a balanced, nonpartisan manner. While these rules did not apply to sports broadcasting, and I felt it was reasonable for the home team presenters to slant their commentary toward the home crowd, I thought the principle behind the doctrine was extremely important. I strongly believe that the removal of this rule in 1987 marked the beginning of a race to the bottom in partisan political broadcasting that has done incalculable damage to the fabric of our nation.

On the field, the Pirates still sucked. 1986 was not quite as bad as '85, but the Pirates still managed to come bottom of the division for the third consecutive year. Despite those results, we closed out the year with our attendance sharply up on '85. The flex books we had introduced proved extremely popular, with roughly 80,000 new tickets sold through this channel over the year (in future seasons, as the team began to win on the field, we were able to grow that number as high as 250,000 flex book tickets sold). I also leaned on the business leaders on the board to fly the flag and use the Pirates as a key part of their corporate entertainment. But most importantly, we did the legwork needed to keep the loyal fans on board first, and to encourage them to grow their engagement with the team and with each other.

Over the next four years, the Pirates went from strength to strength both on and off the field. That first year, we finished forty games behind the New York Mets. Two years later, we were just fifteen behind and placed second in the division. By 1990, we had beaten the Mets and taken the division title, a feat we then repeated twice more in succession. That kind of success naturally has an impact on community engagement and helps to sell tickets. But it goes both ways. More ticket sales and a more enthusiastic crowd gives the team more money to spend and helps add a fierce pride to their play. And boy, did we sell more tickets! By 1988, with almost 1.9 million tickets sold, we had broken the Pirates all-time attendance record, bringing more people through the turnstiles than at any other time in the franchise's more than 100-year-long history. We continued to break the record anew year after year for the rest of my tenure. Following my last year at the Pirates, attendance reached more than two million, 200 percent up on our starting point in 1986. Critically, we had also turned a $10 million deficit into a $10 million profit.

Helping turn the Pirates around felt like a major personal success to me, a vindication of the theories I had developed at UMass and of the risk I had taken to jump into a new career in my late thirties. But more than that, the rapid change I saw in Pittsburgh made me realize that there is no such thing as a team that is too far gone. There is no community that cannot be helped back from the edge by rethinking the things that holds it together and by making it easy and rewarding to participate, even in frustrating times. That, I think, is a lesson worth holding onto in our present political era. We can't just wish away the challenges our country faces, but we *can* rebuild our national community so that it remains robust regardless of the difficulties we are facing.

CHAPTER 7

Rocky Mountain High

The six years I spent in Pittsburgh marked a new high for me in terms of my career. I relished the challenge of turning around the Pirates' catastrophic attendance figures and building a healthy fan community and a highly successful franchise. I was proud of pushing through my fears and anxieties and was developing into a confident and effective leader. It felt as if, by seizing the opportunity and then working on myself, I had opened up new horizons for my personal version of the American dream.

The period I spent in Pittsburgh was not, however, a time of unalloyed joy. My marriage had often been strained and it finally collapsed in 1988, sixteen years after Chris and I had first become engaged. On the one hand, the separation and subsequent divorce was a relief for both of us, a chance to start afresh and rebuild our lives based around a more mature understanding of our personalities, preferred lifestyles, and career goals. But the experience was also painful. Not only was there a sense that our shared struggles and joint achievements in the past were somehow being unwound, but I also felt a great deal of internal conflict as an observant Catholic about where exactly I stood in relation to my faith. All the teachings of the church say that in marriage the husband and wife become one with each other, forming a single unit. This was an idea I seemed to have internalized. As a result, divorce left me feeling broken and as if a large part of me had gone missing. However, our wonderful kids remained a shared achievement that could never be undone. Chris and I were determined that they should feel secure and happy, and that they would maintain a close relationship with both of us, so they continued to live with me in the family home during the week while Chris took custody at the weekend.

Toward the end of 1990, it became clear to me that my time at the Pirates was coming to an end. Doug Danforth, our chairman, had been appointed to head up the MLB committee responsible for choosing the two cities that would get new teams when the National League expanded. I was called on to assist with market research and to help review the applications. But as the process drew on, I found myself in the middle of what became an impossible conflict of interests. As part of my regular duties, I often found myself in conversation with Carl Barger, who had taken over as president of the Pirates in 1987. Carl was very interested in the work of the expansion committee. So, with Doug's permission, I briefed Carl on the committee's progress each time it met. I later noticed that one of the markets the committee was considering seemed to have the uncanny ability to respond immediately to any concerns that the committee had raised about their application.

The Florida Marlins (later the Miami Marlins) had put in a strong bid, but the committee had certain reservations. For instance, several committee members raised concerns about the lack of a purpose-built baseball stadium for the team to play in. A month later, the Marlins' bid was adjusted to announce their plans to retrofit the Miami Dolphins stadium to meet all the needs of a baseball team. Somebody on the committee then stated that this was all well and good, but there was no evidence that the interim stadium was capable of successfully hosting baseball games effectively and drawing large crowds. Low and behold, a month later the Marlins' management team announced that the venue would host a Florida Grapefruit League series between the Yankees and the Orioles, two teams resident in South Florida for their preseason training. My initial reaction was to assume that the Marlins had some forward-looking leaders who were managing to front-run the committee's concerns. It wasn't until I took a business trip down to Florida a month later that the truth came out. Leaving Miami after meeting some of the Pirates' sponsors to play golf at Doral, I happened to run into Carl at the airport. I was shocked to see that he had three senior members of my team in tow, individuals who I had believed would be holding down the fort in Pittsburgh during my brief absence. When I asked what they were doing in the Sunshine State, the story started to emerge. After various evasions, I learned that Carl had long since accepted the role of president of the Marlins from Wayne Huizenga, a client of his law firm. Huizenga, who owned Blockbuster Video, Waste Management Inc. and AutoNation, alongside the Marlins, had been using the information I was sharing with Carl to enhance the Marlins' bid. Worse, Carl had offered my three team members executive positions at the new franchise in exchange for working for him while they were still on the Pirates' payroll.

I was incensed. Not only was this an egregious conflict of interest—Carl intended to continue as president of the Pirates indefinitely after taking on the parallel role with the Marlins—but my team and I had been dragged into the middle of it. I knew immediately that I could no longer work with Carl, but I also knew that giving the board an it's-me-or-him ultimatum could only go one way. Carl was a leading Pittsburgh attorney and had been appointed as president of the Pirates because he was a trusted legal advisor to many of the key firms who owned the Buccos. Since there was little chance the board would remove their handpicked man, it was clearly time for me to go. The meeting was tense, but I had another year on my contract. I agreed to stay on for most of the season so long as I reported to Doug rather than Carl in the interim. When the period ended, I was very pleased to leave the team on a high, with a home attendance record for the season of over two million for the first time in the Pirates' long history.

With the kids splitting their time between myself and Chris, I wanted to find a way to stay in Pittsburgh, as moving elsewhere would mean giving up our shared custody arrangement. However, finding an interesting and challenging job in the sports industry without leaving the Burgh proved harder than I had hoped. Since there were no senior executive roles open at the time, I took a shot at creating a job for myself. I had thought for years that professional soccer was due to take off in the US, one of the few countries in the world that wasn't yet completely devoted to the sport. At the time, I believed that it was the indoor league format that held the most promise for America, as it could use the existing youth sport infrastructure to play in smaller indoor venues and would be immune to the variations in climate across the country. The American public had also shown a real appetite for the format. While the initial attempts to develop outdoor leagues in the United States had all been unsuccessful, the indoor leagues had been a hit. In some major cities during the '80s, indoor soccer consistently drew bigger crowds than either the NBA or the NHL did in those same markets.

With those past successes in mind, I struck a deal to revive the currently defunct Pittsburgh Spirit Professional Indoor Soccer team, with me as general manager and president. Unfortunately, it turned out I was both behind and ahead of the trend line. I was right that soccer would eventually take off again in the United States, but that followed years of success on the international level by the US Men's and Women's National Teams. Indoor soccer, by contrast, was never to recover its former glory. With a poorly thought-out league structure that allowed wealthy teams to spend their way to victory, the crowds soon lost interest. After working hard for nine months on bringing back the Pittsburgh Spirit, the Major Indoor Soccer League announced that they were folding. With no replacement league on the horizon, I reluctantly closed the project down.

With the disappearance of my last option in Pittsburgh, I had no choice but to look further afield. When the MLB expansion teams were finally announced on July 5, 1991, I was far from surprised to learn that one of the spots had gone to the Miami Marlins. I was much more interested to hear that the second franchise has been awarded to the Colorado Rockies in Denver. Not long after, I received a call from the Rockies' new president, Steve Ehrhart, whom I had met when attending a series of conferences on sports law. Steve knew that I had been involved with the market analysis work for the expansion committee, and that I was fully up to date on the situation in Denver. He also knew about my efforts to turn things around at the Pirates. I was thrilled when he told me that he wanted me to head up the business side of the operation for his new team.

Moving to a city 1300 miles away from my children was one of the hardest things I have ever done. There were tears in my eyes on that bright August morning as I packed up the car and filled a trailer with all my worldly possessions. Chris moved into my Pittsburgh house to fully take care of the kids. My family was the focal point of my life, and ensuring they would be safe and secure was what motivated me to work all the hours God sent. Yet, here I was, getting ready to head off to another city without them. The only thing that made it possible was that I was confident we would be reunited soon. If I had not believed that there was some beneficent driving force in the universe that would make things right, I don't think I could have persuaded myself to set out on that new journey west.

While I missed the kids terribly, the edge was taken off the pain by the warmth I found in the people of Denver. I had enjoyed living on the East Coast and in Pittsburgh and had met many wonderful people in the years I spent there. But I missed the friendliness, the instant connections, that had made my time in Kansas so memorable. The culture in Denver, I discovered, was very similar to that which I had left behind in Lawrence: I encountered an open-hearted kindness almost every day in my new home that helped reassure me that I had made the right choice.

The excitement of the job also helped carry me through the heartache of that first year. As long as I stayed focused on my work, I could immerse myself in the daily challenges of building a new fan community from the ground up. Not only did the need to find a constant stream of solutions to problems keep me from thinking maudlin thoughts but tackling them gave me a sense of accomplishment: I felt both confident in my ability to deliver and buoyed up by the enthusiasm of the city's residents for their new team.

Where my work at the Pirates had given me the chance to put my retain-grow-acquire framework into action, the start-up situation in

Denver meant we needed to reverse the order. Obviously, you can't retain members of a community that doesn't exist yet, so, for a new team, acquiring fans is the first order of the day. The second step remains the same: grow the fans' engagement by deepening their connections with the team and each other through attending more games. Then, as the community grows, the focus switches to retaining the fans that you already have.

We worked flat out every day to bring as many people on board as quickly as possible. I was lucky that we were farming fertile soil. While Denver had hosted several successful minor league teams over the years, it had never had an MLB franchise before. The city, and the states of the wider Rocky Mountains region, saw the Colorado Rockies as *their* team. They couldn't wait to compete in the big leagues. Even before we got started that first year, we had deposits for five times as many season tickets as the Pirates had when I started there in '86. So, it seemed obvious that the team was going to have a great start. But that wasn't enough. What would happen to all that enthusiasm if the team was lousy on the field in the first year, as would very likely be the case? It is normal for an MLB expansion team to lose over a hundred games in its first season. If we wanted our fan base to be sustainable, we needed to do more than just tap the pent-up enthusiasm of individuals. We needed to build an enduring community, one that would be able to stick it out together during the rough times as well as cheering the team on when they were doing well.

A key part to building that community spirit was effective branding, which we built around the theme of "Baseball at a Whole New Level." We leaned into the excitement of the ball flying further when hit at a 5,000-foot altitude, the chance for Denver's many transplants to see their home teams visit, and of course, the excitement of Major League Baseball coming to Colorado. We also worked hard to harness momentum, adding extra seating capacity to the interim stadium so that, with 80,277 seats, we would have the largest opening-day crowd in the 124-year history of the sport. Just as important was identifying and building connections with the different groups of fans. The result was a fan community that seemed completely unconcerned by the team's success rate on the field. Whether the Rockies were winning or losing, the fans were having a good time in each other's company.

While I could draw on a deep well of theory and practical experience for the community-building side of the job, there was another aspect that was new to me and that added to the pressure. In my previous role, I had been responsible for stadium ops, the day-to-day business of running the venue in which the team played. But at the Rockies, I was also responsible for overseeing the construction of an entirely new, purpose-built baseball stadium.

While the Rockies played their first two seasons at the Denver Bronco's home, Mile High Stadium, Coors Field was being built to become the team's permanent home from the 1995 season onward. This $300-million construction project involved more than a thousand workmen laboring together for nearly three years to build a state-of-the-art facility. The financing for the project came from a special tax district in the Denver Metro area that levied a 0.1 percent sales tax to cover the cost (notionally for a period of thirty years, although the stadium was actually paid for in just seven). As such, I was answerable not only to the board of the Rockies but also to the Stadium District board, and through them, to several million taxpayers who could call me to account for the outcome of the project. To say that I was a little nervous at first would be an understatement.

I helped create an extra problem for the construction project in the Rockies' first active season in 1993. While the team did slightly better than expected on the field, coming in second from last, instead of the expected bottom of the division, they did not exactly set the world alight. Nevertheless, the fan support from the community we had put together was unshakeable. Despite the lack of success in the ballpark, in that first year we set the MLB's all-time highest attendance record, with more than 4.4 million fans attending home games throughout the season. Not only does this stand as an unbroken record in baseball to this day, but it is also the highest recorded season attendance for any team in any sport anywhere in the world. With an average of more than 60,000 fans attending each of our home games in the early part of that first season, the powers that be decided that the original plans for Coors Field were too conservative, and that additional seating was needed. With just eighteen months more to go before the team was due to move into its new home, significant adjustments to the construction plans were needed. Sadly, by the time the stadium opened in 1995, I was no longer with the team.

Early in the 1993 season, when it became clear just how much of a business success the new team was, Jerry McMorris, the Rockies' chairman, asked me to speak to a guy named David Elmore. David was something of a legend in the world of minor league baseball, founding and owning half a dozen different teams throughout his career. One of these, the Colorado Springs Sky Sox, was the Triple-A affiliate of the Rockies. David was now planning to expand his empire into the world of hockey by setting up a Denver-based team, and Jerry wanted me to share our business plans and market analysis with him. So, I passed on what I thought would be helpful, and in the course of these meetings, David and I became friends. When he saw how unhappy I had become with the executive-suite environment at the Rockies, he gave me some great career advice: if I wanted to achieve my goal of becoming a Major League CEO or general manager, he explained, I needed to gain some experience running the sports side of a team as well as the business side. After a shake-up at the top of the Rockies left me unhappy with the environment there, Dave suggested that the best way to gain that experience would be by taking the job of president and general manager of his new hockey team.

After the last out of the 1993 season, I packed up my office at the Rockies and moved across to my new home at McNichols Arena to begin work on launching the Denver Grizzlies. The Grizzlies would be playing in the IHL, one of the two minor leagues that served as feeders for the NHL at the time. This step from major league baseball to minor league hockey was in one sense a step down. But neither the shift in sport nor the change in tier concerned me. I had long argued that sport business and sport marketing were unified disciplines, with the same rules applying regardless of the sport in question. (This was one of the reasons I insisted on the singular *sport* in the title of the program at UMass and later in the title of my book on the subject.) As for the step from the majors to the minors, I felt that was more than compensated for by the chance to run the whole operation for the first time. After the ugly politics at the Rockies, I was also more than happy to swap major league status for a happy and stable relationship with a single team owner.

The chance to run the whole shooting match at the Grizzlies appealed to the competitive sportsman in me. But more importantly, my success or failure would be critical for my long term career prospects. I knew that I had made my mark on the marketing, revenue-generating, and operations side of the baseball business, and that meant I wouldn't have any trouble finding the same kind of work elsewhere. However, if I limited myself to this field, there were few further steps up I could take. There were, of course, the big city teams in Los Angeles, New York, and Chicago, as well as baseball-mad Boston, with their huge potential fan bases, and massive revenues. But the number of roles like this was very small. Staying in the same lane but looking beyond baseball was another option I considered, with football in particular offering bigger operations to run. But still, it wouldn't be long before I also ran out of road following that route. The Grizzlies, by contrast, offered me a first step on a new career path.

Another important factor in taking the job was that I had two additional strong motivations to remain in Denver. To begin with, for the first time since my divorce from Chris, I was deeply in love. I met Val, the lady who was to become my life partner, during my first year in the city, and we hit it off immediately. We began dating shortly after, and it was not long before we were living together. The other factor was that, by the end of 1993, my kids, one by one, had chosen to come live with me in Denver. One of the most miserable days in my life had been at the end of the Christmas vacation in 1991. I had been in Denver for just three months, and every single day it felt like a large part of me was missing. That year, the kids flew out to spend Christmas with me, and we had a ball together, staying up in the mountains in a hotel with an indoor water park and hitting the slopes to ski every day. But waving them off at the airport as they caught their flight back to Pittsburgh was heartbreaking. As soon as I stepped out of the terminal, I was in tears, feeling as if a part of my soul had been wrenched away. By September 1993, the pieces of my family life had come back together, and I was eager to maintain the newfound stability we had built with Val and my kids all living with me in Denver.

I insisted to David that we should have a full year of preparatory work for the Grizzlies before our first season. I could feel in my bones that the team was going to be a great success. While the city had a top-level collegiate hockey program at University of Denver (DU) that drew good crowds, Denver had been a professional hockey desert for over a decade, since the last NHL team (ironically named the Colorado Rockies) had relocated to become the New Jersey Devils in 1982. David and I believed that there was huge pent-up demand for the sport, although I was warned by local hockey experts to tarp off all the upper-bowl seats of McNichols Arena for home games and to make sure we were never scheduled at home at the same time as the DU team. Unlocking that demand and turning it into an avid fan base felt very natural to me, especially given what I had learned about the local market and fan attitudes over the previous two years. Putting together the team itself and working toward success on the ice was another thing entirely.

The most important step we took as the preparatory period came to an end was to hire Butch Goring as head coach. Butch was a four-time Stanley Cup Winner with the New York Islanders and had coached in the NHL in Boston and New York. He was currently the head coach of the Las Vegas Thunder, where he had just earned the best regular season record in the IHL. Getting Butch on board was foundational for the success of the team, and the addition of Kevin Cheveldayoff as his assistant coach was almost as important. (Butch is now the TV voice of the New York Islanders while Chevy went on to become the successful general manager of the Winnipeg Jets in the NHL).

With Butch and Chevy on board, we were able to sign a minor league agreement with the Islanders to supply us with twelve players, whom our guys then supplemented with some highly talented IHL veterans. The team was phenomenal and our success on the ice reflected its quality. In our inaugural season we had seventy-two wins for just twenty losses and six ties. Not only did we win the regular season by a huge margin, but we also won the Turner Cup Championship and eleven of the twelve trophies the IHL awarded each year. Our success off the ice was just as overwhelming. While Denver's NHL team had drawn 8,180 fans on average in its final season in 1981–82, our minor league team averaged a league-leading 12,094 fans per game.

Despite our achievements, that amazing season and the championship victory that followed were tinged with despair. Even before we raised the trophy, we knew that the magic was going to come to an abrupt halt. The attendance numbers we drew early in the season and the level of community engagement among Denver's hockey fans had attracted the attention of the NHL and the owners of the Denver Nuggets, who also played at McNichols Arena. Seeing how well the market responded to the Grizzlies, the NHL swept in with a plan to grant Denver its own major league franchise. The Nuggets' owners had quietly purchased the NHL's Quebec Nordics, rebranding them as the Colorado Avalanche. They then took advantage of our year-to-year lease to force the Grizzlies out to make space for the new team. We had become victims of our own success.

While David could have fought the move, it would have made little business sense. Instead, we negotiated a large financial settlement with the Avalanche, and David put together a deal to move the team to Utah. I chose not to take up the offer to go with them, as my family's connection with Denver had only deepened during the two years I worked on the project. I was devastated to see the Grizzlies go, but I wouldn't have missed the experience of those incredible two years for the world.

Not only was the deal to move the Nordics to Colorado formulated, signed, and sealed in less than three months, but when the team became the Avalanche, it was able to hit the ground running at amazing speed. There was no preparatory period to build a new community. Instead, the team effectively parachuted into the arena the day the Grizzlies left and took over the existing fan infrastructure. I couldn't help but shake my head in wonder at the boldness of it all, but as we passed the midpoint of the 1990s, this kind of previously unprecedented speed of decision and action was becoming increasingly par for the course across America.

1995 was a tipping point for the digital revolution. Over the previous ten years, the proportion of Americans who had access to an Internet connection had crept up slowly from less than 2 percent to 14 percent. But now adoption exploded, with more than half the nation coming online by the end of the decade. For rapidly increasing numbers of Americans, information could be moved around and accessed almost instantaneously. The world was speeding up, and there was no going back. While my database solution for health clubs in the early '80s had required a human to literally carry the information in the form of a floppy disk from the front desk terminal to the back office for analysis and storage, now we could aggregate data from around the country, indeed the globe, with the click of a mouse button. It was hardly surprising in an age like this that large business concerns could move whole hockey teams thousands of miles with only a few months of planning.

In keeping with the attitude of the times, the prevailing view of what the Internet meant for our future was almost uniformly positive. Instant access to information would make us all smarter, globe-spanning connectivity would bring people together, and we would all move in harmony into a new era of human prosperity and happiness. Of course, the Internet was not the only catalyst for this rosy vision of the future. The fall of the Berlin Wall in 1989 and the collapse of the Soviet Union over the next two years gave the West, and the United States in particular, an unparalleled sense of cultural confidence. The feeling was hardwired into the decade that, now the Evil Empire had fallen, and the threat of nuclear annihilation had dropped away, we could celebrate the freedom and individualism that had brought us this victory. Some even spoke of "the end of history," the idea that we had seen the last of the global political revolutions and that it was now clear which political system would carry humanity through to prosperity and safety. The ease with which the United States and its allies crushed Saddam Hussein's invasion of Kuwait in 1991 only cemented the idea that the power of American-led liberal democracy was unassailable. It took just two weeks of ground action to defeat a million-man army, with the loss of only 147 men to enemy action. The idea that we had moved from dangerous times into a new world of peace and security seemed reasonable to many.

The political situation in America at the time was not exactly a utopia, but it reflected the same optimistic social outlook. An ability to compromise and forge bipartisan consensus was seen as an essential quality for any serious political figure, and, as a result, seats on the federal courts and US Supreme Court, as well as other important appointments, were typically made with the support of large majorities from both parties. Basic politeness and decency were also fundamental expectations in the political sphere, to the extent that the suspicion of inappropriate sexual behavior was enough to derail a presidency.

It is true that members of the Democratic party in Congress often focused on keeping wedge issues alive to divide opinion among their political opponents, regardless of their own views on the matter. At the same time, the Republicans brought a new wave of partisan combativeness to Washington when the 1994 mid-terms delivered success on a platform of shaking up the status quo. But these seemed small waves compared to the positivity that predominated. I, like most other Americans, was content with the country, our society, and our place in the world.

The run with the Grizzlies had been one of the most exciting episodes of my career, a perfect two years in which—thanks to hiring an unbelievably effective staff, great execution and a sprinkling of good fortune—just about every toss of the coin landed the way I would have called it. But it had also opened up a wider set of paths ahead of me than had ever been the case before. I had shown that I could create success on the field of play as well as off it, and I had shown I could operate effectively in sports other than baseball. I was as optimistic about my own future as I was about that of the nation. Now all I had to do was find a new job that used all those skills—without leaving Denver.

CHAPTER 8

Doing It for my Family

For those who had lived through the Cold War, the mid-1990s felt like the dawn of a new age: a more peaceful, more stable, and fundamentally more democratic era. Looking back, it is hard not to wince at the naivety that so many of us shared. The fall of the Soviet Union removed America's only global competitor from the scene, and with that threat gone we all breathed an enormous sigh of relief. But the absence of that great source of fear also meant the loss of a focal point that turned us outward as a nation. With the "Evil Empire" gone, it became all too easy to dismiss the conflicts that continued to rage around the world as minor issues that were irrelevant to the United States. After so many decades as the guarantor of the balance of world power, America was ready for a break.

Of course, those who were touched directly by the violence did not have the luxury of setting it aside as no big deal. The wars that shook the former Yugoslavia in the wake of the collapse of the regime there lasted a decade and killed well over 100,000 people. Tens of thousands died in Chechnya and other regions in the same period as the peoples of the former Soviet Union jockeyed for independence and position. For most in the West, however, these conflicts were just relics of the past, echoes of a world that had slipped away rather than real parts of the new order. Africa, meanwhile, received the same lack of consideration that had characterized Western attitudes for decades, if not centuries: The genocide in Rwanda that killed more than half a million civilians in just three months only received significant international attention when it was too late to stop the horrors unfolding there, while a war in the Congo that was ultimately to leave more than five million dead barely intruded on the public consciousness at all. The smoldering conflicts in Afghanistan and Israel/Palestine would later burst back into flames in spectacular fashion, while wars and civil strife in a dozen other countries led to the deaths of hundreds of thousands more. In reality, the '90s were no safer for many humans than the decades that preceded them, but a sense of invulnerability in the US made these conflicts seem far less serious matters.

At home, as abroad, it is easy to look back now and pick out many of the seeds of future discontents. The progressive liberal consensus in what came to be known as "the mainstream media" accurately represented the evolving attitudes of many Americans, particularly those clustered in big cities and along the coasts. But as that world view took over the airwaves, a large part of the population felt that their values were being neglected, that they were being silenced, driven out of the public square, and treated as if there was something wrong with them. The progressive media consensus helped pave the way for important social advances in the following decades in the fields of gay rights, racial justice, and equality for women. But it did so in large part by simply ignoring the views of many Americans, rather than persuading them. Following the repeal of the Fairness Doctrine, a new media landscape emerged, its contours shaped to reach out to this newly neglected constituency. Highly polarizing talk radio shows exploded in popularity throughout the '90s, while 1996 saw Fox News burst onto the national media scene as the first cable news network to explicitly target the conservative market. This parting of the ways, with one world view represented on mainstream outlets and another on alternative, more conservative, sources of news and commentary has only intensified in the years since, to the point that we now effectively have two competing versions of reality battling for the minds of audiences across America.

There were deeper signs of discontent as well, although, to me at least, they were so strange that they appeared as aberrations, isolated data points rather than identifiable trends. The siege at Waco in 1993, which saw the

Branch Davidians of David Koresh first contained and then killed, was a tragic debacle. Yet it was hard to draw political lessons from these events, beyond the need for the authorities to show great patience in the future when dealing with tense situations. Koresh's cult was not entirely alien—we had seen something similar in the messianic separatism of Jim Jones in the 1970s—but few commentators thought its existence offered any great insight into America's changing society. The Oklahoma City bombing which devastated the Alfred P. Murrah Federal Building precisely two years later offered a clearer indication that something in the American psyche was beginning to turn in on itself. But still, the event was so unprecedented that it was easy to see it as a one-off. The media and the national law enforcement agencies were spurred to take a closer interest in the burgeoning militia movement, but there was little in the way of national introspection. For most Americans, including myself, the bombing was simply a terrible crime carried out by lunatics who stood far beyond even the furthest fringes of mainstream politics. It was not until much later in the decade that I began to feel that these were all pieces of a bigger puzzle, that there was a more deep-seated and destructive malaise threatening to unwind the threads that held America together.

While I followed the story of the Oklahoma City bombing closely on the news, my attention was, in truth, elsewhere. I had known since the beginning of the IHL playoffs in April 1995 that the incredible run we were enjoying with the Denver Grizzlies Pro Hockey Club was coming to an end. Naturally, I started looking around for other positions. One very tempting offer came in from the San Jose Sharks. Having seen what I could do with a hockey franchise, the owners of the Sharks offered me the chance to step up to lead a team in the NHL, initially as executive vice president and then taking over as president two years later when the incumbent retired. The opportunity to head up a franchise in a sport's major league for the first time was extremely attractive, but with my son and daughter happy in high school in Denver, along with Val's son Chad, the disruption to their lives would have been too great. I also received an invitation to work with the Denver Broncos as the team's senior vice president of business, an opportunity that would have let me stay in Denver while gaining some experience working for an NFL team for the first time. Still, I decided to turn it down. Another job that was restricted to the business side of a franchise would be a step back from the leadership level I had operated at with the Grizzlies, and I was determined to keep moving forward. Looking back, I do sometimes wince at an opportunity missed. Val, a Broncos season ticket holder, never tires of reminding me that I could have two Super Bowl Championship rings now if I had taken the job, as the team went on to stunning success in the 1997 and 1998 seasons. Still, I have no regrets about my decision; the job I took instead gave me the chance to work in one of the most intellectually stimulating and most challenging roles I have ever undertaken.

On the face of it, the position of vice chancellor of athletics, recreation, and wellness at the University of Denver (DU) represented a significant departure from my previous work in sport business. However, I saw the return to a university environment as an opportunity to bring together everything I had learned so far across my business and academic careers. On the one hand, budgets in the top athletic programs among the eighteen varsity sports programs at DU were on a similar level to those of many minor league franchises. At the same time, with the university making a push to establish itself as an NCAA Division 1 institution across all its programs, there was a strategic challenge here that was immensely appealing. Not only was the challenge itself something I relished but I was eager to make a lasting contribution to the DU community, which included my daughter, Lara, a political science student, who would shortly be followed by my son, Steven, when he began his digital studies degree.

The sheer variety of hats I would have to wear was extremely attractive to me. But the decisive factor in accepting the offer was that I would have the opportunity to work closely with one of the smartest and most fascinating men I have ever met. Daniel L. Ritchie was appointed chancellor of DU in 1989 after a varied business career that took in banking, broadcasting, and senior roles in Hollywood, with some stints as an entrepreneur along the way. Dan had been on a date with Marilyn Monroe, threatened to fire Marlon Brando, and helped bring the AIDS story to national prominence as a senior news executive. In the course of this career, Dan had become extremely wealthy, sufficiently so that he was able to retire to his ranch to live a life of leisure at the age of fifty-five. When he was invited to take over as chancellor at DU, he gave up the quiet life to devote himself to a job that soon became an extension of who he was as a person. The very picture of the warm-hearted American philanthropist, Dan took home just a dollar a year for his work as chancellor and, in an inversion of the normal relationship, became the university's most generous benefactor. In 1994, the year before I arrived, Dan had helped put the university on a stable financial footing by donating a large part of the land on his Red River ranch, which DU then sold for $15,000,000. He later donated the rest of the ranch, bringing the value of his gift up to $50,000,000. When asked why, he had two replies. On the one hand, he explained, he wanted to prove to himself that he had not become trapped by his wealth, and that he could give away even his most precious belongings. On the other hand, as a chancellor and as a university, "We needed to do things."[17]

The "things" DU needed to do, in Dan's vision for the institution, included achieving excellence in every single aspect of its activities. In part, this meant modernizing the school's sports and wellness facilities and becoming nationally competitive across all its athletic programs. This was not simply a matter of pride. Dan knew that community spirit was essential for creating a successful institution, and that getting people to rally together behind their community's teams was one of the most powerful ways of creating this kind of bond. He also knew that college sports had the ability to elevate a university's brand across the nation, drawing attention and increasing the number and the quality of student applicants.

I was in complete agreement with Dan's views about the power of sports, and I was more than happy to champion them in front of the academic representatives who would have to sign off on his plans. There was, initially, some pushback. New facilities are expensive, and it is perfectly natural for a history professor to wonder why a university should plow resources into building a new gymnasium when they can see more value in endowed chair positions, graduate assistantships, and expanding the university's library holdings. Overhauling sports programs can also lead to worries about cultural changes. This concern proved to be the biggest worry for many among the academic faculty. In particular, there was a fear about the consequences of elevating our basketball program to the Division 1 level.

College basketball is played nationally at a hugely competitive level (matched only by football, a sport in which DU did not field a varsity team). The concern among faculty members was that attracting the best players would mean lowering academic standards, as the best athletes are rarely also the best students. Or, to put it more bluntly, many of the academic staff were worried that we would be bringing in a load of dumb jocks for the sake of sports success, and that doing so would have a negative impact on the academic environment for the other students. Fortunately, members of the professoriate tend to respond well to facts, figures, and reasonable arguments (most of the time, at least). Between the dean of admissions and myself, we were able to provide benchmark data in abundance from comparable universities that had made the step up to NCAA Division I Athletics. This data let us show that the increase in national prominence experienced by other colleges that had made the same move invariably meant much better recruitment results, with a massive growth in the number of student applications and an applicant pool with considerably better academic credentials. With me leading the charge as a former academic, we were able to assuage the concerns and gain the approval of the DU Faculty Senate for Dan's plans.

A key part of my task was ensuring that the facilities at DU were suitable for training at the new levels we were targeting. Our first job was to get rid of the old ice hockey rink that had served the college since the 1940s. This was essentially a large old Quonset hut that had been shipped down from Idaho, where it had served as a drill hall for the US Navy, and then re-erected in Denver with a sand floor under the ice rink. Unsurprisingly, the ice sheet fell far short of the level expected for a leading college team some fifty years later. While this was perhaps the most extreme example, many of the other facilities across campus were substandard in one way or another, and those limitations were holding back recruitment for all our teams and thus acting as a drag on the university's athletics budget. So, the next step after pulling down the old rink was to erect a state-of-the-art modern sports center containing seven separate venues.

Most of the money for the project was provided directly by Dan himself, after whom the building was named, and his multimillionaire cable TV buddies and corporate sponsors, whose names went on the various subvenues within. These included the 6000-capacity Magness Arena, with its hockey rink; the Hamilton Gymnasium, with three practice courts for basketball, volleyball, and gymnastics, and retractable seating for 2000; the Joy Burns Arena, an additional ice rink for hockey practice and other activities, such as a youth hockey program and figure skating; the Olympic-sized El Pomar Natatorium; and the Coors Fitness Center. Then there was a whole floor of offices and meeting rooms to house the staff of the eighteen athletics programs and the 192-foot-high Carl Williams Bell Tower, the third largest carillon in the United States. Additional building projects beyond the Ritchie center included a tennis center, a lacrosse stadium, and a soccer stadium. Of course, none of these buildings was on the same scale as Coors Field, but the incredible range of facilities, the need to ensure that all programs would have access to the venues they needed, and the consequent complexity of decision making made the work much more challenging. I am pleased to say that twenty-five years later these venues still meet the needs of the DU athletics programs seamlessly.

There were many other steps that needed to be executed in a short period to achieve NCAA Division I status. First, we had to apply to the NCAA themselves for the upgrade and undertake an arduous compliance process, which primarily revolved around a three-pronged gender equity test. As the DU student body was roughly 48 percent male and 52 percent female at the time of our application, we needed to demonstrate that our student-athletes were divided in the same proportion. One of the hardest decisions I had to make to ensure we met the gender requirements was cutting our men's varsity baseball program, which had been a DU institution for generations. After spending eight seasons working in MLB, this felt very much like cutting off my own right arm, although many long-time DU baseball fans made it clear that they would be more than happy to carry out the amputation themselves, preferably without anesthetic, as payback for my decision. I also had to tell the reluctant women's soccer and lacrosse coaches to accept as many women into their squads as possible, regardless of talent, to help meet the required numbers, while putting tight caps on membership in the men's squads of both those sports. None of those decisions were well received by the coaches, athletes, families, or fans. I am enormously thankful that I took them in the days before social media. I am certain there would have been online crowds calling for my head if it had been done today.

The next difficult but necessary step was to replace ten of the eighteen varsity coaches in the course of the first two seasons to ensure we had people in place with the experience and ability to lead nationally competitive Division I programs. One of the darkest moments in this period was learning that one of the coaches I had let go tried to kill herself that evening. Fortunately, she went on to recover and to live a happy life, but the episode made me more acutely conscious than ever that the decisions I was taking—and which needed to be taken—had very real human consequences.

While the basketball program did not reach, and has not since reached, the level of success that we had hoped for, in other areas DU's record has been impeccable. In the twenty-five years since we overhauled the sports programs, the university has become home to one of the top ten gymnastics programs in the nation. It has made it to the NCAA men's hockey tournament on twenty occasions and won two NCAA Division I national championships. Along with the University of Utah, DU dominates the

NCAA national competitions in skiing and has since won a staggering ten national championships. The DU men's lacrosse team also won the NCAA Division I national championship in 2015. Perhaps the best measure of the success that sprung from the hard decisions we made is that, overall, DU has won thirteen out of the last fourteen NCAA 1AAA championships (those who compete in all Division 1 sports except football). I am one of many who think that DU has the finest athletics program in the nation on the basis of this record. The long-term success of the program, lasting for many years beyond my own time at DU, is a testament to Dan Ritchie's vision for the university. As predicted, these achievements in sports have driven the volume and quality of applicants through the roof, making the university a better place to study for its students and to teach and research for its staff.

After the initial struggle to gain the faculty senate's approval for the Division I push, I was impressed by how quickly and completely the academic staff at DU rallied together around the expanded athletics program. Of course, there were some who remained unpersuaded, and every university is home to more than a few professors who, quite reasonably, find the paychecks for athletics team coaches absurd when set against their own. Nevertheless, the cultural tension between academics and athletics was largely resolved as the two sides focused on their shared endeavor. That's not to say I didn't find myself rolling my eyes at some of the attitudes and activism that seemed to have become increasingly entrenched in campus life during the two decades I have been away.

In many cases, it was the means used rather than the ends aimed at that I found distasteful. Certain areas of the humanities and social sciences, it seemed to me, had developed what I can only describe as authoritarian streaks. I could agree with the stated goals of some activist students and faculty members, such as increasing the representation of women and people of color on curriculums that had their roots in an earlier era when all the levers of power were controlled by white men. But when the arguments shifted from making a positive case for inclusion to a widespread condemnation of Western thought and history, I found myself recoiling. A discourse that aimed to denigrate, tear down, and replace the cultural world shared by most Americans felt at the time like an act of unwarranted aggression seeking completely unnecessary ends. In the years since, I have come to understand the origins and desired impact of this school of thought a little better, and I now have a rather more sympathetic view. Nevertheless, I continue to believe that the outcomes at which these approaches aimed could be achieved far more effectively through positive engagement and incremental change. Taking constant steps toward a "more perfect union," we can work to build consensus around the changes that are needed, moving step-by-step toward our goal without tearing down everything that has come before.

Instead, the route that is increasingly pursued on campuses around the nation leans into a self-righteous anger and an attitude that the prevailing culture is an enemy that must be brought low. As I read the news and watch the direction of movement in our current events, I cannot see that this is an effective or helpful approach. The kinds of fringe views that were once the purview of a handful of radical campus ideologues have found a new reach through the power of the Internet, which has helped amplify them in much the same way as the views of the extreme right. Positions that could once only be whispered in small groups have now become embedded as central tenets at one extreme of a full-blown culture war. To give just one example, alarming numbers of students on campuses today apparently have no problem with calls for genocide so long as it points in the "right" direction, as determined by those doing the speaking.

I found my own social and political views evolving during my time at DU under the influence of a very different sort of discourse, one that showed how people can be encouraged to discover nuances and to develop new positions without imposing an ideological straitjacket. A key part of this personal evolution came from simply spending time in the company of Dan Ritchie, especially when traveling to schools that belonged to the athletic conferences we were seeking to join. Dan combined a brilliant, incisive mind with a sensitive and thoughtful soul. He was detail oriented and data driven yet had a passion for the arts and the humanities. Dan was a true renaissance man who saw it as his mission to persuade people to change their minds rather than to bully them into conformity. That is not to say, however, that he wouldn't argue with great force for things that mattered to him.

Dan could, and frequently did, cite chapter and verse on America's failure to train and promote members of minority groups to leadership positions. What impressed me most about his approach was the way he connected a commitment to justice with a deep-seated practicality that valued real, measurable change over anything else. When he showed me the figures on just how underrepresented these groups were at the highest levels in the country, I was blown away. I had known that there were issues, but my assumption since I arrived in the United States had been that the country was on a slow but steady climb toward real equality. Learning that were no black billionaires at all in America more than thirty years after the Civil Rights Act was passed shocked me to the core. But Dan's example showed me that it was possible to shift these kinds of stains on our country's history and that we had an obligation to do so; there were solutions we could and should enact at the individual, institutional and governmental levels. And those solutions would start with each one of us committing personally to take action. What was necessary was the matching of principles and practicalities, not the abandonment of one in favor of the other. Dan embodied this balanced approach. After convincing someone that things needed to change, he would immediately pivot to talk about exactly which steps we needed to take, laying out an achievable plan and bringing on board, as a new advocate for fixing the system, the individual who had previously been a doubter. In doing so, he made it clear that it wasn't American society and American values that were at fault, but a fundamental failure to live up to those very ideals. Solving that problem meant bringing about real and effective change from the grassroots on up, not imposing it from the top down.

A key element of Dan's vision for DU was to turn it into a center for developing the next generation of our nation's leaders by providing them with a global perspective on the problems facing society. And as part of that mission, he was dedicated to broadening the backgrounds of those attending DU so that the leaders it sent out into the world would better represent society at large. This was where his practical side came to the fore. Having a broader range of people in leadership positions wasn't just a matter of representation and addressing historical failings. Looking to the future, what was most important for our communities was harnessing all the talent that was currently sitting on the sidelines and going unused. Once we had our values straight and began to live up to them, the best thing we could do, he believed, was use the resources at hand to build our society up rather than pull it down.

My conversations with Dan ignited a spark in me that has since become a burning passion for effecting real and meaningful social change. When thinking about increasing representation in leadership roles, I saw that it was certainly important to adjust attitudes on the recruitment side of the equation that might stand in the way of applicants who belonged to minority groups. But to maximize the pool of future leaders, we also needed to create accessible pathways for those who were growing up in situations that closed off traditional routes for advancement, such as a college education. For many communities around the nation, especially underprivileged or minority communities, a child's chances of success had little to do with their natural talents and much more to do with their parent's socioeconomic circumstances. Real representation at the top of society means bridging the gaps at the bottom to ensure that anyone with the capacity to succeed can forge a path through life on their merits.

Working alongside Dan and hearing him speak so passionately about the need to heal divisions, bridge gaps, and address the inequalities in society had a huge impact on me. Yet just as I began to turn my attention to the divisions that already existed, new fissures were opening up in our social fabric that threatened to undermine the foundations of our whole nation.

When my daughter Lara moved to Denver after her sophomore year in Pennsylvania, she joined Val's son at Chatfield High School. My own son, Steven, followed them just a few years later. Chatfield is a wonderful school, situated in a beautiful setting just east of the foothills of the Rockies. Located in the suburb of Littleton, the school sits on the southwest edge of Denver, in one of the last built-up places before the plains meet the Hogback, the first ridge of the Red Rocks. As a sports fanatic, I enjoyed watching the Chatfield teams play just as much as I loved watching DU. The interschool rivalries that grew up around these games provided a great way of getting to know a little about other parts of town, and it was in this context that I met some of the kids and parents from Chatfield's archrival, Columbine High School, located just a few miles to the east of Littleton.

On April 20, 1999, I was eating lunch in Glendale, a suburb of Denver, with some coworkers. One of our favorite spots was a little Asian place that served fantastic rice bowls. We would huddle round a table in the small dining area, talking and planning and eating while a tiny black and white TV played away in the background. That Tuesday, I was chasing some grains of rice around my bowl when my colleague Mark Ehrhart nudged me and pointed across at the TV. "That looks like Columbine High." I hurried across and crouched in front of the screen, watching as firetrucks and SWAT team members maneuvered into place around the school. I was rooted to the spot as we turned up the TV volume and listened in horror to the reports that were starting to emerge about the carnage inside. The murderous spree by two teenagers had left a dozen students and a teacher dead. I later learned from one of the senior SWAT officers present on the scene that day that the killers had rigged up explosives in the upper floor of the school with the aim of bringing the library, with its heavy book stacks, crashing down into the cafeteria below at lunch time. The goal was to kill at least a thousand of their fellow students, which might well have happened if not for the poor wiring on the bombs they placed.

I was stupefied by the horror of the event, unable to wrap my head around what possible motivation could lead a pair of kids down such a murderous path. A few days later, Val and I went along with thousands of others to listen to Vice President Al Gore give a memorial address in the school's parking lot. I found it hard to listen to his words. My attention was drawn inexorably to the flower-covered cars of the victims that were still parked in the lot, a devastating reminder that a journey to school could be a life-ending one-way trip for some.

The event remained at the front of my mind for weeks after. With Columbine High School still an active police investigation scene, the remaining students were sent across to Chatfield to continue their studies until their own school was ready for them to use again the following year. I thought about them and what they had been through every day. Whenever the newspapers or TV showed pictures of the kids who had been murdered, my heart leaped into my throat. These children would never finish high school, would never go on to live out any version of the American dream that was their birthright. I felt such enormous gratitude that my own children were healthy and happy, that I should be so fortunate to have three such wonderful kids of my own, and Chad as my fourth child through my marriage to Val. I could not dwell for more than a few seconds on the thought of what it would have felt like if the attack had taken place at Chatfield instead, at what it would be like to lose even one of my own beloved family. Whenever the idea intruded into my mind, I had to push it away quickly to prevent the emotions it raised overwhelming me.

In the years since, I have watched my children grow into fine, upstanding citizens, each serving their nation and their community in their own way, and three of them now raising the next generation of Americans to be better than the last. But I still think of the kids lost at Columbine, that appalling waste of potential that robbed both their families and our country of something indescribably precious. Perhaps the most tragic aspect of what took place that day is that the Columbine massacre is remembered now not just as a terrible event in its own right but as the start of an epidemic of school shootings that has since taken the lives of hundreds more young Americans, some as young as six years old.

Four years and a day after the Oklahoma City bombing, the Columbine massacre made it plain to me that there was something wrong in American society that extended further than random acts of violence that had no definable cause. A clear pattern was beginning to emerge of a society in which increasing numbers felt not just apathy but hatred toward their own communities, a society in which some children chose to express their frustration by taking the lives of other children. That pattern has only crystallized in the years since, with mass shootings in malls, churches, bars, movie theatres, and other public spaces. So frequent are these events that we seem to be becoming increasingly desensitized to these horrors, allowing them to become part of a new normal in modern American society. As yet, we have done almost nothing to identify and address their causes.

I suspect that one key culprit is the increasing tide of social alienation that is cutting away the anchors that hold us together as a community. We will not, I think, see the end of this epidemic of mass shootings until we resolve the deep structural tensions that are pulling us further and further apart from each other. Part 2 of this book attempts to move us some way toward understanding these tensions, first by pointing out some of the serious inequities that blight our society and then by offering practical and implementable solutions to respond to these problems.

CHAPTER 9

Big Apple, Here We Come

The turn of the millennium marked the start of my fourth decade in the United States. As is sometimes the way with these things, the universe saw fit to mark the occasion by taking me back to the very beginning of my American journey. After thirty years of moving back and forth across the United States, I found myself living and working in New York for the first time.

I had, of course, visited the great engine room of the American economy many times in the intervening period, both on vacations and for business. While my first experience of New York in 1970 had been terrifying, the city had grown on me in the years since. New York was always vividly alive, a place full of planning and plotting, innovation, and activity. I came to admire the spikey abruptness of the natives, an attitude that seemed designed for getting things done in a city in which everyone lived on top of each other. And the sheer concentration of business and creative talent was breathtaking at times. When I described New York to visitors from England, I would sometimes catch myself sounding like the Uncle Percy of my youth, extolling the virtues of the Big Apple as if it had always been in my blood. However, if I am to be completely honest, the biggest factor that turned around my view of New York was the relative absence of threats to life and limb in my later visits. While my first trip had been marred by a dead body, a police raid, and an armed robbery, the thirty years since had seen an incredible transformation, with crime rates falling to generational lows, and a sheen of respectability settling across most of the five boroughs.

Still, while New York had become one of my favorite places to visit, taking a job there was not on my radar when I moved on from the University of Denver. Instead, I had something very different in mind. The sport business landscape in the United States is a vibrant and constantly evolving world, so when I was offered the chance to head up the league for an up-and-coming new sport I was immediately interested. Roller hockey on inline skates was a high-speed and exciting sport that had similar dynamics to ice hockey but without the expensive infrastructure required to maintain an ice sheet. The blockbuster 1992 movie *The Mighty Ducks* had caught the imagination of many young kids across the country, fueling interest in all forms of indoor hockey. Roller hockey was one of the beneficiaries, riding the wave of a surge of enthusiasm across the country that led to the formation of a professional league the next year. This initial popularity launched over thirty franchises and secured national exposure for the sport through a multiyear broadcast agreement with ESPN. Management problems then led to the league going on hiatus for two seasons toward the end of the decade until I was hired to bring it back into action in 1999.

Critically, the evolution of the Internet had created a new platform we could use to communicate directly with potential fans, and a key part of the challenge for the project was to build the online infrastructure necessary to create an effective marketing channel. While I thought long and hard before accepting the post, I was ultimately persuaded by the enormous signing bonus the league owner put on the table. This cherry on the top of an already generous salary would allow me to fulfil a personal ambition I had been nursing since leaving Pittsburgh: It would give me enough money to purchase and operate my own indoor soccer team, with the resources and local support to put this sport on the map as well.

The package I was offered seemed almost too good to be true, and that should have set the alarm bells ringing. In fairness to myself, the league ownership group had an excellent sport business pedigree, but I should have picked up on the early warning signs that the owners' agenda was not focused on the interests of the community they wanted me to build. In the end, my mercifully brief attempt to re-establish a national roller hockey league turned out to be the single most frustrating business decision of my life. Everything went well on the sports side of the equation. Working with eight operators from around the country, including two NHL franchises and one NBA team owner, my executive team and I got the league back up and running in just a few months. We then completed a successful first season in 1999, growing the fan base to a level that saw almost 10,000 supporters watching the final in person in Anaheim (the home of the Mighty Ducks). But a successful launch was not enough for Raj, the league's primary investor. His goal was to use the initial return season success to bring in the kind of big-league investors who would push the valuation of his ownership stake into the stratosphere. It didn't matter to him how well the league did as a business. His real interest was in maximizing the share value, and if we could not get the bankers excited, the project was a bust as far as he was concerned.

When we took our pitch to the New York banks and investment houses in the summer of 1999, we went equipped with a detailed 100-page plan that outlined the league's almost decade of operation and its broadcast success in its earlier incarnation. We had excellent data showing a stable core fan base and team-by-team statistics documenting the rapid expansion of interest we had achieved in the current season thanks to our strong focus on community-based marketing. We even had an offer to take the league back onto ESPN to put our games on TV screens across the nation. None of this mattered. We had timed our trip exquisitely badly. When we arrived in New York with our pitch, Wall Street was in the grips of one of its not infrequent bouts of "irrational exuberance," with the dotcom bubble closing in on the heights of the insanity it would reach before finally bursting the next year. Companies promising to make fortunes on the new frontier of the Internet were racking up incredible returns for investors with nothing more than a smart domain name and an untested idea. The steady income and solid long-term prospects of our pitch just couldn't compete with the 1000 percent annual returns that some tech stocks were seeing. As a result, the response to the league was lukewarm at best, and we got used to seeing the eyes of the moneymen glazing over as we walked them through our business plan. Nobody, it seemed, was very interested in roller hockey by itself, whatever the business fundamentals said. But that didn't mean the bankers' pocketbooks were closed to us.

While the sport business part of the pitch was met with yawns, when we described our marketing plans, the room would suddenly come alive. One important plank of our long-term marketing strategy was to create an online portal for extreme sports. This would not only allow us to communicate with the growing roller hockey fan base but would also help us get our events in front of the broader extreme sports audience who were willing to look beyond traditional American sports to get their competitive fix. Our plan was to provide a community hub where fans who were into any outdoor or extreme sports could come together in one place to share their interests. The simple fact that we had plans for a website tapping a so-far unserved market was enough to snap the potential investors out of their torpor. The magic words "dot com" were far more interesting to those hooked on the tech boom than anything as prosaic as a potentially successful sport.

Our pitch for the league investment was detailed in a comprehensive report, showing every last detail a diligent investor could ask for. Despite repeated visits to Wall Street, we didn't get a single investment offer for the core business. For the ten-page concept paper outlining the currently nonexistent extreme sports portal, on the other hand, we had two written offers, each for more than $100 million in backing. The amount of money on the table was so absurd that we could have funded the roller hockey league as a side project of the portal. Unfortunately, Raj got carried away by the investing excess of the moment. Instead of grabbing what was on offer with both hands, he continued to arrange meetings with more and more private equity firms, convinced that he could land an even better deal. Eventually, the firms who had made the initial offers got cold feet and backed out, leaving us with no investors at all.

In the end, Raj decided to not only force me to pull the plug on the league, but to walk away without any warning, cutting all ties when there were still many bills to be paid. I had deferred my signing bonus to avoid putting pressure on the league's cashflow in its first year back in front of the crowds. With no money left in the league's bank account, and the season not yet finished, Raj left me with a huge mess to resolve. The office staff I had hired and the suppliers we had made deals with were facing deep financial trouble if their checks did not come through. As I had been responsible for negotiating the deals, I felt morally obligated to clear all the outstanding debt using my own financial resources, so I made things square with the suppliers and ensured that everyone on the team received three months' notice and severance pay.

All in all, the project was a financial disaster for me: between the lost bonus and the costs I shouldered, I was down slightly more than three-quarters of a million dollars. But it was also an amazing learning experience, teaching me several important lessons that have stayed with me since. First and foremost, the blind assumption that every individual will act in the best interests of their community is a dangerous thing. America's economic and social systems are incredible engines for unleashing individual potential, but they are far less effective at holding people to account or restraining unprincipled behavior. Second, the forces that move the financial markets are frequently inscrutable and often irrational. And when the chickens come home to roost, it is typically the average American who pays the price in the form of lost investments, increased taxes, and a significantly diminished economy. Both of these lessons led me to think more carefully about the need for regulation in the commercial field. A commitment to maximizing the range of a company's free action in the commercial sphere has been one of the factors that has helped drive America's economic growth across the last two centuries. But this has never been an all or nothing proposition. Sensible regulations on investment and commerce have been essential tools for developing systemic resilience and a resilient system is essential for avoiding the kind of economic shocks that have shaken the faith of many Americans in their nation over the last two decades.

Despite the unfortunate outcome of my brief roller hockey adventure, the timing left me perfectly placed to take up a once-in-a-lifetime opportunity. Dr. Bill Sutton, my friend and coauthor of *Sport Marketing*, had been engaged by the NBA as a consultant in 1999 while on sabbatical from UMass Amherst, where he been appointed to my old position as professor of sport business and marketing. As the millennium came to an end, the NBA was facing one of the most challenging times in its recent history. The retirement of Michael Jordan in January 1999 had led to a significant drop in basketball's audience and revenue figures, a change in the financial landscape that created a major problem for the commissioner of the NBA, David Stern. Stern had made a promise that the NBA's players would, as a group, be the best-paid athletes in the world, and that their collective pay would only ever increase as the years passed. That promise was now in danger of being broken. Dr. Bill was called in to help develop a response plan that would turn revenues around and ensure that Stern could keep the promises he had made.

One of Bill's central suggestions was that the NBA should set up a department dedicated to creating and implementing marketing and business operations best practices across all the teams in the league. Along with building the necessary support systems, staffing, and resources at the league level. The Team Marketing and Business Operations division (TMBO, as it came to be known) would operate as an in-house McKinsey-style consultancy, collecting data from across the teams, analyzing it to determine what worked well and what did not, and then sharing the best practices across the league to make sure that every team could maximize revenues by optimizing the way it did business. The plan Dr. Bill proposed quickly won David Stern's support. His suggestion that a certain Bernie Mullin should head up the new division received a rather different response: "Who the f*&@ is Bernie Mullin?"

At Bill's urging, I sent in my resume to give David an initial answer to his entirely reasonable question (I had, after all, never worked with a professional basketball team before). A few days later I was invited to put together a presentation to deliver to every NBA team president and chief marketing officer at the association's annual marketing meeting. I started my talk by holding up an invoice I had recently received for a season ticket. The envelope was addressed to Dr. Bernie Mullin. They clearly knew who I was and how to contact me. More importantly, the invoice had my name and address on it as well, an essential element if the team wanted my money! Then I held up the accompanying letter. It opened with "Dear valued season ticket holder" . . . I let the words hang in the air for a moment before asking how valued that greeting would make a season ticket holder feel, *especially* when the team could get the person's name right on all the impersonal elements of the mail. Of course, this was a very small thing by itself, but in the rest of my presentation I went on to show just how much these small things mattered, and how incremental improvements in the team's relationships with their fan communities could have an enormous impact on revenues.

The big point I wanted to make was that small gains could have a much larger impact than one might intuitively think. I gave the example of a team with a hypothetical 90 percent season ticket holder retention rate, which meant that the team could expect to lose one in ten of their most important fans per year. If that retention rate could be pushed up to 95 percent—an apparently small increase when compared to the previous rate—those losses would actually be cut in half, dropping to just one in twenty season ticket holders being lost each year. And the best route, I argued, to making those gains was to ensure that ticket holders felt that they were truly valued members of their team's community, a process that started with including their names properly on all correspondence. I was sure I had gotten the job when David Stern leapt to his feet in the middle of the presentation and shouted, in his inimitable style, "This is f*&@ing brilliant!"

The success of TMBO was nothing short of exceptional. In our first year, across the NBA, we grew ticket revenues alone by $250 million.

By the end of the second year, season ticket retention was up 4 percent and revenues across the league continued to grow. When we turned our attention to growing group tickets and single-game ticket sales, we met with similar success. In my third season with TMBO, we added marketing partnerships to our target list, achieving a 21 percent growth in existing sponsor revenues and a similar figure for new sponsors. In total, this amounted to approximately an additional $100 million per annum in incremental and new sponsorship income.

These gains were by no means easy to achieve. A core challenge we had to overcome was the natural resistance to sharing data between teams. Sports leagues are built around competition, and the teams naturally see each other as bitter rivals for success. A big part of my job was convincing all involved that this competition only extended as far as the boundaries of the court. When it came to *business*, the best route to optimal performance for everyone was through collaboration. The legacy I am most proud of at the NBA is the success of TMBO, with David Stern's vital support, in creating a community that brought all the teams and their owners together around the goal of sharing data. No other major American sport has yet managed to achieve this same level of team collaboration and cooperation despite many attempts.

One of our initial struggles in forging this community-oriented mindset was to overcome the reputation of the NBA's previous Team Services division. Team Services had essentially acted as cops or auditor, checking that teams were conforming to the league's rules and issuing fines to those who failed to do so. Like TMBO, their mission was to raise standards across the organization, but they operated as if the NBA and the individual teams had competing agendas. One of my first goals with TMBO was to demonstrate to the teams that we were on their side, and that our job was to help them make as much money as possible. A key component in this strategy was making sure that the credit for running successful initiatives went to the teams, even if the plan came from TMBO. But we also had to change attitudes from the ground up, and that meant building personal relationships with the management team at every franchise so we could hear what they needed from us and then deliver it.

That step was much simpler for the teams whose attendance and revenue figures were near the middle or bottom of the league. With few exceptions, the executives at those teams were open to pretty much any and all ideas and systemic changes we could offer them. In a few cases, we came across insecure executives who were resistant to our ideas, but most of them came around when they saw the effectiveness of the programs we put in place. And for those who wouldn't jump, David Stern was there ready to give them a push. I have a vivid recollection of an owners' meeting at which I was called on to present some of the new sponsorship concepts TMBO had developed, along with data on how successful they had been at the teams that had implemented them. Just as I was about to start speaking, David stood up and, with a dramatic flourish, informed the owners of two teams that they would have to leave the room. Since these two franchises had refused to share key sponsorship contracts, he informed them, they could not expect to benefit from the analyses we had conducted on the data from the rest of the teams. Unsurprisingly, the embarrassment of being thrown out combined with rumors about the value of the insights they had missed out on soon brought these two last holdouts around.

In my first year with the NBA, I assumed that getting the teams to see how their interests aligned would always be my toughest challenge. My guess was proved tragically wrong in 2001, when we were forced to tackle a situation that was unprecedented in modern sporting history. For myself, as for many other Americans, September 11, 2001, was a truly devastating day. I had traveled into Manhattan early that morning from my home in Hastings, Westchester County, on what seemed a perfectly normal fall Tuesday. As I did on any other day when I wasn't on the road, I took the 7.50 a.m. express train from Greystone Station into the city, arriving at Grand Central Station around 8.20 a.m. From there I walked the few blocks up Madison Avenue to the NBA's Olympic Tower offices.

As a good Catholic boy, I passed through St. Patrick's Cathedral as I did every morning, lighting a candle, taking communion, and saying a few prayers before heading directly across Fifty-First Street to my building. When I walked inside, it was a regular day in New York. By the time the elevator reached my office on the fourteenth floor, the whole world had changed.

The first sign that something was wrong was the sound of my executive assistant, Joanne, crying uncontrollably while struggling to speak on the phone. I had hired Joanne away from the investment bank Cantor Fitzgerald shortly after I moved to New York. I later learned that when I reached the office that morning, she was on a call with three of her best friends, all trapped in the North Tower with almost the entire Cantor Fitzgerald New York staff. Joanne's three friends were among more than 600 of her former colleagues who tragically died that day. I rushed down the hall to the corner conference room that provided views down Fifth Avenue to the World Trade Center. Even from three miles away, I could see the damage that the first plane had done to the North Tower.

Over the next ten minutes, the room began to fill with the attendees for our daily rapid-response communications meeting. Very little was said as we stood together in a huddle, staring at the TV on the corner wall. We were listening to the morning news and trying to understand what was going on when the second plane struck. As I turned to the window and looked down Fifth Avenue toward the Twin Towers, I saw an enormous cigar-shaped plume of fire and smoke erupt from the north side of the South Tower. Like many others, I handled the horror of the moment by entering a state of detachment. From that second until I finally reached home in the late afternoon, my memories are eerily distant, almost as if I had been watching myself in a movie, observing from the outside. The later collapse of the towers . . . the roiling clouds of dust in the street . . . the ghostly sight of an unmoving man in a business suit, covered head to toe in grey-white ash as he sat across from me on the train home . . . it all appears flat and faded in my mind.

Trauma followed all of us home that day. Many Americans already lived precarious lives, lacking economic safety nets or exposed to crime and other dangers in their communities. But 9-11 brought a sense of fear to everyone, the feeling that nowhere was truly safe, that even in the very heart of America's largest city, lives could be extinguished by the thousands because someone, somewhere, wished us ill. For me, the aftermath was, if anything, even harder to bear than the pain of the day itself. When we returned to the office a week after the attacks, the funerals began. St. Patrick's was the chosen venue for many of the Catholic victims of the attacks, including many of the Irish, Italian, Polish, and Hispanic Americans who made up such a large part of the heroic first-responder teams that were lost when the towers came down. The funerals continued seemingly without end, day after day. And every day I looked down and watched from my office window, pausing to say a prayer for the fallen. I used to love bagpipe music, and the skirl of the pipes as they struck up "Amazing Grace" in particular. But since those grey, mournful weeks across September and October 2001, I cannot hear that hymn without being reminded of all those lives lost, all those dreams cut short.

Like the rest of the country, I was determined that the terrorists should not be allowed to win. There would be no going back to normal—not for a long time; not for months or even years—but it was clear to me that we had to start living our lives again, refusing to allow the attackers to steal the joy and pleasure we found in the rituals of American life.

As head of TMBO, David Stern charged me with leading the group that would bring together the thirty NBA teams to set our joint strategy for the start of the 2001–02 season in October. One of the first things we did was carry out a security assessment of all NBA venues. This led to the shocking discovery that twenty of our sites were vulnerable to a poison or toxic chemical attack through unguarded air intakes located within easy reach at ground level. The result of the assessment was that our venue entrance security protocols immediately became far stricter. But while we all accepted that we had moved into a new world in which much tighter security would be the norm, we were determined that our events should be symbols of American strength rather than fear.

Our country was hurt and angry. In New York, the smell of smoldering rubble and toxic fumes hung in the air for weeks, a constant reminder of the devastation that had been visited on the city. I felt that as we restarted league play, we needed to respect those feelings but also work through them by helping Americans channel their grief in a community setting. That meant acknowledging the pain with a moment of silence before each game and then letting the competitive fun carry our audiences away once play began. We made sure to provide complementary tickets for first responders to say thank you to them on behalf of the nation, and once military operations began, we extended the same gratitude to members of our armed services. But more than anything else, the goal was for our games to go on as normal, to support our collective return to the regular rhythms of life as soon as possible. This, I was certain, was the best way to give Osama Bin Laden and his evil crew the biggest middle finger possible.

For a time, 9-11 touched everything we did at the NBA, as it touched every other part of American life. Even as a semblance of normality began to return, it was clear that something profound had changed in America, perhaps permanently. The optimism and the sense of invincibility that had been a constant presence throughout the '90s was gone, as was the economic confidence that had been undermined by the bursting of the dot com bubble and the recession that followed. And yet, in the face of tragedy, the country came together to an extent that I had never seen before. For months, no one honked their horn on the streets of Manhattan, even as more and more vehicles returned. People stepped aside for each other on the streets and angry words were a rarity. It was as if New York had become another world.

There was something deeply noble and touching in the unquestioning support Americans showed to each other in the aftermath of the September 11 attacks. But in the long term, this pause for breath in the brewing culture war only served as an accelerant. Unfortunately, the geopolitical and legislative decisions we took as a nation following 9-11 were not always wise. For nearly twenty years afterward, America was engaged in foreign conflicts that achieved very little at enormous expense, in terms of dollars spent, Americans lives lost, and worse yet, the animosity and long-term hatred across the Arab and Muslim communities. Our choices shook international confidence in our strategic and moral leadership while funneling trillions of dollars into futile causes abroad that could have been transformative if spent at home.

One of the two most dangerous consequences of what came to be called the global war on terror was the erosion of trust in our government and media that came from the questionable decision to invade Iraq and the failure of the press to hold decision makers to account. The other, I believe, was the normalizing of anger and emotion over dispassionate rationality in the political arena. Initially, this was a unifying force. Our anger as a nation was righteous; our emotion at the murder of thousands of our fellow Americans was heartfelt. But after the period of unity that followed the attacks, when the politics of division resumed as usual, it did so, it seems to me, with greater violence and a greater willingness to set aside reason than had been the case before. Over the past twenty years, first gradually and then like a dam collapsing, extreme feelings, words, and attitudes have pushed their way into the mainstream on both sides of the political debate. We have entered a morally polarized world in which activists and politicians stand behind symbols and causes, dividing Americans into us and them, the good and the bad, with no nuance and no room for the many shades of gray that are a feature of the real world. If we are to bring America back together in an enduring way, if we are to get past the divisions and come to love each other once again, or at least not hate each other, then we need to take conscious action to find a new way forward. And that means laying to rest the bitter ghosts of the past.

CHAPTER 10

Southern Hospitality and a House Divided

One of my personal responsibilities at TMBO was to provide a two-day session for the new team owners whenever a franchise changed hands. The goal of this "owners 101," as we called it, was twofold. On the one hand, as the NBA's representative for all things business, I would break down for the owners which rights belonged to the individual team, and which belonged to the league. So, if the team wanted to do an advertising deal with their local beer distributor, that was fine. But if they wanted to sign a deal with, say, a major Chinese beer brand to create a campaign across China, that was out of bounds. Those rights and revenues belonged to the NBA. (The Houston Rockets attempted to do just this after drafting Chinese sensation Yao Ming in 2002.) The other thing I would do was provide the new owners with a detailed analysis of how effective their business staff and operations were in comparison to the other teams in the league. This was often an eye-opener for those on the other side of the table. When purchasing the team, the buyers would have had access to the team's own internal accounts, but TMBO's vast data sets would only be made available after they had signed on the dotted line. While the owners for the most part had a good handle on what their ticket, sponsorship, and broadcast revenues were, it was only at this point that they would learn whether these figures were good or bad in relation to the rest of the league when factoring in the team's market size. Drawing on these figures, I would go on to provide a detailed analysis of the team's operational practices, highlighting where they were doing well and where they were falling short.

The NBA was in a unique position on this front because, unlike other major national sports leagues, our system was highly centralized. Every marketing and sales initiative, advertisement, promotion, or online campaign that the teams wanted to use had to be preapproved by TMBO to ensure that they were a good fit with the NBA brand and complied with our marketing policies. As a consequence, we gathered a huge amount of data about each team that we would then analyze and feed back to the team's personnel. We also had an unparalleled view of the wider market conditions the teams were operating in. We knew, for instance, what each beer sponsor was paying in the different markets, itemized for each piece of sponsorable inventory (such as courtside signage). By sharing that data with the teams, we could blow away a lot of the fog that normally shrouds corporate negotiations. For example, by arming a team with the knowledge that Budweiser was already paying X hundred thousand dollars for signage in a comparable market, we could ensure that our franchises maximized their revenues rather than leaving money on the table.

Toward the end of my fourth year with the NBA, I sat down with the new owners of the Atlanta Hawks to run them through their owners 101 analysis. At the time, the Hawks were one of the worst-performing clubs in the league, both on the court, where they were exceeding the salary cap yet still managing to lose fifty-four games in a season, and on the business side, where they placed in the bottom four teams in terms of revenue and attendance. The new owners were, unsurprisingly, eager to shake things up. The issues with the Hawks were only part of the portfolio of problems they were facing. The owner's consortium had also purchased an NHL team, the Atlanta Thrashers, and the operating rights to the relatively newly constructed Philips Arena (now State Farm Arena), which served as a home to both teams. When I took a close look at the figures, it turned out that the combined operation was losing $47 million per year across all three of its components, with none of the parts of the business turning a profit. After hearing me outline a plan for turning the Hawks around, the owners asked me if I would consider leaving TMBO and coming on board as their new CEO to try to salvage the whole concern.

I can't pretend that the offer didn't excite me. Ever since I had left academia for my first executive job with the Pirates, I had dreamed of heading up the leadership team at a major league US sports franchise. Now I was being offered two teams at the same time, and a world class arena to run on the side. I was on Cloud 9. Still, I made an effort to play it cool. Yes, I would be interested in discussing the offer, I said, but I couldn't begin talking about it until they received clearance from David Stern. Starting even exploratory discussions behind the back of the NBA commissioner was a line I wouldn't cross.

David didn't want me to leave, but he knew that the offer that was on the table, including a seven-figure salary, was the fulfilment of a decades-long dream for me. As commissioner, he was also keen to see the Hawks pulled out of their consistently underperforming hole. It helped that I had been careful about succession planning at TMBO, hiring an outstanding deputy who was a great fit with the NBA's culture. Scott O'Neil was an extremely talented Harvard MBA who was very similar to David in work ethic, outlook, and temperament. David was more than satisfied with the idea of working with Scott as my replacement, so he gave me the green light to accept the offer. The five-year deal I negotiated met all my needs, including my requirement that I have full control of both teams, with the general managers reporting directly to me. After all, as I explained, there was no point appointing someone to be CEO of a brewery if they weren't going to be in charge of the beer. I moved to Atlanta on April 1, 2004, with Val following in June once the construction of our house in Chastain Park was finalized.

I fell in love with my new home almost immediately. Georgia is one of the most beautiful states in the union, with a combination of eye-catching countryside and historic towns. Georgia also has a climate that spoke to something deep in my soul. Having spent my first eighteen years growing up on the wind-and-rain-swept coast of north-west England, the consistent sunny days, hot summers, and mild winters were almost magical.

Throughout the state, a deep-rooted sense of history collided with a genteel modernism that had very few of the rough edges I had become accustomed to in New York. There was an ongoing negotiation between past and present here, rather than a simple overwriting of the latter by the former. It seemed as if there was a natural continuum, a kind of geographical harmony that ran from the antebellum grace of Savannah and through the unspoiled beauty of the state's rural areas to Atlanta's gleaming downtown.

After four years in New York, the traditional Southern hospitality I found everywhere was a revelation. The warmth and kindness of strangers immediately made me feel at home. There was something about the politeness that reminded me of the UK, including the familiar way in which the most sweetly charming language could conceal steel within. It took me a little while, but I eventually came to see that a phrase like "Bless your little heart" could smuggle razor blades into a conversation under a cozy quilt-like cover.

While I loved the charm of Georgia's countryside and old buildings, it was the spiky, modern energy of Atlanta that really stole my heart. When Val and I moved to Atlanta, the city was in the middle of a period of rapid growth. In the preceding twenty years, the Atlanta metro area had more than doubled its population. During our nineteen years in the city, the population grew by another 60 percent, to just under 6.2 million residents, a total addition of 4.5 million new inhabitants in less than forty years. What was drawing all these people together was an incredibly dynamic local economy and the diverse Southern culture.

The traditional heart of the Atlanta economy, all the way back to its founding as a railroad terminus, has always been its position as a logistics hub, and that tradition continues to this day. But from the '90s onward, Atlanta also reshaped itself into a business-friendly, low-tax, low-cost-of-living city with the world's busiest airport. These conditions made it the ideal home for a host of American giants, including Coca Cola, Home Depot, UPS, Chick-fil-A, and Delta Airlines, along with dozens of medium- to large-sized financial services companies. These traditional industries were soon joined by a vibrant technology sector, which has now grown to more than 700 tech companies, all providing well-paid jobs and acting as a supercharger to the local economy.

Atlanta is a great place to do business. But it is also a unique cultural center that shows how creative America can be when it rises above the divisions of history. In the 1960s, an alliance between Dr. Martin Luther King and Ivan Allen, the white mayor of Atlanta, ensured that the city remained largely peaceful despite the tensions of the era. This foundation provided a platform for stability and investment that has more recently seen Atlanta become the base for some of America's most prominent black movie and TV documentary producers, along with many hip-hop artists, musicians, and record labels. Tax-free grants and other incentives have led to Georgia competing head-to-head with California for the largest number of TV and movie productions and the highest budget spends. For sports fans like me, the fact that the city is home to many graduates of two prominent college athletics conferences—the Atlantic Coast Conference (ACC) and the Southeastern Conference (SEC)—alongside its MLB, NFL and NBA franchises, means that there is always a game to get excited about. And for foodies, the evolution of Atlanta's restaurant scene into one of the best in the country, with the second highest restaurant spend per capita after New York, is another great attraction.

So much for the Atlanta Chamber of Commerce pitch. But there is another side to the city, a side that taught me a great deal about the divides that have come to shape America's politics. In a very real sense, the city is a microcosm of modern America, a dramatic reflection of our nation in miniature, with both the good and the bad cast in high relief in a way that makes our national virtues and vices easier to see. Many of the structural forces that divide America are so visible in Atlanta that it is impossible to ignore them. On the one hand, the rapid growth of the city has brought together people from different backgrounds to create a tolerant and diverse environment that offers rich opportunities for pursuing the American dream. On the other hand, those same forces of rapid change and expansion have created a stratified economy in which those who do well do very well while those who are left behind experience some of the worst conditions in the country.

Atlanta is a study in contrasts, the focal point where Georgia's past and present meet. The bulk of the population is split fairly evenly between black and white residents. In the city itself, the black population is slightly bigger than the white population, while in the metro area overall, the split leans the other way, becoming more pronounced in the less urbanized areas.[18] These figures tell a story in themselves, reflecting the white flight and racist redlining policies that emerged in many US cities in the aftermath of the civil rights movement. But despite this history, Atlanta is one of the most fully integrated cities imaginable. In its arts, politics, and professions, especially sports and entertainment, the idea that race would prevent someone rising to the top is almost unthinkable (which is not to say that it couldn't still make such a rise harder than it needs to be). Where Atlanta displays America's divisions in sharpest relief is on the economic front, and for many younger Atlantans, this economic divide has a radical impact on their opportunity to share in the American dream.

In 2004, the year I became a resident, 15 percent of Georgia's population lived in families with a collective income below the poverty line, a figure that climbed rapidly to just shy of 20 percent following the global financial crisis of 2008.[19] In Atlanta itself, the child poverty rate in 2004 was an astonishing 49 percent.[20] That figure has since been cut in half—a remarkable achievement—but this still leaves around a quarter of children in one of America's biggest cities being born into circumstances that dramatically diminish their chances of future success.

Socioeconomic mobility was once one of the defining features of American life. Throughout most of the twentieth century, we took it for granted that, in contrast to the class-bound social structures of the Old

World, Americans could rise easily from poor backgrounds to the highest income brackets based solely on their abilities and performance. Our history books are full of stories that reflect this key feature of our culture. Sidney Weinberg famously left school at thirteen and rose from assistant janitor at Goldman Sachs to become the CEO of the storied banking institution. John D. Rockefeller grew up in a poor family yet went on to become the richest man in the nation, if not the world. In the years since, millions of immigrants have come to these shores seeking a similar path, with each generation surpassing the previous one for decade after decade. But in the last forty years, the proportions of Americans who exceed their parents' earnings has fallen precipitously. Where 93 percent of Americans born into the fiftieth income percentile in 1940 would go on to outearn their parents, for those born in 1980 that figure has dropped to just 45 percent.[21] And the trend appears to be accelerating.

What this means for those born into poverty is that an unfortunate economic start is increasingly likely to trap them and hold them back for the rest of their lives. We can see what this lack of mobility does to our society when we consider two high-paying professions that should be accessible to anyone who has the raw intelligence and talent to succeed: medicine and the law. A 2019 study found that, across America, those in the lowest 30 percent of earners produced just 6 percent of our nation's med students. Families in the top 20 percent of incomes, by contrast, produced 60 percent of our future doctors while the top 1 percent was responsible for more med students than the bottom 30 percent combined.[22] The picture is much the same if we look at America's lawyers. According to the *American Bar Association Journal*, citing a UCLA study, "More than three quarters of the students at the nation's top 20 law schools come from the top one-fourth of the socioeconomic population, and well over half of the students at these schools come from the top 10 percent . . . Just 2 percent come from the bottom quarter."[23]

For children born into poverty in Atlanta, this lack of mobility means that opportunities to live out the American dream in full will be available to only a small number. As part of our community outreach and desire to create new Hawks and Thrashers fans, I had the very good fortune to work with many children from underprivileged backgrounds during my time leading several teams. Rewarding as this work was, seeing so much potential being squandered, whole swathes of the next generations being held back by circumstances beyond their control, was life-changing for me.

Over time, the desire to do something to effect some real change on this front became a burning passion. I eventually came to see that the root of most of these social problems was the politics of division, the force of which pulls groups away from each other, setting up boundaries between them in a way that breaks up our national and local communities. But during my first years in Atlanta, my mind was focused on a divide of a different sort. In comparison with childhood poverty, it now seems a trivial matter, but for many months, it was the center of my attention from the moment I got up in the morning to the time I went to sleep.

I knew that my job with the Hawks and the Thrashers was going to be demanding. I had worked on turnaround projects before, but the scale of the Atlanta Spirit's challenges was like nothing I had encountered before. Still, I walked into the role with my eyes fully open about how much we would need to change. Unfortunately, my enthusiasm for the job had blinded me to the depths of one particular challenge, something that fell outside the management of the teams or the internal functioning of the combined business operation. This was the difficulty of dealing with the owners themselves. While I had dealt with large ownership groups in previous jobs (the Pirates had fourteen owners while the Rockies had a group of nine), the Atlanta Spirit owner's consortium was another beast entirely. David Stern had warned me that the disparate groups of owners that made up the consortium had never worked together before and had no prior association at all until they invested in the teams, so their ability to cooperate was a major unknown. In my haste to accept the job, I failed to think through exactly what this would mean on a practical level. It wasn't long before it became abundantly clear that cooperation was not something we could expect. Even armed neutrality was more than we could hope for most of the time. I soon learned that an ownership group riven by internal conflict would be devastating to our management team's attempt to effect far-reaching change. As Lincoln so eloquently put it (borrowing from the gospels of Matthew and Luke), "A house divided against itself, cannot stand."

The Atlanta Spirit LLC had paid about $100 million in cash for their purchase, in addition to taking on just under $200 million in debt. This was a steal given the potential value of the teams once they were turned around (some twenty years later, NBA teams can fetch $3–4 billion by themselves), but the purchase price was still a large amount of money. Unsurprisingly, all the members of the owners' group were united in their desire to see the operation move from loss into profit as soon as possible. Unfortunately, it soon became evident that this was just about the only thing they agreed on. A big part of the problem was that the owners had so little in common. While the Pittsburgh Pirates had a complex shared ownership structure when I ran the business side of the operation there, the fourteen companies were united by a common purpose that transcended their individual interests: each business contributed to the purchase because they wanted to save the team for their home city. Most of the Atlanta Spirit owners, by contrast, saw their purchase as partly a business proposition, and partly a chance to live out their individual fantasies of owning a major-league team. One consequence of this was that there was no shared vision regarding either how the teams should be built up to a competitive level or how the business should be run to increase long-term asset value.

The ownership consortium consisted of nine wealthy individuals, split into three distinct groups, with each group having a single vote when it came to board matters. The largest individual shareholder was Steve Belkin, a Boston businessman with a long track record of building successful businesses. Steve was a first-class singles tennis player at Cornell who remained competitive into his fifties, competing nationally with some success in national senior's competitions. I had no problem with Steve himself, because he was very clear about what he expected from me: deliver the bottom line on the court and on the financials. However, his penchant for going it alone when it came to both sports and business proved to be a key sticking point in my attempts to run the Atlanta Spirit on behalf of the broader group of owners.

While Steve owned his slice of the Spirit consortium outright as an individual, the other two ownership groups each had several members. The Washington, DC, group was composed of three executives at a very successful business intelligence company. These guys were all smart people and delightful individuals to spend time with, but they did not make decisions quickly. They were also sports fans first and foremost. As such, the fiscally conservative long-term plan we had developed sometimes chafed. While my goal was to ensure that our general managers could patiently build up both franchises through careful trades and the draft, I was constantly worried that the Washington group would push me to hire high-priced free agents who could get us ahead on the court and the ice more swiftly. The Atlanta group was the only part of the consortium that was actually based in the city and had an emotional and personal stake in the success of the city's teams. Spearheaded by Michael Gearon Jr., a Hawks fan from birth, this group felt every loss as a personal affront. Neither the Washington nor the Atlanta group had the deep pockets necessary to fund an expensive short-term turnaround. While the Washington group were extremely well-paid executives, they were not the kind of corporate titans who could throw around hundreds of millions of dollars without a care. And while Michael later went on to become extremely wealthy by building a company—American Tower—that played a major role in expanding the US cellphone infrastructure, at the time we worked together his group appeared to have even shallower pockets than the group in Washington. As far as I could tell, Steve was probably the only person who did have the personal resources needed to pursue an aggressive team development strategy, but this kind of approach was simply anathema to his way of doing business.

As the CEO, I was answerable to what was essentially a committee with no meaningful connections between the members, no shared vision, and no unity of purpose. Even the way they distributed the ranks and titles among themselves set them up for further division rather than providing a platform to bring them together. As the owner of the single largest stake in the consortium, Steve received the title of governor of the Hawks. Steve was happy to let the Washington group have titular control over the Thrashers, while the Atlanta group played a supporting role across all three parts of the enterprise, with a particular focus on the many concerts and events held at Philips Arena. Even in the best of times, this would have been a difficult set-up for me to navigate as CEO. But these were far from the best of times.

The basketball team that I inherited at the Hawks was the worst in the NBA. I was stuck with the existing roster for the year I came on board, so it was no surprise to me or anyone else when we ended the season with some of the worst results in the franchise's history. My main focus at the time was supporting Billy Knight, our general manager, in hiring a new head coach for the Hawks and changing out as many of the older high-priced players as we could. There weren't many members of our current team who would be good role models for the promising young players we aimed to draft, so it was important to prepare the ground and make sure we had the framework in place to enable the young draftees to eventually elevate the team and start winning some games. We all agreed that this was the most powerful way both to build a quality team and to drive fan engagement. Unfortunately, within two months of my arrival, the unified front the owners had constructed around this point of agreement fell apart in spectacular fashion.

As part of our strategy to replace the team's older players, we decided to arrange a trade with the Phoenix Suns. Despite the board's majority vote in favor of the trade, Steve was unwilling to accept a player trade (Boris Diaw and two draft picks). Instead, he attempted to use his position as governor of the Hawks to veto the decision, filing an injunction in a Boston court to prevent the board from completing the transfer. This marked the start of a months-long legal saga that drained money, time, and goodwill before the court finally upheld the trade. Steve was then removed as governor for refusing to act in accordance with the vote of the board.

What followed was a long and unrelenting nightmare for my senior management team. Open hostilities broke out between the different factions of the ownership group, leading the press to dub the consortium "the Atlanta Dispirit Group." Our weekly board-level conference calls became the front line of this war, with each decision turning into a battleground. The most mundane management issues were debated in minute detail again and again as each side looked to gain leverage over the other rather than making decisions for the sake of the business or the teams. These meetings were followed up by long lists of information requests—some reasonable, most trivial, all time consuming—from Steve Belkin's lawyer, again seeking to identify disagreements, minor breaches of procedure, and anything else that could be turned into a weapon. The net effect was that my staff became increasingly demoralized as their time and energy were wasted by this conflict. To insulate my team from this impact, I made sure that I was the point of contact for anything contentious. This gave the team space to do their jobs, but it meant the bulk of my own energy disappeared into the black hole created by squabbling owners.

Despite these difficulties, I was able to work with my group of mostly talented executives to turn both clubs around and set the business on a more stable and prosperous course. When I arrived, the Hawks had not made it to the playoffs in the previous five seasons and the Spirit's business was collectively losing $47 million a year. With our five-year plan for building up the Hawks through the draft, it would be three more seasons before we could expect to be competitive again. The Atlanta Thrashers had a slightly different but no less troubled story. An expansion team that had joined the league in 1999, they had never had a winning season prior to my arrival. In my first year, a labor dispute between the NHL and the players' union led to the entire 2004–05 hockey season being cancelled, decimating the Thrashers' season ticket base. We quickly rebuilt, with the Thrashers rocketing to their best season ever the next year, and we followed this up in 2007–08 by winning the Southeastern Division and making it to the playoffs for the only time in the club's history.

By the end of my tenure, we had brought the collective operating loss of the company, in four years, down from $47 million to $13 million, with both the Hawks and the arena becoming profitable ventures when taken individually. Work on the Thrashers had been delayed due to the lockout in the first season, but I was confident that a couple more years of staying the course would see it move into profit as well. Sadly, I also knew that I would not be able to see that part of the project through to completion. The burden of running a company while the owners were at war with each other had become intolerable. I was expending more time and energy managing relations between the owner groups than I was managing the business itself. The inability to get agreement on even the simplest decisions came to a head for me while I was on vacation in Europe. I spent hours on a conference call, one morning, discussing our capital expenditure budget in minute details while driving along a crowded autobahn in Austria. My frustration came to a head when I found that the board could not even agree on the purchase of a few thousand dollars' worth of rope tensa barriers to manage the lines at the concession stands without butting heads. After wasting nearly half an hour begging the owners to agree on something so basic, I felt completely drained. As soon as I hung up, my wife, Val, who had been forced to listen in to every minute of this idiotic conversation, turned to me and said, "You need to quit."

The clarity of the words and the conviction with which they were spoken were a wake-up call. If I wanted a respite from the disputes and the division, it was up to me to act. If I wanted my workplace to be a genuine community that was unified around a shared vision, I would have to build it myself. I realized that it was time to grasp the final part of my long-held American dream: it was time to build a lasting business of my own.

CHAPTER 11

Final Chapters and New Beginnings

The decision to hand over the reins of the Atlanta Spirit and turn my attention to building a business of my own was both liberating and terrifying. After two decades as a senior executive in roles across the sport business sector, I had become used to solving problems for other people. Now, I would be answerable for my decisions to nobody but myself.

When I first arrived in America, the idea of building and running a business that would survive the test of time seemed like the highest summit of the American dream. I held onto this vision of success during my time as an executive, and on several occasions was nearly drawn away from my career by the chance to build something of my own from scratch. I saw constructing a business from the ground up as the ultimate challenge. Building a lasting business is about more than just making money. It is an opportunity to create something that extends beyond the person of the founder, weaving together the personalities, hopes and dreams of many different individuals into something solid and coherent. Some of those people will stay with the company for years while others will just be passing through. The challenge is to create something stable that will endure through those changes, to grow an organization into an institution.

Over the next sixteen years, I put everything I had learned as an athlete, academic, and executive to work as my team and I grew the Aspire Group from a sport marketing start-up into a mature business that generated more than $1.5 billion dollars in revenue for our partners. As a consulting practice, Aspire has helped install the TMBO model I pioneered at the NBA in eleven sports leagues around the globe, including the NHL, all three Canadian hockey leagues, the Australian Football League (AFL) and Australian National Rugby League (NRL). At home in the United States, our ticketing and community-building program for collegiate athletics worked for Georgia Tech, Rutgers, Maryland, Arizona State, Purdue, Minnesota, and my alma mater Kansas, among many others, to build fan communities and maximize revenues. We produced renewal rates in the Mid-90's range along with related ticket donation levels that broke all-time records. Aspires company growth was second to none.

While the group's financial success has certainly been gratifying, the most rewarding part of my work with Aspire has been growing the business without compromising my values. Building the Aspire company culture so that we walked the talk rather than treating our values as a branding exercise has been a genuine challenge. I would love to say that all the moral and social lessons I learned in my journey across America just happened to be the perfect ingredients for optimizing profits and supercharging corporate expansion. The reality, of course, is messier. By the end of my almost sixteen years leading the group, we had hit our long-standing diversity target of ensuring that at least half our workforce came from underrepresented parts of the population. I was very grateful for the breadth of perspectives and ideas this brought to the team, but it is hard to put a measurable dollar value on the initiative. Our commitment to developing talent internally rather than routinely hiring for the roles from the external market gave more than a hundred of our staff the step up from entry-level positions to managerial jobs. This approach certainly helped with retention, but I don't have a data set that proves that it was better for our bottom line than widening the pool we could draw on (although my gut says that it was). Similarly, implementing a minimum wage of $15 an hour whenever we could get the agreement of our clients undoubtedly helped motivate and energize our staff. But did doubling the federal minimum wage lead to a 100 percent increase in output? It's hard to quantify, but I feel confident in saying it did not. I can also confidently say that this doesn't matter in the slightest. I chose to set our minimum pay level at Aspire not based on the least I could get away with paying but based on the minimum that team members would need to feed, cloth, and house themselves and their families.

As I got closer to the final realization of my own American dream, I found myself spending more and more time reflecting on how much my understanding of that dream had changed during the half a century I had lived in the United States. When I arrived on these shores, I was focused on succeeding as an individual, first in business and then, after I began my PhD, in academia. The arrival of my children expanded my definition of success to include my responsibility to provide them with the best possible start in life. This role had a financial component, of course, especially as far as providing a good education was concerned, but at its center was the challenge of raising them to be good members of society with strong values and the desire to help others. The year I spent twisting and turning on the brink of bankruptcy when I moved to Massachusetts deepened my understanding of how dependent we all are on circumstance, luck, and the support of those around us.

I carried these lessons with me as I moved on to executive roles in sport business, first at the Pirates and then with the Rockies. Yet during this time I still saw my own version of the American dream as fundamentally rooted in individualism. The romance of the American frontier and the archetype of the hardworking immigrant pulling himself up by his bootstraps still lay at the center of my ideal vision of America. It was only during my time at the University of Denver, under the influence of the remarkable Dan Ritchie, that my view of the American dream began to focus less on the heroic journey of the outsider or the pioneer at the edge of society and more on the struggles of those who were born and would spend their whole lives within America's communities. Here, it seemed to me, we had something of a blind spot as a nation. On the one hand, we proclaimed and wholeheartedly believed that America was the land of opportunity, a place where anyone could make it whatever their background. Yet on the other hand, attitudes toward and conditions within some of our communities not only limited the chances many Americans had of achieving that dream but went so far as to make that birthright seem like an impossible fantasy, a future that belonged exclusively to other people.

In the ten years that followed, I fervently hoped that this imbalance in American society would right itself. With the nation buoyed up by the optimism of the '90s and the economic power of the digital revolution, it seemed to me that we had all the resources needed to make progress on this front. Yet instead of coming together, reshaping our communities, and refreshing our understanding of the American dream, we have moved in the opposite direction. This is not because we have become worse people. If anything, I believe that most Americans have become more thoughtful, kinder, and more concerned with doing what is right than ever before. And it is not because some evil genius has sought to bring our society low. The forces that have come together to power this shift arose from a nexus of events and technological developments that I do not believe could have been predicted. Nevertheless, the result is that division and conflict have intensified in America to a level I have never seen before in my time here. And this division makes it impossible to reach a consensus about how the American dream needs to change to ensure that it is accessible to all.

The appetite of Americans for hope, change and a shared vision that will bring the nation together was evident in the enthusiasm for Barrack Obama's first election campaign. But despite some notable accomplishments, I believe that the Obama administration manifestly failed to reforge the connections needed to unite America once again (or was prevented from doing so, as some would argue). In fact, the political rhetoric has only intensified in the years since, with extreme views, hateful language, and a refusal to cooperate becoming standard features of American life. The election of Donald Trump eight years later was a pivotal moment, showing just how disillusioned many Americans had become with their political system. The four years that followed, with numerous undignified moments, only made matters worse, eroding trust in Congress, the Senate, the presidency and the Supreme Court to an unprecedented degree. While the Biden administration has thrown less fuel directly onto the fires of discontent, it has, in my opinion, also done little to change the direction of travel, especially when it comes to the question of the mental competence of America's commander in chief.

As my own career moved toward its summit, I increasingly felt a sense of slippage, as if I was fortunate enough to be traveling in one direction while the country on which my success relied was moving in reverse on a parallel track. This feeling that things have come unstuck, that the ties that bind us together have come loose, helped me realize that I have one last chapter to add to my own American dream.

In 2023, I sold the Aspire Group and retired from my career in business. I had achieved all I hoped for as an individual and as a businessman. But there remains much more to accomplish if I am to live up to my own reimagined view of the American dream as something that must extend outward to embrace the wider community. A key part of this new chapter will be the development and growth of the Aspire Difference Foundation, a charity that aims to support the physical and mental health and wellness of single parents while ensuring that their children receive an excellent early-years education. Through this vehicle for change, I will do everything I can to make a direct difference in the lives of others. To that end, all net proceeds from both this book and my consulting work will go to The Aspire Difference Foundation to fund its work.

Still, there is much more to do than I can hope to achieve alone. My amazing wife Val, who has served brilliantly as Senior Vice President of Business Administration for Aspire for more than fourteen years, stayed on with our old company after the sale but will soon be joining me in the next phase of our life together as we spread the message of *Reimagining America's Dream*. The goal of this book is to reach out further than the Foundation, to seek a wider community whose members will join together in committing themselves to fighting for a better America. If we are to pull the nation through this moment of peril, it is essential that America's moderates fight to retake the center ground and push back the influence of the extremists in both political parties. We can do this together by working toward a version of the American dream that prioritizes both the individual and the community, balancing the one and the many to form a harmonious whole.

To make this vision a reality, the moderate majority need to start making changes. Some of these changes can begin the moment the reader puts down the book (see chapter 12). But others require more far-reaching changes (chapters 13–21) that will re-lay the foundations for a society in which that which unites us once again becomes more important than that which divides us.

Part 2

CHAPTER 12

A Dream for Our Times

My fifty years in America have taught me more lessons than I imagined I could learn in a single lifetime. Most of these have been lessons about myself that will be of interest to few people beyond my immediate family. But some have a wider relevance. I came to live in this country pursuing a vision of the American dream that had built up slowly, layers of fact, meaning, and fantasy growing slowly into something concrete. I pieced together my American dream from Hollywood movies and enthusiastic uncles, from warm-hearted mentors and the chatter of kids at camp during long, hot summers. This patchwork understanding gave me a sense of not just what life was like in America but what life in America made possible. And those possibilities were intoxicating to me.

The American dream I absorbed from these disparate sources was almost identical to the classic version of the dream that had inspired generations of immigrants and native-born Americans before me. It was a dream of freedom: freedom from the constraints of class and the expectations of others; freedom from a small world in which opportunities were narrow; freedom to dream on a scale that matched that of America's landscape; freedom to create, and build, and grow without the government, or anyone else, getting in the way. In short, the American dream seemed to offer me the freedom to build a better life and make the most of my potential.

Of course, every ideal runs into reality at some point. Even a limited government has some rules you have to follow; a lot of that magnificent landscape is already taken by others pursuing their dreams; some people will always have a jump on you thanks to the circumstances of their birth; and each individual must somehow reconcile their freedom to pursue their own goals with that of others who might want to compete or might want to steer the world in another direction entirely. These are the lessons every adult learns as they grow into themselves and their society. They don't sink the American dream; they just pull it down to earth, bringing it out of the imagination as fantasy turns into reality. Some of these limitations and compromises take a little of the shine off the dream, but they are also necessary. For instance, if you want the opportunity to earn advantages for the next generation of your family, you can't complain if it's tough to outcompete someone who was born with wealth and connections. There's a little unavoidable friction in the system, but that just means sometimes you need to work a little harder to attain your goals. Perfectly fair? No. But it's a price worth paying for the opportunities the system yields up.

There were also harder problems to reconcile, as I soon learned after arriving on these shores. Historic injustices meant that some communities were held back by a lack of financial and educational capital. Redlining and other racist policies directly denied opportunities to some Americans because of the color of their skin. Educational opportunities could vary enormously from one school district to another across the country, giving children advantages or disadvantages that went beyond their natural talents and willingness to work hard. Nevertheless, for the first two decades I spent in the United States, I saw these as legacy problems, issues from an earlier age that America was working together to overcome. I could point to huge leaps forward over time that showed we were moving in the right direction as a nation, great steps being taken to right wrongs and reduce racial inequalities. As I entered my third decade in the country, I came to realize that the progress we were making was often not as fast as it should be, and that this lack of speed in correcting matters represented an injustice in itself. Nevertheless, I was sure that we were still traveling in the right direction in most, if not all, of these areas.

And then something changed. Or rather, a bunch of interconnected things changed, some for obvious reasons and other for reasons I still struggle to understand. From the late 1990s onward, the people of our country have seemed to be drifting apart from one another. Even as we continued to make important progress in many areas, views that were once confined to the fringes of our social and political lives started to take on a new prominence. At the same time, previously unthinkable behavior began to become commonplace. While crime was falling across the nation, the unspeakable evil of school shootings became a regular news item. While acceptance and tolerance became ingrained popular values, a new maliciousness entered the political arena. While we preached peace and the value of human life, our nation engaged in a war of choice that led to hundreds of thousands of direct and indirect casualties.

I often wondered when I thought about these changes whether they were really changes at all. Perhaps I was just noticing things that were perennial but unfortunate constants in the messy reality of our national life. We had known epidemics of senseless violence before while another failed war of choice, the conflict in Vietnam, overlapped with my own early years in America. It was tempting to recall the old biblical line that "There is no new thing under the sun" and chalk my changing perceptions up to an earlier naivety on my part. But the more I looked, the more convinced I became that this was not the case. Yes, some unfortunate elements recur again and again throughout history. But there were also new things here, from the 24/7 media cycle to the digital revolution and our new hyperconnected world, which combined to make this modern age something genuinely different. We can see that this is the case in the many long-term trends that have slowed or begun to reverse over the last twenty years. Social mobility is down; life expectancy is falling for many; trust in each other, in our politicians, in our system of government, and all of our pillar institutions, such as schools and religion, are at lows that have never been seen before. These aren't just blips in the data; these trends reflect real changes in how we live and how we relate to each other.

So, where does this leave the American dream? Parts of it are still intact. Indeed, in many senses many Americans have more opportunities than at any point in the past. Gender equality is closer than it has ever been to a reality, with American girls growing up with the belief that there is no door that will remain closed to them, no glass ceiling that they can't shatter. Racial equality has taken enormous steps forward over the last twenty-five years, with America electing its first black president, the first black billionaires breaking through old economic barriers, and black music culture not just becoming mainstream but defining the mainstream. Asian Americans and Hispanic Americans are increasingly prominent in business and politics, and that trend looks set to continue, while Native Americans are now receiving some measure of respect and restitution for what they lost as the United States expanded across their territories. Gay rights have also stepped into a new era with an unprecedented degree of acceptance of different identities and lifestyles. In all these areas, more Americans have more freedom to build the lives they wish to live than did their parents or any earlier generation.

On the economic front, the picture is much less rosy. For me, America has always meant *more*: more opportunities than anywhere else, with every generation surpassing the last as they climb toward greater prosperity and higher standards of living. But the economic engine of the American dream has stalled for many. America itself continues to be a global powerhouse of economic growth and innovation. But the upward path on which the American people previously traveled together has now split into two branches. Well-off Americans continue to prosper, tracking the path of ever-increasing wealth that has been central to our national self-image for many decades. However, those in the bottom 50 percent of incomes have seen wages stagnate, with many now earning less than their parents did at the same age. This economic parting of the ways is one of the most fundamental divisions in American society today. For many Americans, the expectation of economic progress has stalled or disappeared entirely, and that means the American dream of securing more than the previous generation through hard work is disappearing as well. This is the key fault line in American society today, dividing our nation into those who can expect to enjoy the benefits of our national dream and those who cannot. Importantly, this line also divides Americans in two other critical areas that determine quality of life: education and health care. We will look at these divisions in more detail in chapters 13, 14, and 15.

The other great polarizing force in America today is political division. Just like the economic divide, our political strife is pulling Americans apart from one another and setting them on very different trajectories. This may initially seem like a much more tenuous threat to the traditional version of the American dream. After all, it is not the case that opportunities to achieve economic success are cut off if you support one party and boosted if you support the other. But the danger in this area is both equally real and fundamentally connected to the economic divide. If we cannot gather the fraying threads and pull the people of our nation back into a single harmonious unit, we may end up without a recognizable America in which to live out the dream.

Our political divisions are being driven first by the culmination of long-term trends in the American two-party system and then supercharged by developments in the media and technology landscapes. The result is that our politics have increasingly become a tug-of-war between those on the extreme right and the extreme left, while the moderates—both those with party affiliations and those who identify as independents—are frozen out of the debate. Sensible, centrist positions are rarely able to gain traction because the party machines are captured by those on the fringes, leading to a sense that our politics are broken and that the country is being run in a way that satisfies nobody. The result is that many Americans feel alienated from each other and from their national community, fracturing the unity that is necessary for any sort of national dream or ideal to have true motivating power. The social and political paralysis this division causes also shuts off the path to any kind of solution to the economic divisions that deny access to the American dream. Chapters 16 to 19 take a closer look at some of the key points of political dispute in our current era and outline the contours of solutions that may be achievable if the moderate majority can reclaim both its voice and its central place in our system.

If we are to start moving forward together again as a single nation gathered around a shared national goal, we need to reimagine the American dream in two different ways. First, we need to adapt it to reflect the reality of the world we now live in, a world that is more connected than ever and yet riven by deeper divides than this country has faced for a long time. To achieve this, we need to recalibrate the values that underpin the American dream. The dream has traditionally focused on freeing individuals to maximize their individual potential, a worthy goal and one that must be maintained. To this we need to add a greater focus on the community and the place of the individual within it, a recognition that nobody succeeds in a vacuum, and that it is our society as a whole that provides the stable foundation on which each of us can build our lives. We must reimagine the dream as something essentially shared, something that connects us to each other and acknowledges the value of a higher power that lies outside ourselves. Chapter 20 sets out where we can find such values. Then, with that reimagined dream before us, we must take a second step, turning outward and focusing our attention on making the dream attainable for all.

There are some immediate steps we can all take toward these goals. It is our duty as moderates who care about our country to refuse the easy path of ceding the political arena to extremists of either sort. There are two dimensions to the actions we all need to take here. On the one hand, to fulfil our responsibilities as a moderate majority that has the interests of our whole nation at its heart, we have to commit to being properly informed and educated about the key issues of the day. That means refusing to accept our news from the easiest sources, such as our social media feeds, and instead, devoting time and effort to informing ourselves about the nuances of what is really going on. What will inevitably emerge from such efforts is a recognition that no party, interest group, or other political team has a monopoly on the truth. As such, we need to do the hard work of rejecting partisan political participation and instead think about and engage with specific issues. If we ever find ourselves in full agreement with party spokespeople or political commentators from any wing, that is a good guide to tell us we are almost certainly not thinking adequately about the issues. At a practical level, we need to set the value of community coherence above and beyond any other individual issue, refusing to donate to, or support in any other way, politicians or movements that seek to create divisions in our nation. This is particularly true when we agree with key elements of their policy platform: This kind of agreement is precisely where the temptation to allow destructive forces into politics comes from and it must be resisted.

However, we should also recognize that we cannot just click our fingers and turn the tanker around in a few easy steps. If we wish to reclaim our country from the extremists, we must be willing to put in the effort to make our voices heard and to step up and fight for what we believe in. And that requires both individual effort and thoughtful consideration of policy positions we can unite behind. In the second part of this book, I analyze our current situation in eight key areas and offer some suggestions for how we might find a path through them together. The final chapter, then, sets out a far-reaching program for both fixing our politics and making the American dream attainable to all. The only way we will achieve long-term change is by focusing our efforts on the living future of America: our children and grandchildren.

My hope is that this book will serve as a wake-up call for those of us in the middle. We need to stand up and shout out to America that we are no longer willing to accept the extremism, the nastiness, the hatred, and the disinformation that has flooded into our politics from the fringes. If we refuse the call, this country will only become more fractured, more dissatisfied, and more violent. If we are unwilling to use our time and energy to preserve our nation, we may soon find that we have ceded it to the extremists forever.

CHAPTER 13

It's the Economy Stupid

The story of America's economic rise in the nineteenth century is an epic for the ages. From a population of just 2.8 million in 1780,[24] the United States expanded at a historically unprecedented rate, housing no less than 76 million by 1900.[25] In the same period, the land area under US control expanded from 430,000 square miles at independence (already nearly four times the size of Great Britain) to just under 3.8 million square miles. And this enormous increase in population and landmass had a similar effect on the economy. While the United States accounted for less than one percent of global economic output in 1800, a century later that figure was 23.6 percent,[26] making the US the largest economy in the world by a considerable margin. In just a hundred years, America was transformed from a backwater colony of Great Britain to an unstoppable economic titan.

The story of the "American century" that followed is just as impressive. The United States has retained its spot as the world's leading economy for more than 140 years now, posting growth rates that are the envy of every other industrialized nation. While China has recently emerged as a potential challenger, the US economy is still 50 percent larger than its nearest rival, with Chinese growth now slowing considerably. A commitment to free trade has seen US products reach out to penetrate markets across the globe while the stock market at home has consistently offered investors both a safe harbor and excellent returns. It is no surprise that more than half of the world's largest companies are American.

Despite these successes, the picture is more mixed if we look to the recent past and the future. America stands at the forefront of the economic boom unleashed by the digital revolution and our companies are the most innovative, the most efficient and the most competitive in the field of technology. The gains in this area have rippled out across the economy to boost the value of businesses in almost all industries. And we are far from done. Looking ahead, we seem to be on the cusp of another wave of high value innovation, with AI, big data, and the next generation of connectivity coming together to make new heights of economic growth attainable. But while these kinds of gains yield huge benefits for many Americans, especially those with the resources to invest in the stock market, many others have been left behind.

As the United States has stood at the forefront of the increasingly globalized economy, we have enjoyed access to new markets for our goods and services. But the flip side of the equation is an increasing reliance on imported goods and the offshoring of the manufacturing operations of our own companies. Since 2000, more than a quarter of US manufacturing jobs have disappeared,[27] while competition with less expensive workers elsewhere has held pay down in those jobs that remain. One result is that the American middle class has been shrinking. While some of this change has resulted in more higher income jobs, the rest of the movement has been downward, increasing the number of lower income jobs, which now provide work for 29 percent of the population.[28] Wage growth for low- and middle-income families has also dramatically lagged that for upper income households over the last fifty years, with total earnings for these two groups falling from 70 percent of national income to just 50 percent.[29] After adjusting for inflation, typical worker pay has only increased by 17 percent over the last 50 years, while productivity has grown at more than three times this rate;[30] house prices are up 118 percent; and college tuition has increased by 169 percent since 1980.[31]

The aspiration to own a home and help your children get ahead by putting them through college have long been core parts of the American dream, but these goals are now increasingly out of reach for many people. And with these key steppingstones to a better life becoming harder and harder to achieve, it is no surprise that social mobility has dropped to historically low rates over recent decades.[32] The gap between those at the top and those at the bottom of the economic pile is now enormous. At the time of writing, the top 50 percent of households in the United States own 97.5 percent of the nation's total household wealth, while the bottom 50 percent own just 2.5 percent.[33] For the top 10 percent, the average wealth per household is $6,500,000;[34] for the bottom 50 percent, it is just $50,000;[35] while 20 percent of Americans have either zero or negative wealth.[36] One of the key forces driving division in America is the sense that Americans are increasingly no longer living in the same worlds as one another. Economically, this is unquestionably true.

The dilemma we now face cuts to the very core of our identity as a nation. Can we create an economy that not only continues to power world-leading growth but also fosters unity and inclusivity? I believe we can. But if we are to have any hope of achieving this goal, we must first step away from the divisive rhetoric that dominates our current discourse, a rhetoric that leans into and feeds off people's fears and differences. The suggestion that any sort of government intervention sets us on a slippery slope toward socialism is, frankly, nonsense. So, too, is the demonization of the wealthy as the primary architects of inequality. This kind of extreme framing of the problem not only oversimplifies the issues but also polarizes the nation, pushing Americans into two camps that are set against each other.

My experiences across different states, sectors, and roles have taught me the vital importance of having nuanced conversations. The hardworking entrepreneur in California who risks everything she owns to innovate and create jobs deserves recognition and reward, just as does the single parent in Georgia working two jobs to make ends meet. At the moment, our economy is only geared to rewarding one of these individuals. But this does not have to be a binary choice. We don't have to tear down the former to raise up the latter. We don't have to choose between extreme socialism and unbridled capitalism. Instead, we need to find a balance that reflects our most cherished ideals and that gives everyone the chance to chase their own American dream.

Consider the debates around the national minimum wage, a policy often simplistically viewed through a binary lens that contrasts economic freedom with government control. The reality is far more nuanced. A minimum wage that aligns with living costs isn't a handout; it's a recognition of the fundamental principle that hard work deserves fair pay and that every working American should be able to support their family without the specter of poverty looming over them. The argument that market forces alone should dictate pay simply does not work. We have already made certain moral commitments as a society. We will, rightly, not allow people to starve. We won't permit American children to go to school barefoot and in rags. And we insist that nobody should be turned away from a hospital in an hour of need.

As a nation, we have built systems—often imperfect but frequently effective—to prevent these outcomes from happening. But in many cases, building these systems on a national, state, or city level simply means that the community as a whole is subsidizing employers who refuse to pay a fair wage. We all end up paying more in taxes, health-care costs and philanthropic donations to minimize a type of working poverty that is both unnecessary and immoral. There is a much simpler system available to guarantee that everyone who works can live free of the fear that they may fall over the financial precipice. And that is a national minimum wage that fixes minimum earnings at a level sufficient to survive and thrive in our shared society. At the time of writing, this level hovers around $15 per hour for the United States, equating to a basic annual salary of $30,000 for a full-time job. The dignity of labor is not just an abstract idea and a minimum wage that aligns with the basic costs of living isn't just an economic policy. An honest paycheck for an honest day's work is much, much more than that. It is a recognition of the value of each person's contribution to the tapestry of America, of our value in the eyes of each other.

The economic disparity in America divides us. In truth, it will never be possible, or even desirable, to flatten the economic pyramid. The rewards at the top are one of the key features of our free-market system that drives people to strive for and achieve as much as they possibly can. These rewards motivate us and act as a key accelerant for the economy as a whole, helping to make the pie bigger for everyone. But we can acknowledge this fact while also acknowledging that the gap between the top and the bottom has become unsustainably large, severing some of the core bonds that hold us together as a single national community. A modest contribution from business owners—not a handout, but a fair recognition of the value of the work performed by their teams—can help smooth the edges of our economy, removing much of the roughness that chafes against so many. It can ensure that the American dream does not become an exclusive privilege but remains a shared aspiration.

But the story doesn't end with adjusting fiscal policies. It's also about the narratives we choose to tell ourselves. Across America, every community from the smallest heartland town to the largest coastal city is tied together by a common identity. The story of any one person's success is not just about rugged individualism; it is about working within and building on that shared story. From its beginnings, the story of America has been a story of communal support and interdependence, a story of how we can work together to ensure that every individual can maximize their potential. Success often involves individual grit and resilience, but it also depends on the networks of support that buoy us through the tough times.

Ensuring that our communities flourish is essential for our success as a nation. In part, that means protecting them from the worst excesses of global market forces by legislating to not just keep American jobs in America but to bring back many of those that have gone abroad. This will also protect our workers from a race to the bottom that they can't win against nations with poorer safety standards, fewer worker protections, and lower economic baselines. We must also take steps to remove unnecessary economic divisions *within* our communities, and that means getting rid of insurance and bank and mortgage lending policies that discriminate against those who live on the wrong side of the tracks. As a nation, we need to help those living in underprivileged areas to find their way up the economic ladder, not put additional obstacles in their way. Finally, we need to institute national programs to ensure that every young American can access the kinds of advantages that currently belong only to those lucky beneficiaries of intergenerational wealth. (In chapters 2, 3, and 4, I discuss how much difference a bequest from my father made to the course of my own life, allowing me to take the first step onto the property ladder many years earlier than would otherwise have been possible.)

Our future as a cohesive and connected nation hinges on our ability to weave these strands together. But before we can set about securing that future, we must first set aside the extremism that colors our current debates. The health of our union, our community, must be our starting point. It is only when we seek solutions that work for all of us that we can build an economy in which every individual American can flourish.

Recommended Action Points

- All Americans who work a full-time job should be able to support themselves and their family above the poverty line without requiring support from the state. As an important step toward this goal, the federal minimum wage should rise to $15 an hour, with annual cost-of-living adjustments to maintain that baseline going forward. I know from first-hand experience that this is possible. There has been an awakening on this front in the aftermath of the COVID-19 pandemic, with both my own company and those of our client partners gaining the awareness and motivation necessary to drive this policy through.

- A single-minded commitment to free trade suited America in certain periods of our economic development. But we should not confuse an approach that is beneficial in certain situations for an absolute moral principle. Where free trade undermines whole segments of our society, we need to take action to protect American workers and American communities. As a first step in this direction, we need to enact legislation that strongly disincentivizes American companies from offshoring jobs and that incentivizes onshoring jobs that had previously been moved abroad. We also need to take urgent steps to onshore industries that are vital to our national security, in particular expanding the work of the 2022 CHIPS (Creating Helpful Incentives to Produce Semiconductors) Act.

- Even though redlining has been outlawed since 1968, the historical weight of discriminatory practices that denied services to those living in poorer, predominantly minority neighborhoods has left scars on our communities. Firmer regulation is needed to overcome the remaining vestiges of these practices along with policies for regenerating areas that have suffered as a result.

- The final chapter of this book outlines an innovative "American prescription" that sets out a far-reaching solution for many of the ills that currently assail our nation. A key feature of this prescription is an increased investment in youth education, including a four-year program of guaranteed paid work for high-school students over the summer vacation along with the creation of a special high-interest savings account to hold the earnings from this work. Any student participating in the complete program could leave high school with as much as $25,000 in the bank (the exact amount depending on interest rates and how little capital is withdrawn). This will provide a nest egg that can be used to support living expenses at college or provide the seed for the downpayment on a home in early adulthood. This program will ensure that all Americans can earn access to the benefits previously reserved for those fortunate enough to be born into wealthy families. For the other elements of the prescription, please see chapter 21.

CHAPTER 14

Education Is Expensive, but Ignorance Costs Much More!

Education has long been a key component in America's success as a nation, acting as a critical tool for tapping our country's economic potential and an engine for increasing the wealth, health, and happiness of all Americans. Our universities do not just lead the world; they dominate the global rankings for teaching quality and research output. We invented the science of business administration, have won more Nobel prizes than the next five countries combined,[37] and the output of our top schools sets the global agenda in both the sciences and the humanities.

Yet while the impact of our higher education system has been immense, the view is less rosy when it comes to primary and secondary education. Education at this level is phenomenally important for both individuals and society as a whole. It socializes children to the idea of being part of a community, with the rights and responsibilities that membership entails. It encourages aspirations for the future and offers a sense of possibility and opportunity. And it provides the knowledge base and cognitive tools that will allow our children to reach their fullest potential. I don't believe it is an exaggeration to say that childhood education is the single most important key for unlocking access to the American dream.

Effective education is the ultimate leveler, a force that can lift people from the most extreme poverty and give them access to opportunities they could otherwise never dream of pursuing. But our primary and secondary school system is currently failing many young people catastrophically. The goal of our schools should be improving social mobility so that every individual can live a life commensurate with their fullest potential. However, the reality is that disparities in the provision of education intensify pre-existing divisions: Those who start out with the fewest advantages fall further behind during their school years. The reason for this is that the schooling and preschool options available to disadvantaged families tend to be less effective than those available to middle- and upper-class families, a disparity that is often amplified by attitudes toward education at home. Instead of easing the path to participation in the American dream, attending an underfunded school located in an already underprivileged area entrenches inequality. While great steps have been made toward closing the funding gap in recent years,[38] inequalities still remain in many places.[39] And even where funding is equal, this does not mean that the educational provision is. For instance, inner-city school districts can find it much harder to attract the highest quality teachers than schools elsewhere,[40] while the concentration of parental fundraising in already wealthy neighborhoods provides a hidden financial advantage for the students who attend these schools.[41] Instead of empowering aspiration, these disparities fuel feelings of alienation, futility, and a sense that society is only geared to work for other people.

The long-term effects are huge. The median lifetime earnings for someone with a bachelor's degree are almost double those of someone with only a high-school diploma.[42,43] Individuals with college degrees now own 74.1 percent of the total wealth in America,[44] yet only a third of Americans fall into this privileged class.[45] And before we start kidding ourselves that this is actually a merit-based division, we need to look at the impact a child's background has on their likelihood of making it to college. Children of college graduates are almost twice as likely to gain a degree as those whose parents did not have a college education. And when it comes to the elite schools that offer the greatest opportunities, the proportion is even more skewed: only 15 percent of Harvard undergraduates are first-generation students,[46] which means the other 85 percent come from the much smaller group of families in which the parents already have degrees.

It can sometimes be hard to see how stark this division is. Americans with a college education tend to move in similar circles, have friends who also have degrees, and work alongside others with similar qualifications. And this social and professional circle does not feel small or limited in the slightest. Here, the sheer scale of our nation acts as a distorting lens. With a US population now north of 330 million, the college-educated slice of the country has more members than the total populations of Italy and Spain combined. With such a large group membership, possessing a college degree certainly does not feel like having an entry ticket to a tiny elite. Yet, despite the large absolute size of this demographic, the group of Americans that sits outside it is twice as big. And increasingly these two groups live in completely different worlds.

Of course, these different worlds are visible in the fact that college graduates earn so much more than those whose education ends with high school, but educational attainment can have other important effects on quality of life. In the last fifteen years, average life expectancy in America has stagnated, falling behind the continuous growth posted in other industrialized economies. But this average conceals a more dangerous divide. While life expectancy for college graduates has actually continued to rise, for the two thirds of the population without a degree it has been falling since 2010.[47] A college graduate is now likely to live eight years longer than someone who does not earn a degree, to say nothing about the comparative quality of life across those years arising from the income differential.

To ensure that everyone has a real chance to pursue the American dream, and even just to live for roughly the same amount of time, we must bring the standard of education everywhere in the United States up to a higher national baseline. An essential first step is ensuring that funding per student in all areas of the nation reaches the levels found in middle- and upper-class districts. The injection of large amounts of federal funding over the past two decades has done much to close this gap, but the job needs to be completed. We then need to turn our attention to a second problem: Despite the provision of new funding, average student test scores have not increased in proportion, which strongly suggests that either this funding is not being deployed efficiently or that there are other important underlying issues that need to be addressed as well.

I believe a whole suite of measures will be needed to level the educational playing field. One critical area will be the provision of high-quality preschool options to all American parents. By ensuring that all children can read, write, and do basic arithmetic before they enter the school system, we can guarantee that every child can make the best possible use of the educational resources available to them. In the final chapter of this book, I will also outline a national program for American high-school children, designed to increase civic engagement and provide a common foundational experience for all children. Completion of this four-year summer program will entitle the student to four years of college education, or completion of a professional certification paid for by the federal government, ensuring that all American children, regardless of their background, will have the resources to pursue a degree if they are willing to commit the necessary time and effort.

These programs will inevitably require a significant increase in the federal tax burden to cover the funding gap (for full costings, see appendix A), but the huge increase in capability and drive in the workforce will bring enormous benefits to the economy. A shortage of skilled workers has long been touted as a vital factor holding back growth in the tech industry, to give just one example. By improving educational levels across the country, we help not only those who will now receive the education all Americans deserve, but also those who innovate, build companies, and drive the economy forward.

More resources, and the more effective deployment of those resources, will go a long way toward elevating our primary and secondary education systems to the world-leading standards that Americans are entitled to expect. However, if we are to rally the nation behind these changes, we must also increase the confidence of parents in the ability of their children's schools to deliver appropriate teaching materials and the confidence of teachers in their freedom to exercise their professional competencies while being properly remunerated for their work.

Our schools have recently become battlegrounds in the culture wars that are dividing our nation. On the one hand, academic views that depart from those of the American mainstream are comparatively common in our classrooms. On the other hand, attempts from outside the teaching profession to control the curriculum have led to increasingly frequent campaigns to ban books as well as highly questionable decisions about what should be included in course materials. One way to pour oil on these waters will be to recruit teaching staff from a broader cross-section of society with a more representative spectrum of political views, a possibility that opens up with increased pay for the teaching profession. This will act as a brake on the tendency of many educational establishments to act as an ideological vanguard for views that have not achieved broad consensus in the communities they serve. At the same time, while parents have the right to expect that their children are not being taught fringe views, the ability of PTAs and elected school board officials to guide the teaching practice of qualified professionals must be limited. Professional standards should be a matter for the professionals themselves, in the same way that the medical and legal professions oversee their own practices.

Recommended Action Points

- First, we need to pay our teachers more. Teaching our children is clearly one of the most critically important jobs in America. The average public-school teacher's pay is currently $60,000 per annum. I believe that this should be raised to $75,000, a 25 percent increase, with the goal of attracting and retaining better teachers, especially in poorer school districts. According to the National Center for Educational Statistics, in 2022, there were 3.2 million public-school teachers in America.[48]

- Free preschool for all American-born children and children of permanent residents is essential for providing a true head start for every child in the nation. Free before-and after-school care for the children of parents who have to work early or late shifts is also a necessity if we expect parents to be active in the job market without negatively affecting their children's educational achievement.

- We also need to raise the level of financial support provided to underfunded schools to the same level as schools in middle- or upper-class areas. The current average spend per student in the United States is \$14,347 per year.[49] While important steps have been made to bring funding across the country up to this level, we now need to take the final step to eliminate all lasting disparities.

- A greater degree of professional status and oversight in the teaching profession will make it possible to demand greater accountability when it comes to delivering results. When children move on from grade school or middle school to high school, we need a proper system of assessment for testing that they have been suitably equipped for the transition, and that they have all the intellectual tools they need to benefit from the next tier of education. Assessing results and holding teachers and schools accountable is critical for ensuring that funds are properly distributed. And that means measuring outcomes so the teaching profession can model success and cut the dead wood. At the institutional level, schools need to adopt tools used by businesses, such as key performance indicators, to ensure accountability to stakeholders. The mission these organizations are responsible for is too critical to the health of our nation to allow them to muddle through in an unsystematic manner. There have been steps in the right direction in this respect, but the failure of educational cultures built around "teaching to the test" shows how much more work is needed. The future of our children depends on every school performing at an appropriate level.

If we are going to turn the educational key to the American dream, we need to make sure that key fits the lock.

- The environment in which a child is raised plays a critical role in determining their educational outcomes. Studies have consistently shown that children who grow up in single-parent homes are less likely to achieve their full potential at school than those from homes with two parents (it is less clear whether this effect arises from the financial constraints many single-parent families face or from a lack of strong role models). Unfortunately, young black Americans are disproportionately likely to grow up without one of their parents, and this is most frequently the father. To counteract this effect, we need a national Fathers Stand Up campaign to encourage and support absent fathers from all backgrounds, but especially within the black community, to take full responsibility for their children.

CHAPTER 15

Health Care in the United States: What's Wrong with This Picture?

In 2022, health-care spending in the United States hit a new high, as it does every year. Following a 4.1 percent rise in expenditure, total spending across the nation reached $4.5 trillion.[50] It is worth pausing for a moment to consider just how large that sum is. It is twice as big as the whole world's annual defense spending.[51] It is enough to pay off 15 percent of the total US national debt.[52] It is more than the gross domestic product of Germany, the fourth largest economy in the world, and 50 percent higher than the entire GDP of France.[53] It is possibly the largest single economic line item in world history.

Not only does health-care spending dwarf any other area of expenditure in the US economy but it continues to grow at an extraordinary rate, outpacing our national economic growth almost every year and thus forming a larger and larger part of the economy. In the last fifty years, health care has gone from constituting approximately 7 percent of our economy to more than 17 percent, with inflation-adjusted expenditure per person increasing more than sevenfold.[54] This trend is expected to continue and even accelerate, with predictions for growth in the near future ranging from 4.8 percent[55] to 7.1 percent a year.[56]

Unsurprisingly, these enormous sums buy a lot of health-care services. The United States prides itself on having the best hospitals and doctors in the world, the most advanced pharmaceutical and medical tech industry, and the leading research universities. But while we get a lot of facilities and expertise for the $13,500 we spend, on average, per person per year,[57] we don't do so well on what should be the key metric: health-care outcomes.

It is certainly true that our health-care system can deliver world-class health care to those who have full and unencumbered access to it. But for many Americans, the experience is devastatingly costly and delivers outcomes far below of other developed nations.[58] A recent Commonwealth Fund report studying health care in eleven industrialized nations ranked the United States highly (second) for its care process (preventive medicine; engagement with patient preferences; safety of care; coordination of care) but last in every other category: access to care; health outcomes; and administrative efficiency and equity. Two charts from the report paint the picture with exceptional clarity.

Here's what our health system costs us compared to other countries:

Health Care System Performance Compared to Spending

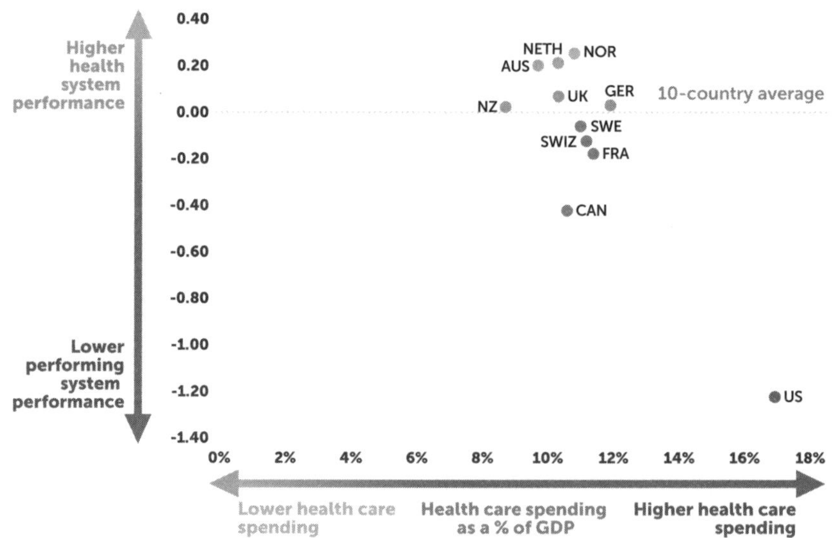

Note: Health care spending as a percent of GDP. Performance scores are based on standard deviation calculated from the 10-country average that excludes the US. See *How We Conducted This Study* for more detail.

Data: Spending data are from OECD for the year 2019 (updated in July 2021).

Source: Eric C. Schneider et al., *Mirror, Mirror 2021—Reflecting Poorly: Health Care in the U.S. Compared to Other High-Income Countries* (Commonwealth Fund, Aug. 2021). *https://doi.org/10.26099/01DV-H208*

And this is what we get for our investment:

Comparative Health Care System Performance Scores

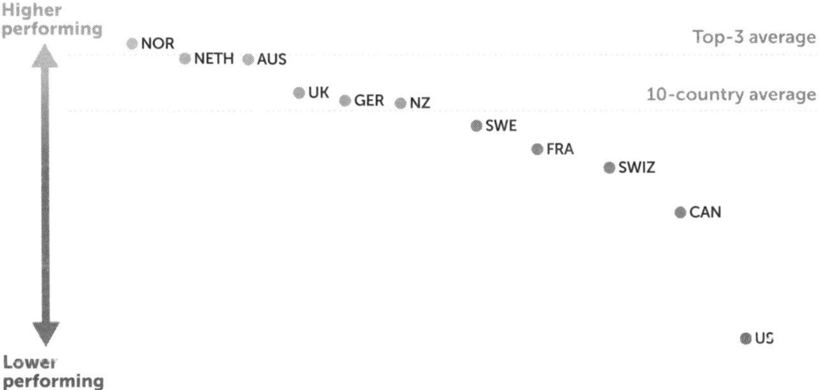

Note: To normalize performance scores across countries, each score is the calculated standard deviation from a 10-country average that excludes the US. See *How We Conduct This Study* for more detail.

Data: Commonwealth Fund Analysis.

Source: Eric C. Schneider et al., *Mirror, Mirror 2021—Reflecting Poorly: Health Care in the U.S. Compared to Other High-Income Countries* (Commonwealth Fund, Aug. 2021). *https://doi.org/10.26099/01DV-H208*

This failure to deliver anything remotely resembling value for money is bad enough. But our system manages to fail the American people in another, equally devastating, way. Of all the world's industrialized nations, America is unique in having high levels of bankruptcies arising from medical debt. Medical expenses cause approximately half a million Americans to fall into bankruptcy each year, a figure that amounts to nearly 60 percent of all bankruptcies in the nation.[59] And these are just the most extreme cases. One hundred million Americans, including 41 percent of all adults, are now burdened with at least some medical debt.[60] For the 27 percent of Americans who have less than $1,000 in savings,[61] almost any uninsured medical expense can plunge them into debt. And even for the next 29 percent who have between $1,000 and $50,000 put away, any major illness, or even a pregnancy with complications, can be financially devastating. For more than half of Americans, then, a major illness represents not just a health emergency but also a potential threat to their long-term financial well-being.

The result is that many Americans live with a sword of Damocles hanging over them. Even those with good jobs and stable finances cannot feel relaxed about their future because they cannot predict the effects of an illness. This sense of financial insecurity, of a merely conditional stability, divides Americans into two very distinct classes, with all the consequences this has for our long-term political stability. Americans who feel that they live precarious existences despite residing in the richest nation the world has ever known are more likely to look to the political extremes for answers when the politicians in the center fail to deliver solutions. After all, if our country is unable to preserve the health and life that is necessary to enjoy liberty and the pursuit of happiness, then it is quite reasonable to ask whether the community truly operates in the interests of all its members. If it does not, then that system faces a crisis of legitimacy, at least in the minds of those who do not have the resources to enjoy its benefits.

The rising cost of health care is not only outstripping the growth of our national economy but also wage growth and inflation. (2023 was a rare exception on this latter front).[62] This places an extraordinary burden on millions of ordinary working Americans. The financial risks that accrue with medical problems can not only send a family that has done everything right from prosperity to poverty through no fault of their own, but also have broader systemic effects. The risks created by our system dampen individual economic dynamism and act as a barrier to new opportunities through the phenomenon known as job lock. The fear of losing insurance coverage affects the employment decisions of many Americans,[63] because the dangers involved in giving up stable health insurance are simply too high in many cases to make it viable to pursue other opportunities. And while working Americans grapple with the failures of this system, so, too, do small businesses, which find it increasingly difficult to meet the expenses of providing quality health-care benefits, to the advantage of their larger competitors.[64] At Aspire we made the conscious choice to cover

100% of our employees medical benefit costs for all of our staff. The annual cost exceeded $600K, which is a major expense for a company of less than 200 full-time employees.

The differences in health outcomes for different economic groups is stark. While life expectancy follows the decades-long trend of continual increases for the wealthy, it has actually begun to fall over the last decade for less well-off Americans. The difference in life expectancy between the highest and lowest income groups in the United States is more than fifteen years for men and more than ten years for women.[65,66] This pattern is repeated across many domains of health outcomes, from infant mortality[67] and childhood obesity[68] to cancer survival rates[69] and prevalence of chronic conditions.[70] In short, Americans are divided not only by the number of years they can expect to live but also by their quality of life in those years.

The impact of these unequal outcomes unsurprisingly feeds into feelings of anger and alienation, supporting the view that the system doesn't work for the average American. I believe that it is time to recognize the right to a healthy life as a basic feature of this country's social contract, a crucial contributing factor to equal access to the American dream. When we see basic health as a privilege rather than a right, we effectively say that the less wealthy should have less time to spend in the pursuit of happiness and less happiness in the time they have. We say that a cast of the dice should be able to sweep away a family's future, not just undermining the health and finances of the person who becomes ill, but shifting the next generation of the family into an economic group in which their own outcomes will be worse. And we say that it is acceptable for our system of government to fail to deliver a solution that is enjoyed in the rest of the Western world.

Perhaps the most damaging feature of our health-care system is that it simply does not have to be like this. Our system is the result of political choice rather than necessity. And that is why its failures sting so badly.

Recommended Action Points

- The government should introduce a fully funded American health insurance program that automatically enrolls all US citizens. Variations on such a system have been adopted by every other industrialized nation, and it is long past time that the United States caught up. The persistent inability of politicians to implement health policy that aligns with the public's will is a central example of the failure of our current political class to deliver effective governance. With the exception of a brief period during the debates around Obamacare, since the beginning of the century a majority of Americans have consistently held the view that the government should ensure full health-care coverage.[71] The gap between public opinion and political action not only exacerbates societal divisions but also feeds into the increasingly intense public dissatisfaction and mistrust of the political establishment. Achieving the goal of universal coverage will require moving past the political and ideological divides that define the current health-care debate. We need to foster a nuanced discussion about what works, and the practical steps we need to take. A health-care system in which costs do not threaten the economic stability of individuals is vital for the collective well-being of the nation as it provides a shared foundation for the pursuit of a shared dream. Without it, a critical part will be missing from our national fabric: the element that shows that we value the lives and well-being of every American equally. According to a recent Yale study, moving to a single-payer system will reduce America's health-care costs by some $450 billion a year.[72]

- I believe as much as anyone in the importance of market forces and the power of market demand in driving efficiency. But I do not believe that health and life should be subject to these forces without restriction. Having grown up in the UK, and with family members and friends still living there, I am well aware of both the benefits and flaws of Britain's National Health Service (NHS), which provides world-leading care to every British resident, free at the point of delivery, and paid for through taxation. The medical care the NHS delivers is truly excellent, but follow-up, support, and administration all show the negative effects of a lack of market forces to weed out inefficiencies. The ideal solution, I believe, is a hybrid public/private model for the delivery of care, ensuring universal provision for everyone but in a system that includes privately run health-care providers to drive efficiency.

- Eighty-two percent of Americans believe that the cost of prescription drugs is unreasonable, and 73 percent support government regulation to place caps on drug prices.[73] There is a clear national consensus in this area and it is vital that we act on it.

CHAPTER 16

We the People: The Changing Face of America

The United States is famously a nation of immigrants, and as a first-generation migrant of fifty years' standing, I am proud to be part of that long tradition. Yet ironically, despite a unique historical background that makes more than 98 percent of American citizens the descendants of families with their roots in other lands, immigration is currently one of the most contested issues in American politics. In the last annualized period for which we have data, 2.5 million immigrants were apprehended after crossing the southern border, with hundreds of thousands more evading border patrols and moving directly into the interior of the United States. This staggering number amounts to more than the populations of San Francisco, Denver, and Seattle combined. Indeed, there are fifteen US states that have smaller populations than the number of known migrants entering the country in just one year and through just this one route. Given these figures, it is unsurprising that the subject of immigration is crystallizing debates around what it means to be American and what our nation should look like in the future. What is more worrying is that immigration has become a central focus for some of the most divisive and nasty rhetoric and decision making in US politics. To give just two examples, governments in several states have taken to bussing or flying undocumented migrants to sanctuary cities without any real informed consent, while some at the other end of the political spectrum use the absurdly emotive label of "concentration camps" to describe standard border security measures.

As in many of the other areas we explore in this section of the book, discussion of immigration has largely been captured by voices at the political extremes. On the one hand, we have those who think that immigration is a threat to America's essential identity. The underlying assumption, sometimes explicit and sometimes implicit, is that any shift that makes America less white (when put in terms of race) or less "European" (when framed in terms of culture) is an existential challenge that threatens the very foundations of our nation. This view grounds the American identity in an important but narrow slice of our country's history, seeking the roots of that identity in the founding of the thirteen colonies and then their fight for freedom from British rule. It sees the expansion of that state and the swallowing up of most of the North American landmass not just as legitimate but as determining which race and culture stands at the center of the American story. Native American stories are treated as marginal, relevant only where they intersect with the growth of the United States, and the same is true for the histories of the land that was once Mexican, Spanish, French, Hawaiian, or Russian. The story of "we the people" then becomes the story of the white Anglo-Saxon settlers, at least at first, with the gradual absorption of certain other European identities into the mix (normally after a period of exile on the fringes, as the Irish, Jewish, Italian experiences attest). Those with clearly and *visibly* distinct histories—African Americans, Chinese Americans, Indian Americans, Arab Americans, Hispanic Americans, and so on—are granted a place in the picture only when we talk about the great American melting pot, with their identities and values falling away to become aligned with those of the stars of the story. Ultimately, these identities are positioned as a supporting act to what it *really* means to be American. And that is to look a certain way, have a certain family history, hold certain religious beliefs, and pursue certain cultural practices. Ironically, as a first-generation migrant who ticks all these boxes, I am often treated as more authentically American than a descendant of one of the hundreds of thousands of Chinese Americans who emigrated to the country in the late nineteenth century.

To the people who believe that the American story is essentially a white European story, current demographic trends seem like a threat to both their culture and their personal identity. And these trends are changing the makeup of America very rapidly indeed: the US Census Bureau currently predicts that the non-Hispanic white population will become a minority by 2050, just twenty-six years away. In the context of this story about what America was, is and should be, the current extremely high rates of undocumented immigration pose a clear and present danger to the identity, and thus the survival, of the United States.

At the opposite pole of the debate, we have the view that there is no amount of immigration that could be too high. Proponents of this position reject entirely the idea that American identity should be anything to do with the white, European history of the state. Indeed, in today's America, that history is often depicted as a historical sin, with the people who have previously been marginalized deserving a greater than equal say and greater than equal opportunities now to redress the balance of historical injustice. On this account, the American story needs to be retold, with the previously dominant group relegated to a secondary status, at best, or assigned the role of villain, at worst. America, for those who hold this view, has no essential identity at all and is nothing beyond the people who happen to live here now, wherever they might have come from and however they might have entered the country. Traditional American values, such as those enshrined in the constitution, are not viewed as sacred, and nor are the Founding Fathers held up as great examples of humanity. Instead, they are typically castigated for regressive political views that seem abhorrent by the standards of the modern day. The constitution itself is depicted as stained with the blood of the oppressed, the result of a Faustian pact that wrote the horrors of slavery into the legal and moral code of the country at its birth. On this account, there is nothing special, nothing inspiring about America, and therefore nothing to protect from the changes that would inevitably stem from uncontrolled immigration. It follows that those who have entered the country in contravention of America's laws should never be referred to as illegal, should never be denied essential access to certain essential services, and more generally, should never be treated in any way that is distinct from a citizen of the country.

The majority of Americans roll their eyes at the excesses of both of these views. Eighty percent of Americans, for instance, think that local governments should cooperate with federal law enforcement officers when it comes to turning over undocumented migrants who are arrested for other criminal acts, a key point rejected by the sanctuary city idea.[74] But that does not necessarily mean they would prefer a zero-immigration approach aimed at preserving a white, Christian, European American identity. It turns out that most Americans hold far more nuanced positions than this, even if there is not a perfect consensus on every point. Sixty-one percent of Americans think the falling share of the white population is neither bad nor good while just 13 percent think it is somewhat bad, 9 percent very bad, and 15 percent either somewhat or very good.[75] Yet somehow our debate about these topics has come to be framed as a battle between the two extremes rather than as a search for sensible and balanced policy making in the middle ground.

Here are a few points that I believe most Americans can agree on, and that we should *insist* on when fringe activists from either end of the political spectrum start banging their drums.

There is nothing essentially white about America. The story we tell of our nation needs to do far more to acknowledge the mistreatment of the Native Americans at the hands of settlers, including the massacres, displacements, and breaches of the treaties agreed with the US government. Similarly, we must ensure that the traumatic experiences of enslaved Africans, who were chained and sent into a brutal servitude are just as much a part of our American history as the Pilgrim Fathers and the Revolutionary War. The effect of these moral abominations still taints our contemporary society hundreds of years later. However, this recognition of the breadth of the

American story does not mean we should deny the contributions of those with European heritage or the many benefits that have accrued from the transmission of strands of European culture and science to North America. While these benefits were reserved solely for white Americans for far too long, they are important factors that feed into much of what now makes America the most powerful and vibrant economy and research center the world has ever seen.

We can accept that the scientific and industrial revolutions, the energetic spirit of the early pioneers, and an open-minded humanism that has been shaped by a gentle Christian ethos have all provided valuable gifts to our modern America. And we can do so while acknowledging that more extreme versions of these views and ideologies have been damaging, and that this damage is often manifested in the marginalization of minority groups. The task for our modern age is not the simplistic picking and choosing of one history or the other but the careful curating of positive impacts while we work to undo the injustices and biases that still remain. America is an essentially complex and evolving community, and the story we tell about it should match that complexity and that ability to change. Polarizing accounts that set modern Americans against each other, or that define our nation by fixing it in place in relation to the goods and bads of the past should not be allowed to pass unchallenged.

America exists as a legitimate nation made up of its current citizens. The colonial origins of our state, historic injustices to racial groups, and the supplanting of the Native Americans all need to be recognized, addressed, and appropriately apologized for. But they do not undermine the reality of 330 million people in the modern day exercising their national self-determination over the land in which most of them were born. Nor do I believe that financial reparations for descendants of slaves is an answer for our country going forward. The idea that history can be unrolled, and that modern Americans should be held responsible, individually or collectively, for injustices committed before they were born is both naïve on a practical level and fundamentally corrosive to our national community. Not only does such an approach divide America today into oppressors and oppressed based on the actions of those long dead, but I do not believe the transfer of unearned lump sums from one part of the population to another is compatible with our national ideals. Nor will it lead to real change in the communities on the receiving end, as handouts will never be treated with the same reverence as wealth that has been earned. Rather, as this book advocates throughout, and especially in its final chapter, the creation of new programs to ensure that every American child can achieve as much as their talent permits is the best way to level out historic imbalances. The answer to the problems of the past is to build a better future that unites us, not to create, entrench or intensify prior divisions. Any policy that seeks to separate Americans into an *us* and a *them* should be wholeheartedly rejected.

No noncitizen has any fundamental right to residence and citizenship in this nation through any route other than that laid down by the law of the United States. Immigration can have both positive and negative effects, and it is perfectly reasonable for America to actively seek a balance that works for its citizens, even if that balance does not suit every noncitizen who wishes to come here to live and work. Racism and prejudice against any type of ethnic, national, or religious identity should have no place in our immigration policy. However, there is nothing essentially racist about enforcing our immigration laws. Increased security at our southern border is an important tool in the enforcement armory, and seeking to control our borders is a fundamental part of being a nation state. At the same time, we need a careful and honest assessment of the amount of legal immigration we require and of how to facilitate it. Our economy currently relies on a growing population and this growth depends heavily on healthy immigration figures. The current system for legal migration is inadequate to its task. So, to manage this inflow, we need to create robust routes for legal migration that can accommodate high volumes as needed.

I am confident that a clear majority of Americans will agree with almost everything I have outlined in these three points. If that is correct, then these are the discussion points we need to force to the forefront of the national debate about immigration and identity. We should set them up as the main line of argument against both extremes, rather than allowing extremist views the oxygen of publicity that comes from duking it out with each other in the town square.

I would like to add two further suggestions for the reader's consideration. These views do not reflect the current majority consensus, but I believe they can help us move forward toward a more *united* United States.

Recommended Action Points

- The classic image of America as a melting pot has served our nation well in many senses, providing an important and valuable way of thinking about the coming together of cultures into a unified whole. However, I believe it is time to retire this metaphor, or rather to adapt it for the modern era. The image of the melting pot suggests the gradual annihilation of differences, the removal of division through a process by which we all become the same. We have a long enough history to look at now to know that this is really not what happens. A more useful, and accurate, way of thinking about the ongoing evolution of America is to see the nation as a great mosaic in which each individual tile remains well defined and unique but becomes part of something greater through its combination with its neighbors. This does not imply that there is no change when a new tile is added. It might offer contrast, or shading, or sparkle to the tiles around it and to the picture as a whole. And it takes on new significance in its own right by its juxtaposition with other tiles. We should not, I believe, aim for a culture that will ultimately become uniform and homogenous. Not only is it likely that we will fail in our goal but the outcome if we succeed will be less desirable. Yes, those nations with homogeneous cultures are more stable and consistent over time, but they also lack the dynamism that comes from difference. The rich cultural differences we enjoy in the United States add variety, cognitive diversity, and spice to our lives.

Let's celebrate that difference even if we have to work harder at making all the pieces of the mosaic fit.

- Finally, to help unite our nation going forward, I believe we need to create a national campaign that identifies and communicates our shared identity. The people of Costa Rica offer a fantastic example of the way in which a few words can transmit and embed a shared ethos. The positive approach to life in this small but dynamic country is summed up in the philosophy of *pura vida* (pure life). Pura vida is both a mindset and a motto, a phrase used as a salutation or a mark of happiness or satisfaction. It reflects and encourages a lifestyle that is relaxed, carefree, and optimistic.

- I believe we need a similar motto in America, a phrase that consciously and explicitly frames the goal of moving past the current era of division and nastiness that is pulling our country apart. This national branding campaign will need careful thought. However, to get the ball rolling, I would like to offer an initial idea for consideration.

- So much of how we relate to each other is conditioned by the language we use to address each other. To focus attention on what connects us, what holds us together as a single people, I would like to encourage my fellow Americans to address one another as "pal." As US citizens and permanent residents, we are *all* pals and we should all seek to find the friendly basis for coexistence that the word implies. On a more symbolic level, PAL also serves as an acronym for two things we desperately need in our political discourse: peace and love. With a little more effort to demonstrate our love for one another and our goal of coexisting in peace, I am confident we can move forward into a new, more friendly era.

- The US needs to remain a safe haven for those seeking asylum. However, I believe that we need to begin that process outside our borders. In 2023, the US Border Patrol processed almost 2.3 million initial applications from asylum seekers at the southern border alone, temporarily admitting this huge number without any finality and with many given court dates as far as four years in advance. The good news is that more than 80 percent of such individuals are currently showing up for their hearings. However, even just 20 percent of initial applicants slipping into the population with no intention of following the legal procedure amounts to almost half a million undocumented migrants a year. These numbers are unsustainable. I believe we should thus create overseas processing centers to ensure that all those who wish to claim asylum can do so more easily and in the correct way, entering the country only when their application has been finalized. At the same time, we need to make it much harder to follow a path to asylum that involves breaking our laws by crossing the southern border illegally.

CHAPTER 17

Crime, Justice and Quality of Life

Crime, law enforcement, and gun ownership have become three of the most politically explosive issues of our time. Public debates on these issues tend to be highly polarized and emotionally charged, with advocates on either side taking up entrenched positions that are as much a reflection of their identities as they are of any relevant facts. Unsurprisingly, party affiliation provides an excellent indicator of likely views on each of these subjects. Our views on these topics are particularly important because they directly shape our quality of life, increasing levels of fear are leading us to see fellow Americans as threats to our well-being and property. Unfortunately, here as elsewhere, it is the loudest, most passionate and most unyielding voices that dominate the discussion when nuance and a careful analysis of the data are vital to any real understanding of the issues.

As individuals, very few of us sit down and crunch crime data every day to assess whether crime is rising or falling. Instead, we tend to form our opinions at one remove, based on personal experiences, the anecdotes we hear from neighbors, the volume of reports we see on the news or the emphasis that politicians place on the topic. These are not rigorous or reliable sources of data. As a result, our assessments about whether crime is rising or falling tend to be extraordinarily poor.

As 2023 drew to a close, 77 percent of American believed that crime rates were rising across the country.[76] The truth was that crime had fallen dramatically over the previous year, with violent crime down 8 percent and property crime reaching its lowest levels since the start of the 1960s.[77,78] Across twenty-six Gallup surveys over the last thirty years,[79] there has been only one occasion on which more Americans thought that crime was falling rather than rising. Most years (twenty-one out of the twenty-six annual surveys), the number of Americans who believe crime is rising exceeds 60 percent,[80] with those who think it is falling hovering between 15 percent and 25 percent. Yet across this period, crime in America has been slashed dramatically. Violent crimes have been cut in half; homicides are down nearly 40 percent; property crimes have more than halved.[81] After two decades of dramatic falls, the last ten years have seen crime rates stabilize at a new low level in some categories (e.g., homicide, violent crime) or continue to fall in others (e.g., property crime), giving us some of the lowest levels we have seen in the last half a century. And yet in that time there was not a single year in which a majority of Americans believed crime was falling (the figures for the single year in which those who thought crime was falling exceeded those who thought it was rising were: 41 percent rising; 43 percent falling; 10 percent the same).

It seems obvious that an important factor contributing to the widespread disconnect between perception and reality is the frequency and tone of media reporting on the subject. "If it bleeds, it leads" has been a key editorial policy for many news outlets for over a hundred years now. Conflict, drama, and tension are central elements to successful storytelling, and crime stories have these features in abundance. Since news organizations are businesses that make their money by keeping audiences reading or watching, it is no surprise that coverage of crimes remains consistent even when the crime rate is low. And this, of course, impacts the audience. In a 2018 study, around 70 percent of Americans stated that the reports of crime they encountered on media and social media channels influenced their perception of how much crime there was in America.[82]

The media and social media are not the only factors amplifying this disconnect between perception and reality. At least since Nixon, the promise to clamp down on crime, and on the threat of violence in particular, has been a powerful electoral tool, and it is one that politicians continue to exploit today. Of course, Americans do indeed suffer from criminal behavior, with rates of homicide in particular far exceeding those of any other Western nations.[83] Too many individuals throughout the country have their assets, their earnings, or even their lives damaged or destroyed by criminals. But the sensible answer to these problems is to improve policing, deter cybercrime, and ensure the criminal justice system works effectively and efficiently. Instead, many politicians prefer to spread a low-grade miasma of fear that encourages Americans to look at their fellow citizens with suspicion. When figures at one extreme speak of "American carnage" while those at the other demonize communities in which legal gun ownership is a part of life, it is because they find political advantage in fostering division rather than seeking sensible solutions that will work for all Americans.

It is no surprise that Americans tend to associate communities other than their own with crime. In 2023, 63 percent of Americans described the problem of crime in America as either "extremely serious" or "very serious," with only 8 percent saying it was "not too serious" or "not at all serious." But when asked about crime in their own areas, only 17 percent of respondents said the problem was extremely or very serious, while 47 percent said it was not too or not at all serious. This pattern has remained consistent for over twenty years now, ever since the data started to be collected.[84] Only a small proportion of Americans experience crime as a major problem in their own area, but vast numbers assume that things are terrible across the country as a whole. These opinions foster an us-versus-them dynamic when the happy truth is that the long-term trend shows crime becoming less of a problem, not more.

I find it extremely interesting that the only year in the last thirty in which Gallup's annual survey found more Americans perceived crime to be falling than rising was 2001. Gallup conducts its surveys in October, with 2001's data being gathered almost exactly thirty days after the September 11 attacks.[85] This was a time of heartbreak and tragedy for America, but it was also a unique moment of national unity and resolution. I cannot help but wonder whether that brief window in which we came together as a country impacted perceptions of how likely Americans were to commit criminal acts against each other. It is at least a startling coincidence that this unique data point aligns almost perfectly with that unique time in our nation's history. Since then, the increasing vehemence of the view that crime is rising has almost perfectly tracked the increasing political division in our nation, detaching almost entirely from actual crime data trends.

Whether this relationship is causal or is merely coincidental, there are two distinct but related issues we need to tackle as a nation when it comes to crime. On the one hand, it is vital that we address the imbalance between perception and reality when it comes to crime rates. These misapprehensions about crime are destructive: They lower our quality of life by making us more fearful than is necessary; they give power to those who should remain on the political fringes by suggesting that American society needs to be upended to fix a problem that does not exist in the form that they claim it does; they push us apart from one another by drawing dividing lines between communities and framing other Americans as threats; and they feed into a narrative of national decline that only emboldens the extremists. We should all, then, make an effort to ground our views about crime rates in the evidence rather than in impressions we gain from media sources or politicians. And when we do use the media for statistical evidence, we should always take a moment to follow that data back to its source and confirm for ourselves what it actually says. The issue is too important to accept second-hand information that may have already been spun for political gain.

Nevertheless, it would be wrong to say that falling or stable crime rates mean there is no work to be done on the reality as well as the perception of crime. There are genuine problems with the way we manage criminality and serve as sources of national division. Critically, they also act as obstacles that block access to key features of the American dream for some groups of Americans.

One of the key focal points for tension in America today is the widespread perception that black Americans, and to a lesser extent, members of other ethnic minority groups, are treated unfairly at all levels of the criminal justice system, from policing and the courts through to the carceral system. Over the last decade, the proportion of Americans who believe that the police treat black and white citizens equally has fallen to a historic low of just 41 percent.[86] These views are reflected in the stark figures for fatalities in interactions with the police. A 2014 analysis showed that black teenagers are twenty-one times more likely than white teenagers to be killed by the police.[87] Similarly, while twice as many unarmed white men are killed by the police each year as unarmed black men, when adjusted for population size this means that black men are twice as likely to die in these circumstances.

A similar statistical imbalance appears in the data for our court and prison systems. While black people constitute just 12 percent of the US population, they make up 33 percent of those in prison.[88] A 2023 report by the United States Sentencing Commission found that "Black males received sentences 13.4 percent longer, and Hispanic males received sentences 11.2 percent longer, than White males."[89] The data for variance in state sentencing is less robust, but given the racial disparities in the make-up of prison populations in many states, it seems likely that the same or greater difference in sentencing outcomes exists at this level.

We need to be careful about the conclusions we draw and the policies we recommend on the basis of our current information. At one political extreme, this data leads to the conclusion that police departments across the United States, as well as the justice system more broadly, are institutionally racist, and that we should therefore burn the current system down (literally in some cases). This line of thought manifests in calls to defund the police, to ignore organized, flash-mob shoplifting and looting, and to accept violent rioting and zones of lawlessness as a natural response to systemic injustice.

Extreme responses like these have no place in the political discourse of a moderate society. The acceptance of violence against individuals and property in support of political ends can never be condoned, regardless of how noble the underlying goal might be. But before we even think about what type of response might be appropriate, we need to consider the facts in more detail to establish what really requires a response of any sort. Because once we move beyond the headline figures, the picture that emerges is much more complex and nuanced.

Let's start with sentencing. While it is clear beyond a shadow of a doubt that there is a racial disparity in sentencing, it is far less clear that this arises from any structural racism in the court system. Unfortunately, while we have very good data for the disparity itself, there has been much less research on the more complex question of the sources of this disparity. Prosecutors argue very reasonably that these differences are invariably driven by the backgrounds to the specific cases in question, reflecting the fact that a previous record of criminal behavior tends to be more common in the case of minority perpetrators. It also seems likely that a considerable part of this imbalance arises not from the courts themselves being racially biased but from the system failing to deliver equal justice to those who lack the financial means to defend themselves, a socioeconomic group to which black people disproportionately belong. However, more fine-grained research is clearly needed in this area.

When it comes to policing, we first need to start with an acknowledgement that institutionalized racism is part of the history of American law enforcement, just as it is part of our history as a nation. Even in the aftermath of the civil rights era, there is a plausible argument that some of the legislation that leads to disproportionate numbers of black men being incarcerated was initiated and entrenched for at least partially racist reasons. If we are to take Richard Nixon's domestic policy advisor John Ehrlichman at his word, the War on Drugs had its origins in part in a desire to target and disrupt the black communities that consistently voted for Nixon's political opponents. As Ehrlichman put it in a 1994 interview, "The Nixon campaign in 1968, and the Nixon White House after that, had two enemies: the antiwar left and black people. You understand what I'm saying? We knew we couldn't make it illegal to be either against the war or black, but by getting the public to associate the hippies with marijuana and blacks with heroin, and then criminalizing both heavily, we could disrupt those communities."[90] It also seems clear that at least some police officers today have explicit or implicit racial biases and carry those biases into their work. And sometimes, these prejudices lead to fatal outcomes for unarmed black people who come into contact with the police.

All this can be true, and all this can require urgent attention, without validating many of the extreme attitudes toward the police that have become commonplace among some political commentators and activists. Here the situation increasingly seems to mirror that of the beliefs about crime rates that we looked at above. An increasing media focus on certain dramatic issues in our society is making unacceptable but rare behavior appear to be far more common than it is. There is certainly no factual basis for suggesting that racist attitudes are held by the majority, or even a significant number, of officers across our nation. I passionately believe that we are making important steps in the right direction as a society when it comes to issues of racial justice. And I believe equally passionately that it is vital to shine a spotlight on unacceptable or criminal behavior by police officers and other law enforcement officials when it occurs. But in rightly seeking to address these issues, some of the loudest voices in our society have now swung too far in the opposite direction, leaving critical thinking behind. The result is an impression that things are getting worse when they are getting better, leading to an entrenching of difference and a deepening of divisions that has too often spilled over into violence. As a consequence, other sources of danger that deserve as much or more publicity, such as the more than 600 homicides in South Chicago in the course of 2023, are starved of the attention they deserve.

The response to the death of Michael Brown in Ferguson, Missouri, is a case in point here. After Brown was shot by a police officer in 2014, a wave of rioting and discontent shook the nation. Three months later, when a grand jury determined that the officer responsible should not face criminal charges in the matter, more unrest broke out across the country. Protestors focused in particular on the claim that Brown had his hands up at the time of the shooting and had been heard by witnesses saying, "Don't shoot!" While these claims about the events have become deeply rooted in the public consciousness, very little attention was paid to the results of an exhaustive Justice Department investigation into the events commissioned by the Obama administration and Attorney General Eric Holder, which was published in March the following year. This inquiry by a body with no connection to local law enforcement found that there was not a single credible witness who claimed that Brown was trying to surrender when he was shot. Instead, the report found that "Not only do eyewitnesses and physical evidence corroborate [the officer's] account, but there is no credible evidence to disprove [his] perception that Brown posed a threat to [him] as Brown advanced toward him."[91] The evidence here stands in stark contrast to that in the case of the murder and manslaughter convictions of multiple police officers for their part in the death of George Floyd, and yet the two cases are frequently treated as if they should be given equivalent weight.

Police officers in America at the moment face a demoralizing and difficult task, seeking to keep communities safe while trust in their motives and actions deteriorates. I admire those who take on this task, and I believe we would all benefit from walking a mile in their shoes before adopting excessively critical views. Nevertheless, I also think that we need to fundamentally rethink our approach to policing in this country. While knee-jerk reactions in the absence of real evidence—as well as rioting, looting, and other destructive behavior—muddy the waters and encourage defensiveness and the adoption of entrenched positions, policing, for many, is an important source of the feeling that this country does not work in their interests. A greater focus on collaborative, community-based policing can help those in underprivileged communities feel that the system is working for them, not against them.

Recommended Action Points

- Attitudes to cash bail provide a useful testcase for calibrating balanced policies that meet both the needs of the public and those of individuals who interact with the criminal justice system. Historically, the requirement to provide cash bail after an arrest has been highly prejudicial to those in lower income brackets, with the effects falling disproportionately on black and Latino Americans. Forcing those who have few assets to sit in jail while awaiting trial leads to a two-tier system that pushes those in need further into poverty, leading to the loss of much-needed wages and potentially the loss of jobs, housing, and even custody of their children in the case of single parents. In response to these outcomes, some states have almost entirely removed the requirement for cash bail, meaning that only the most dangerous alleged offenders will remain in jail before their trial. However, this means that most of those arrested are sent back onto the street within days, enabling the genuine criminals among them to continue their illegal business. There is no simple solution here, but what emerges from experiments with these policies in different states is that if the pendulum swings too hard in the opposite direction when attempting to solve a problem in the justice system, it can create entirely new problems. As ever, what is needed is balanced discussion and judgment rather than ill-thought-out policies that are swayed by political talking points.

- The police have frequently been tarred with an unfair brush in our recent national conversations due to the despicable actions of a small number of individuals. Policy platforms such as Defund the Police only add to the weight of pressures placed on those who already have to deal with physical violence and traumatic experiences on a regular basis. But if we strip away the terribly divisive branding, there are some nuggets of sense in the underlying ideas for police reform. It seems clearly correct that our law enforcement officers are not the right people to deal with certain issues, such as welfare checks and mental health callouts. It is not fair to expect the police to act as a public-service Swiss Army knife that can backstop failures to provide adequate resources to other services. So, the call should not be to defund the police, but rather to take a load off their shoulders by adequately funding other public services that work closely in tandem with the police.

- Policing is increasingly a highly sensitive and sophisticated profession. As such, I believe that all new law enforcement officers should hold a college degree, ideally in a criminal-justice-related subject. This will both improve base levels of education and maturity among new officers while also serving to balance attitudes that seem to increasingly align with those appropriate for military operations. Officers with college degrees should receive a 25 percent pay supplement to reflect their investment in their education and the additional value they bring to their communities.

- The adoption of a "warrior mindset" from the 1990s onward,[92] the increasing use of surplus military equipment, and the recruiting of many veterans has led to the embedding of an attitude that police officers are marching out to war each day, with the civilian population around them a potential threat. Tempering this worldview with a renewed commitment to community-based policing that sees more officers of the same ethnicity patrolling the streets and developing relationships with residents, will go a long way toward healing divisions.

- Discussions about the Second Amendment and the right to bear arms are some of the most tangled and emotive in US politics. Any engagement with the topic runs into deeply entrenched and divisive positions. On the one hand, these can be abstruse technical issues of textual interpretation regarding the intentions of the Founding Fathers or the rights of the courts. On the other, they can devolve into shouting matches in which supporters of gun control blame school shootings on gun rights advocates while gun rights advocates paint supporters of gun control as paving the way for tyranny. I have no illusion that we will resolve these issues here, but it is nevertheless worth outlining a few points on which I believe there is majority agreement in this country.

- Regardless of the intents of the founders, we need to have a sane and balanced discussion about how to apply rules around individual possession of firearms in a world in which weaponry has evolved in ways that would have been inconceivable to the original framers of those rules. There is clearly some line to be drawn about which arms can be borne—a nuclear weapon is obviously not okay—so absolutist views are of no use when asking where that line lies.

- A strong and consistent majority have favored stricter gun laws for more than thirty years. There is broad agreement (in excess of 75 percent in each case) that the gun show loophole for evading background checks should be closed, that those convicted of violent crimes should not be permitted to own guns, that there should be a combined national database of gun sales across all federal and state agencies, that red-flag laws should be strengthened, and that there should be a thirty-day waiting period for any gun purchase.[93,94] None of these requirements would prevent Americans from exercising their historic gun rights, yet these issues have become politicized. As a result, lines have been drawn over issues for which a cross-party consensus should already have been reached. This cannot be allowed to continue. We must demand that our political leaders put the clear will of the people into action in the form of these limited and sensible changes.

CHAPTER 18

Public (Dis)service Broadcasting

Across my career I have had the good and bad fortune to work with TV channels, radio shows, the print media and websites, blogs and podcasts. I have watched as the media landscape has changed and evolved from the simpler world of the 1970s to today's complex and multilayered web of content. From this personal and professional perspective that has been more than forty years in the making, I can confidently state that the current media landscape is one of the most important factors magnifying the divisions that are pulling apart the social fabric of America. We have never before had access to so much information so easily and so inexpensively. And yet, instead of leaving us better informed, the sheer quantity of facts and opinions overwhelms us. Nobody can possibly read and understand it all, so we tend to pick and choose from sources that feel socially and ideologically sympathetic. The result is an increasingly fractured experience of reality in which many Americans are unable to agree on even basic facts about the world, such as who won an election or whether climate change is real. Bad but easily digestible information increasingly displaces information that is of a higher quality but is harder for audiences to process. At the same time, a range of factors are leading our political discourse in increasingly aggressive and confrontational directions, with the result that the language of political violence has become almost mainstream in modern America.

In some cases, the traditional media has become a direct source of divisive opinions. Many news outlets now present their stories in a way that is framed by a partisan slant. Sometimes this is implicit, but the political biases and social values of media organizations are increasingly out in the open. MSNBC, CNN, and FOX News, for instance, make no pretense of hiding their political positioning and all three serve as campaigning platforms for the views they support. In other cases, a news organization's commitment to a political party may be less secure, but the output will still broadly reflect a particular world view. *The New York Times*, for example, can be relied upon to amplify and boost progressive views and causes while *The Wall Street Journal*'s opinion pages will almost invariably offer a conservative perspective on current events. Regardless of whether the outlet pins its heart to its sleeve or seeks to present itself as neutral, it is rare to find a truly balanced take on any noteworthy social or political event or trend.

As our society becomes more polarized, so the commercial imperative mounts to pick a side, which only serves to further fan the flames of division. But commercial forces also amplify differences in another way, providing the fuel of publicity that feeds and encourages toxic behavior. The shift to a twenty-four-hour news cycle that began in the 1990s is now complete. For news outlets to secure their financial survival, they have to focus on what is eye-catching. Dramatic news, angry outbursts, and convention-breaking behavior all grab more attention than reports of sedate procedural progress, polite discussion, and predictable words and choices. As a result, all news outlets are financially incentivized to maximize their coverage of the one and minimize the other, prioritizing coverage using the political version of the "If it bleeds, it leads" mantra. But where once sufficiently outrageous behavior would be enough to kill a political career, the current trend toward the extremes becomes a self-reinforcing spiral. Insults and unpleasantness now rile up the activist base and secure the oxygen of publicity, meaning politicians are incentivized to behave in increasingly divisive ways, just as media outlets are incentivized to cover this behavior. Unfortunately, no one appears to have grasped this strategy more effectively than Donald Trump.

Problematic as these trends in the traditional media landscape are, social media and other online "news" sources present an even greater danger. Here, too, we find that provocation is rewarded, with mechanisms such as Likes not only driving user engagement but also encouraging the underlying algorithms to increase the visibility of the bite-sized analysis, the hot take, the shocking or unpleasant comment. Lengthy posts and reasoned engagement with issues attract fewer thumbs up from the user base and so are distributed less widely, leading to them receiving less attention, and so on, in a vicious feed-back loop that punishes depth and thoughtfulness.

Not only do the mechanisms of these platforms promote shallow analyses but they also have an even more pernicious effect. A technology that was originally designed to connect people by helping them find social groups now serves to divide them with the very same tools. Social media algorithms are trained to group people together and create interactions based on the similarity of views. This would be fine if the grouping mechanisms just sought out radio-controlled plane enthusiasts or fans of square dancing and helped them build communities around their interests. But by applying the same approach to political views, these platforms create echo chambers in which partisan positions get recycled and intensified without fact checking or any force of moderation. In the worst cases, extremist views and conspiracy theories are entrenched, amplified, and then spread, where previously they would have died on the vine as the crazy views of a handful of kooks.

The anonymity of online forums for discussion is a further contributing factor. First, people feel able to say anonymously things that they would be unwilling to say in public because such views are so far from mainstream acceptability. As other users read these comments, their own view of what is within the bounds of public discourse begins to shift, with the end result that public, in-person pronouncements begin to approximate in their extremism, hatefulness, and mean-spiritedness the views that could initially only survive anonymously online. The cloak of anonymity thus not only provides cover for people to say terrible things but also acts as a slow poison that seeps into real-life, in-person discussions.

Anonymity also provides cover for bad actors who are intent on fomenting division in American society in order to weaken our nation's global power. Russia's use of troll farms and online personas to intensify and amplify extremist and divisive messages on both sides of the political divide is well documented and ranges from the organization of Black Lives Matter protests with no stewards on the ground in the hope that they turn violent to supporting fringe, but potentially dangerous, views such as the secession of Texas from the union,[95,96] all while pretending to be voicing the opinions of concerned American citizens. While the weight of evidence for Russian involvement is extremely high, we would be foolish to assume that no other geopolitical competitors are willing to use the same tools.

We are moving into an age in which these dangers will only increase. The ability of AI to mimic human writing and to manipulate texts, images, and videos threatens to supercharge the volume and effectiveness of disinformation campaigns. The World Economic Forum's 2024 *Global Risks Report* identifies misinformation and disinformation as the most dangerous threat to global stability in the next two years,[97] and it is certainly one of the most important risk factors for the stability of the United States as well.

So, how do we solve these problems? There are no easy answers, but the first step is for moderates to recognize that we *must* treat these issues as one of the greatest challenges of our time and that we *must* start a robust conversation aimed at finding a resolution. I believe that many of the resources we will need will come out of our organizing ourselves as a community with the shared goal of responding to these threats.

Some of the trends that are undermining our national unity involve a conscious or unconscious weaponization of one of our most important national values: freedom of speech. The First Amendment is a vital force for good in American society. It is not something that we can simply toss away as we respond to these challenges, and we must think with the greatest care and clarity before suggesting any policies that might undermine its force. It may become necessary to look again at the question of whether online anonymity should really enjoy constitutional protection, or whether legislation is needed to force social media platforms to police misinformation. But there are already many steps we can take collectively to improve the situation without butting heads with the First Amendment.

The free flow of information is something that is fundamental to our national identity, and we should neither take it for granted nor seek to impose curbs on it. Instead, we need to be courageous, organize and find tools of our own to ensure that good information and polite discussion drive out disinformation and discord. These are complex questions, but we cannot afford to wait before tackling them. If we leave it too late, there is a very serious risk that there will be no coming back from the looming precipice.

Recommended Action Points

- As individuals, we can begin by taking responsibility for calling out unacceptable views when we see them. The easy option is to let divisive, aggressive, and hate-filled talk pass in the hope that it will simply fade away. But we can now see perfectly clearly that this does not work. If we want the public square to be a place for the majority, then we will have to muster the courage to confront dangerous speech when we see or hear it, making it clear that it is unacceptable.

- Given the sheer quantity of dangerous and divisive views now circulating, we need to work together as a community to develop resources to stem the tide and make sure that it is the voice of the majority that rings out the loudest in our public spaces. Volunteer and professional organizations are needed to monitor, assess, and clarify the information that flows through our various on- and offline media channels. Adding layers of clarificatory information is a powerful way of disrupting misinformation and disinformation without limiting freedom of speech. Some have also called for a return of the Fairness Doctrine to better balance media commentary. While I do not think it necessary at this time, I do believe that we need to monitor social media very closely and act quickly and decisively in reaction to clearly harmful posts such as those that encourage criminal behavior or teen suicide. An alternative approach for the modern world would be to assign fairness ratings to media and social media outlets each year based on a rigorous assessment by an independent professional association.

- With the proliferation of polarizing echo chambers that push participants to the extremes, we, as moderates, need to create spaces for discussion that are militantly rational and pluralistic, and in which extremist views are not permitted to shout down or silence those who are willing to compromise and find a middle path. That puts the onus on the community of moderates to organize ourselves, creating a powerful combined voice. Only by doing so can we ensure that activists on the left and right are unable to take sole control of shaping the national debate.

- While the courts have ruled that online anonymity for humans is protected by the First Amendment, we need to push for rapid legislation to bar AI bots from representing themselves as real people. As the founder of Google's DeepMind has argued, AI agents should be forbidden, globally, from engaging in public discourse unless they identify themselves as nonhuman.[98] The right to know who is on the other side of the conversation should certainly go at least as far as knowing that they are a real person and not just a program pretending to be human as part of a deliberate bad-faith program to corrupt our public discourse.

- Finally, and perhaps most importantly, we need to make explicit efforts to see both sides of the argument on contentious issues. In the abortion debate, I am both pro-life and pro-choice simultaneously: I know not everyone shares my view as a Catholic that I would prefer there be no abortions, but I understand when a woman makes that decision. I just hope it is an informed one. As a Christian, I believe that God gave everyone free will, and it is certainly not my place to force my values onto women who find themselves facing difficult choices. I strongly believe we need to start becoming more open in such difficult areas and more willing to accept that what we think is right will not necessarily be the best policy for others or for the nation as a whole.

CHAPTER 19

A Wake-Up Call for the Tired Giant

The first half of the twentieth century was a period of unprecedented economic and social development for America. With the expansion westward across the North American continent complete and the fratricidal Civil War era a distant memory, America was the most dynamic financial and industrial power in the world. In the fifty years to 1940, the population of the United States more than doubled, from 63 million to 132 million.[99] Staggering industrial growth propelled America to become the world leader in steel, automobiles, aircraft and shipping, while American oil companies flourished both at home and abroad. At the same time, a dazzling cultural renaissance saw the US shake off the last of its colonial legacy, becoming a research powerhouse and the world center for new forms of art, music, and film. And yet, as our nation dreamed the American dream into reality at home, on the world stage it slumbered.

From time to time, when America turned its eye outward and set its thumb on the scale of world affairs, it would tilt the balance decisively. The decision to join the Allies in the First World War, for instance, helped bring that devastating conflict to a close, while the pioneering of modern arms limitation treaties at the Washington Naval Conference made a significant, if temporary, contribution to peace. But most of the time, the United States showed little interest in becoming embroiled in world affairs, focusing instead on its internal development and only showing an interest in foreign policy insofar as that policy might open up new markets for its goods. This inconstancy led to other powers of lesser strength dominating the world stage, with America considered to be unreliable at best and impotent at worst. The most damaging effects came from indecisiveness, as when America first led but then withdrew from international initiatives, with one administration proposing a new policy while the next fatally undermined it. The disaster that was the League of Nations was probably the most important failure of America's international will in this era.

The Second World War changed everything. It had been raging in Europe for more than two years when Japan attacked US sovereign soil at Pearl Harbor. This act of aggression, followed by Nazi Germany's declaration of war on America, gave the country no choice but to turn its gaze outward. The alternative was to allow the rest of the world to fall under the jackboot of fascism, leaving the United States isolated, at risk of invasion and, even if it could secure reasonable peace terms, cut off from its vital global markets. Despite some residual resistance to "foreign adventures," the nation rallied around the need to secure its global position by defending its allies and ensuring that its ideological enemies were unable to conquer the globe. In the years that followed the decisive victory against the Nazis, America secured its position as the dominant superpower by matching economic might with military power. As the leader of various alliances in Europe and the Asia-Pacific region, America's power has been responsible for a lasting peace. For nearly seventy years there has been no great power war to match the destruction of the global conflicts that caused so much damage in the decades before the United States stepped up to the plate.

The cost of maintaining this position as the global cop is immense. The US Department of Defense requested nearly $850 billion for the 2024 budgetary period alone,[100] an annual cost of $2,500 for every woman, man and child in the nation. A single US Navy carrier strike group has enough firepower to overwhelm the defenses of most nations around the world; America possesses eleven. The US Air Force is not only the largest but also the most advanced air force in the world by a very significant margin, while the US Army and the US Marine Corps have a tried and tested battlefield capability that is second to none. In exchange for this huge military investment, the United States can leverage its power to shape global policy in all sorts of ways that are unavailable to other countries, from securing the borders of friendly nations to guaranteeing the free flow of trade and having an effective veto on military coups or land invasions anywhere we consider to be within our sphere of interest.

Until very recently, there has been a solid cross-party consensus that America should maintain its leading place on the global stage rather than retreating back into isolationism. And this position still receives extremely strong support from a large majority of Americans. Sixty-eight percent of the population actively approves of continued membership of NATO, while 19 percent are indifferent, and just 7 percent are opposed.[101] And yet the position supported by a tiny minority is increasingly pushed by leading figures at one end of the political spectrum. Similarly, there is a broad consensus among Americans both in support of maintaining or increasing defense spending and for arming our international allies,[102] albeit with some doubts about the precise levels of spending.[103] Yet the loudest voices at the extremes seek to reduce spending for Ukraine (Republicans) or Israel (Democrats), based on politically led talking points.

Despite the firm agreement in the political center that America should maintain its position on the global stage, domestic infighting and congressional paralysis is leading to an international view of the United States as an increasingly tired superpower, a nation in retreat, politically hamstrung and the victim of inevitable decline. Where just twenty years ago commentators talked of America as the sole global hyperpower, the discussion now tends to focus on a giving way of the American century to one that will see the rise of new powers, and of China in particular. In this context, the risk of a retreat into isolation is increased by major policy failures of the last twenty years that have done huge damage to the credibility of American power.

There are two related pressures here that threaten to undermine our security by acting on public opinion both at home and abroad. On the one hand, the perception of America as falling short of its own stated moral values has led many to feel that taking on the role of global cop has a fundamentally corrupting effect on the national psyche. From the bombing of civilians in Vietnam and Cambodia during the 1960s and 1970s to the removal of democratic governments in South America and the more recent assessments of the invasion of Iraq after 9-11, the feeling that we have come to equate might with right strikes at the heart of our national self-image and our confidence in the just wielding of power. At the same time, and often in parallel with the questionable morality of some of America's overseas entanglements, a perception of strategic failure has also led to the view that a huge investment of blood and treasure has been wasted on endeavors that have led to shameful retreats, most notably in Vietnam and then again, fifty years later, in Afghanistan.

Despite the remarkable consistency of support from America's centrist majority, the calls to give up the role of global cop and retreat into isolation are only growing in volume. As someone who is fundamentally opposed to violence of any sort, I feel the pull of these ideas. The dream of taking some of the money from our defense budget and putting it to other uses, such as providing better quality education for our youth, is tantalizing. We could spend just half of our current defense budget and still have a military expenditure that would be higher than the next three countries combined while at the same time virtually eliminating our budget deficit. Or we could pump that money into directly saving American lives by funding new health-care initiatives. But tempting as these ideas sound, they are filled with enormous danger. Giving up our uncomfortable position as the dominant global power and reducing our defense spending to fit a posture based solely on protecting American soil would create a vast power vacuum in world affairs. The old truism that "nature abhors a vacuum" is just as salient in geopolitics as it is in physics. As soon as we step off the world stage, other nations will rush in to fill the space we once occupied. And when that happens, we will find ourselves back in the position we were in prior to WWII. China has made much of its so-called peaceful rise, but if there is one thing that history teaches us, it is that despotic regimes only remain peaceful so long as they are scared of the results of their violence. We can be certain that a China untrammeled by any fear of consequences would rapidly start to force its control over not just neighboring states—including a near-certain takeover of Taiwan—but anywhere it has an economic interest. The withdrawal of the United States from key institutions such as NATO would further embolden dictators like Vladimir Putin, who, as we have seen in the last two years, is more than happy to return to the dark days of wars of conquest in Europe.

Some might say, "So what? Why should we really care in America if other nations fall under the control of unpleasant regimes? So long as US citizens remain free in their homeland, why should we expend truly extraordinary sums of money to protect people who can't protect themselves?" These are perfectly reasonable questions, but there are clear and decisive answers to them. First, I believe we have a moral obligation to ensure that the rest of the world does not fall into darkness. America is more than just a collection of people living within certain lines on a map. It is an idea, an ideal, a beacon of democracy that stands as a symbol of the potential of humankind to live freely in the pursuit of happiness. If we give up our moral obligations to other people, I strongly believe that we give up a key part of our own identity.

The second reason is that maintaining global peace is critical to our own interests. Ever since the advent of nuclear weapons, the threat of an actual invasion of our shores has become infinitesimally small. At the same time, we are uniquely blessed in terms of the natural resources we have available to us as a nation of continental scale. Yet trade is still a vital part of our country's lifeblood. US exports to overseas customers account for more than 10 percent of national GDP, amounting to approximately three trillion dollars of value produced for our economy,[104] enough to pay for our current defense budget three times over. Of course, that is balanced by our imports, but even when imports and exports are cancelled out, and even if we assume that we could, tomorrow, meet all the needs of our national market from purely domestic production, we would still suffer a huge economic blow. A 2018 analysis estimated that the benefits of trade could be as much as 8 percent of GDP, based on the efficiencies the economy gains from bringing in goods and services that cannot be produced at the same favorable prices at home.[105] If we were cut off from global supply chains, we would all suffer significantly. The fuel price shocks of 2022 and 2023 have shown clearly that, despite our position as the largest oil producer in the world, we are still highly vulnerable to what goes on elsewhere. We also need to bear in mind that the United States was extremely fortunate in the resources discovered on the North American landmass during the twentieth century, with plentiful supplies of everything we needed to drive the development of our industrial might, from timber to iron ore to coal and oil. Other places around the world were not nearly so fortunate, and we cannot assume that every future resource needed for each new economic advance will be present locally and in abundance.

The third reason is that the globalization of our interests is not simply a matter of choice. Some problematic behaviors can cross borders, and we must retain the ability to carefully and selectively impose our will in case we need to act against serious, or even existential, threats. Overfishing or pollution with sources in other countries, for instance, could have major impacts on our national well-being. Global geopolitical instability can and does drive massive waves of immigration, with problematically large numbers finding their way to our shores. And as the power of new technologies such as artificial intelligence increases, we need to retain the capacity to strike back at those who would threaten us with digital attacks. While it would be nice to think that all these problems could be resolved diplomatically, the inability to impose our will, if necessary, could potentially be devastating.

A final point is that the defense budget may not be quite as expensive as it seems. It is impossible to quantify exactly how much defense spending helps the broader economy, especially in comparison to other hypothetical cases for using that money. However, in the field of technology in particular, defense spending acts as an important accelerant to innovation and technological breakthroughs. From jet engines to satellites and the Internet, the technical needs of the military have led to new technologies that have reshaped economic life in the civilian sector, and the enormous spending of the United States on this front—the defense R&D budget alone is higher than the entire defense budgets of most European nations—appears to be one of several contributors to our world-leading technology sector. While this is not in itself an argument for maintaining defense expenditure at its current high levels, it is at least worth considering when looking holistically at the big picture.

The United States is blessed with the largest and most dynamic economy in the world Although 3.1 percent of our national GDP is a huge amount when looked at as a dollar figure, when we consider our expenditure in proportion to the size of our economy, the size of our responsibilities, and the importance of protecting our global strategic and economic interests, it is, if not a small price to pay, then a price that is well within the bounds of reason.

Recommended Action Points

- As a nation, it is vital that we maintain our leadership of NATO and retain our bilateral alliances with our allies in the Pacific region. Ad hoc arrangements in times of need are no substitute for combined command-and-control, shared doctrines, and ongoing training based around the assumption of fighting together. Pulling back from our international military commitments significantly undermines our own defense capabilities, so we must insist that our politicians heed the will of the majority of Americans and reflect that will in their policies. The legislation passed in December 2023 to prevent any US president withdrawing from NATO without the consent of Congress is an excellent step toward ensuring stability on this front and the achievement of bipartisan support for this measure can serve as a valuable model for other measures to solidify our defense posture.

- Our commitments to our allies are not a one-way street. Some members of NATO are content to live under the umbrella of the America's military might, slashing their own defense budgets on the assumption that we will always provide for their needs. We should use every tool in our diplomatic and economic armory to pressure all NATO members to meet the commitment to spending *at least* 2 percent of their GDP on defense so that they can meet their own obligations to the alliance.

- We must always fight the good fight. One of the greatest dangers to our ability to use our military effectively abroad is a lack of support at home, and there is no better way to lose that support than to engage in wars of choice that do not serve fundamental ethical ends. If we are to be the heavyweight on the block, the guy with the big stick, then it is incumbent on us to be exceptionally careful about how we throw our weight around. We cannot be the incarnation of "the ugly American" in our military policy, asserting that our culture is superior or that might makes right. We can only have legitimacy in our international role if we act in the interests of both ourselves and the wider world. Part of taking a moral stance in world affairs involves taking a scrupulous approach to the protection of noncombatants, both in our own military actions and in our reaction to those of our allies. For instance, while I am convinced that America was right to stand firmly behind Israel in response to the heinous attacks by Hamas in October 2023, by failing to insist on a balanced response from the onset of the Gaza war, America not only ceded much of our moral authority on the world stage but also contributed to the future dangers that will inevitably arise from the reaction to so many civilian deaths, in the Middle East in particular.

- If we are to serve as the military leader of the free world, we have an obligation to clean up our act at home in parallel. The American crown has slipped in recent years, leaving our allies and opponents on the world stage questioning our internal cohesion and our right to serve as an arbiter of justice. Much of this slippage in global perception lies in the perceived treatment of minorities, especially black Americans. Despite the fact that we still have millions of immigrants willing to risk their lives daily to enter the United States, we need to be much more proactive in resolving these tensions. To be worthy of our role, we must aim to become a shining example to the world by living up to what have always been America's ideals. Whether or not we think that these ideals have been achieved in the past, there is no better time to set things aright than right now.

CHAPTER 20

A Higher Power: Community and Morality in Modern America

Religion in America is in decline. In 2022, the number of those who believed in a deity fell to 81 percent, a rapid drop from 92 percent just a decade earlier.[106] And of those who do believe, increasing numbers do so outside the framework of any organized religion.[107] As a result, church membership is dropping fast, falling below 50 percent for the first time in 2021.[108] Younger Americans are considerably less likely to believe in God,[109] so we can expect this trend to accelerate in the future, although it will be slowed slightly by immigration, as newcomers to the United States are slightly more likely to be religious than those recently born here.[110,111]

In parallel to these falls, Americans are increasingly turning inward, focusing on themselves as individuals rather than seeing themselves as part of a wider community. Staggering numbers of Americans now no longer feel a sense of belonging in their workplace (64 percent), their local community (74 percent), or the country as a whole (68 percent),[112] figures that are reflected in the epidemic of loneliness across the nation, especially among the young and those with low incomes.[113] It is perhaps unsurprising that these high levels correlate with an era in which technology draws us increasingly into private thought worlds, locked in by algorithms designed to provide a constant stream of dopamine hits so long as we remain attentively focused on our screens.[114] The COVID-19 pandemic served as an accelerator, forcing

Americans to stay away from one another for unprecedentedly long periods, although the retreat from social engagement pre-exists both our current era of hyperconnectedness and the pandemic.[115] The loss of access to the American dream for many in our society is a critical factor that has also contributed to this trend.

It is not clear whether these two trends are causally connected. Data from other Western countries suggests that the United States is an outlier when it comes to religion, and that the current decline may simply reflect a broader trend that impacted other nations much earlier.[116,117] Nevertheless, both trends feed into what I, like many others, believe is a crisis of values in America.[118,119,120] This crisis arises from the elevation of the self to the position of the highest power and the increasing rejection of the idea that there is anything beyond us as individuals to which we are responsible. People run stop signs more frequently, low-level rule breaking is accepted and even praised in sports as a winning tactic, politicians condone theft and violence as acceptable responses to social conditions, tax evasion is rife among the wealthy . . . I could go on, but the clear direction of travel when it comes to seeking advantages for the self at the expense of others is to push it just a little further . . . and a little further . . . and a little further. As a result, more and more Americans are now disappearing into their personal me-verse, a place in which the defining criterion of value for every choice is, "What can I get out of this?"

It is undeniable that individualism has always been a key American value. But when that individualism loses its connection to the wider community and becomes pure selfishness, it turns from a virtue into a national vice. As my father used to say, "There's no such thing as a self-made man." We are all the products of our creator, first and foremost, and our environments next, and we all rely for our success on the network of social relationships in which we are embedded. When we forget this and come to believe that it is only ourselves and our own decisions that matter, we set ourselves on a very dangerous path. Not only do we damage ourselves in the long run by undermining the communities that are essential for our own lives, but we inevitably end up treating other humans as nothing more than tools to be exploited and then cast away when we are done with them. These kinds of attitudes represent a critical obstacle to any attempt to make the American dream attainable to all; we cannot hope to have a level playing field if everyone is trying to skew that field in their own favor.

Let's be clear: equality of outcomes across individuals is not a realistic or, in most cases, even a desirable goal to aim for. We are all born into this world with different talents in different degrees, and our upbringing and other factors outside our control also shape who we are by the time we emerge into adulthood. I grew up wanting to be a professional soccer player, but I wasn't born with the physical gifts and talent of a Pele, Messi, or Ronaldo. On the other hand, I suspect that my sport marketing gifts may be greater than those of any of these three superstars. So, we do not all embark on our life's journey with the same resources to draw on, and nor can we all expect to achieve the same levels or types of career success. But what everyone *is* entitled to is equal dignity as a human and an equal chance to do as much as they possibly can with their talents, each in their own unique way. But we can only create the kind of environment in which this is possible if we accept and adhere to a shared national value system.

This does not, of course, mean that we must all agree on every point of moral debate. Nor does it mean we must all share the same religion or accept that our values are rooted in the same foundational beliefs. But there are certain minimal values, certain basic moral building blocks, without which a shared, egalitarian society cannot hope to flourish. Sadly, I am convinced that America is losing touch with these values at present, and I firmly believe that we need to actively plot a course back to them as a nation. The core principle from which all other central values flow is that life is not just about you!

Communities are built on concern for others, and from this concern flows respect for life, respect for property, respect for our neighbors, and respect for the rules that keep all those other things in equilibrium. It is not enough to hold onto these values as some vague idea that we wave toward but then ignore when they run counter to our personal interests. If they are to be anything at all, they must be a firm and conscious presence in our lives, the anchor that grounds us, the pillar that we lean on in trying times.

The recognition that there is something bigger than the self is critical for the survival and well-being of our nation. For many, myself included, this view will be rooted first in a religious belief, in faith in a divine higher power, a driving force of the universe that creates us and brings us into communion with each other. As a Catholic, I have found my faith challenged over the past three decades as I have learned about the long history of appalling actions by some members of the clergy against the most vulnerable of their flock. My confidence in the church as an institution has been shaken by its failure, even now, to deal fully and transparently with the perpetrators and the victims of these many scandals around the world, and my heart goes out to all those who have been harmed. Nevertheless, my faith anchors and amplifies my belief that to love God and one's neighbor first and oneself only second is not just desirable but necessary if we are to hope to live together in harmony.

Organized religion manages to be at the same time one of the great unifying forces on the planet and one of the greatest dividers. It brings people together in enduring communities of national and international brotherhood and sisterhood. Yet it also frequently becomes a dividing line that people use to separate themselves into factions rather than seeking the common threads that tie us together and unite us across doctrines. This division has been one of, if not the, most common causes of conflict across the history of civilization. The unfortunate truth is that whatever divine inspiration we are lucky enough to be granted as humans, we cannot help but interpret from our flawed and limited human perspective, and we bring those flaws into the practice of religion as we do into everything else.

However, these challenges and all-too-human failings should not be treated as a reason for rejecting the values that religions can impart. The Christian faith forms a key part of America's history. This faith was central to the stories of the first European settlers. It remained central to the shared values that underpinned the early republic and the drafting of the US Constitution and Bill of Rights. Christian values that emphasize the dignity of the individual, that preach kindness and tolerance and love for one's neighbor, are foundational values for America. But despite the Christian path by which these values found their way into our communal history, accepting their importance does not require any belief in Christian theology. These values are available to anyone as a simple moral code that is completely detachable from Christian dogma, or from the views of any form of religion.

This is a critical point to understand as America evolves. While our communal values may have been rooted in religion in the past, and while many, like me, still see their own religion as the pre-eminent source of their values, there is no need to be a Christian or, indeed, a believer in any faith in order to accept the values that are needed to hold our community together. Not all Americans are members of churches or believers in a god or gods. But this does nothing to stop them being good people and good citizens. My own children stand as an example to me of this simple fact. While I would have preferred them to follow me in my faith, their adult decision to take another path has not prevented them from becoming deeply moral individuals who value their nation and local communities and who give of themselves to serve others. The point is not that we must be religious or atheist or agnostic; it is that we must believe in the value of something beyond and bigger than our individual selves. *That* is the currency that buys connection and community.

Recommended Action Points

- Those of us who wish to bring our nation together once again must spread an important message in both our words and our actions. That message is: Believe whatever you choose to believe, so long as you accept that there is a force within the universe that is bigger than yourself. I believe that we were not put on this earth to be alone; we were put here to live alongside others, to foster new life, and to help others fulfil their potential. This is best evidenced by the fact that nobody can create human life alone. A power beyond that of the individual stands at the root of the very existence of the human species.

- We can all find a higher power to guide us outside ourselves so long as we consciously seek it out. A well-balanced life is much like a stool with four legs. Each of those legs represents a source of connection to something greater than the individual.

  For me, the first leg of the stool is the values and principles that serve as my rock, my foundation. This encompasses the set of beliefs that serve as a beacon or guiding light for my actions. In my own case, these beliefs spring from my Catholic faith, but for many other Americans they will be rooted in other religions, in humanism, or in simple fellow feeling. What is most critical is that this belief system is not self-centered. I believe that this is the anchor that will see us all through the storms of life.

  Leg 2 is family, or rather F.A.M.I.L.Y. ("Forget about me; I love you"), a concept I have borrowed from Rutgers University Football Coach Greg Schiano. Your family is your immediate community, your nation in miniature, your first circle outside you. It is the first and most important domain within which we each learn our values, form relationships, and discover how we can serve the interests of people other than ourselves.

  Leg 3 is your career. Your career takes you out into the wider world, connecting you to colleagues and clients, the people you work alongside and the people you serve. It is a forum for putting your values to work in a way that immediately touches the lives of a broad swathe of humanity. For many, our career gives us our life's purpose in the wider world beyond our families.

Leg 4 is community. First locally, then nationally, and finally, embracing all humans, our communities are where our values are called on to do their hardest work, treating those who are distant as if they are worthy of the same consideration as those who are close. It is the playing out of our values at the level of our national community that will make it possible to see ourselves as a truly United States once again.

- As a community of Americans, we must put a final stop to a pernicious idea that has proved a divisive battleground in American life. While I am religious and ground my values in my religion, there is no place in our country for the view that my religion, or any other, should be elevated in any way and established as having any official status. To quote Thomas Jefferson, in his letter to the Danbury Baptists:

> Believing with you that religion is a matter which lies solely between man and his God, that he owes account to none other for his faith or his worship, that the legislative powers of government reach actions only, and not opinions, I contemplate with sovereign reverence that act of the whole American people which declared that their legislature should "make no law respecting an establishment of religion, or prohibiting the free exercise thereof," thus building a wall of separation between church and state.

This "wall of separation" is essential to our ability to each choose our own moral foundations and values. Without it, America becomes an exclusive club, not the inclusive community that has always been our imperfectly realized national ideal. Attempts by some of my fellow Christians to insist that America was, is, and always will be a Christian nation are fundamentally misguided. It is true that Christian values played a vital role in the foundation of our country, but those values can stand alone, independently of any theological commitments. So clear were the founders on the need to separate church and state and to prevent the establishment of any official religion that I cannot see arguments to the contrary as conducted in anything other than bad faith. As to the claim that the constitution did not prevent individual states from establishing an official religion, this does indeed seem to have been accepted in the early years of our nation. However, the passing of the Fourteenth Amendment gave the constitution primacy over state law in this matter as in many others. The Supreme Court settled this issue decisively in 1947 in *Everson v. Board of Education* and attempting to turn the clock back will do nothing at all to bring our nation together once again.

- Just as the constitution makes it clear that there is no room in our nation for an established faith, it is equally clear that the founders did not envisage that religion should be driven from public life. From the swearing of oaths on the Bible to the celebration of Christmas or Eid at the community level, there is no reason that religion should be confined to the home. What is critical is that each American citizen should have the choice as to which symbols and ceremonies they choose to uphold or participate in.

- The Pledge of Allegiance is part of our nation's history and a valuable symbolic tool for tying us all together. The controversy over whether it should be retained in schools can be overcome by simply reverting to the words of the original version and removing "under God," which is a modern accretion that was only added by Congress in 1954.[121]

CHAPTER 21

The American Prescription

This final chapter outlines an innovative and far-reaching program that aims to inoculate the next generation of Americans, and America itself, against many of the ills from which our society currently suffers. Much of the division in our society is the product of the EPH cycle (education, poverty, hopelessness). Lack of educational attainment is responsible for holding many Americans back from achieving their full potential and living out the American dream, particularly by limiting the development of cognitive skills and making college inaccessible. This leads to low wages and often a life at or below the poverty line. The feeling of being unable to participate in the good things our society has to offer then contributes to a sense of futility, a lack of hope for the future, and often, anger. These feelings can manifest themselves in mental health problems and irresponsible behavior, sometimes rising to the level of criminality. Poverty and hopelessness then go on to create conditions that can make educational attainment difficult for the next generation, as well as ensuring that no financial equity is passed down from one generation to the next to provide a foundation for young people to build on. And so the cycle repeats itself. Breaking the EPH cycle will set America's youth onto a hopeful path that leads to wealth and achievement thanks to a strong educational foundation. This will help heal the divisions in our nation and make the American dream attainable to all.

My American prescription outlined below targets each element in this cycle to ensure that every American child not only receives an adequate education but has all the tools required to make the best of that education. It seeks to break the cycle of poverty by giving every young American the opportunity to earn what were previously privileges reserved for the wealthy. A core feature of my American prescription is the provision of a common experience for all American teenagers, a shared touchstone that will spread more understanding and mutual respect across our nation. It is an investment in the future of our entire country that will ultimately have an enormous impact on all segments of the population.

Goals

- Improve educational outcomes by giving all American children the resources they need to gain the greatest possible benefit from the educational opportunities available to them.
- Provide support services to ensure that no American child lacks supervision and support while their parents are at work.
- Instill the values appropriate to pursuing and participating in the reimagined American dream.
- Offer all American children the opportunity to enjoy the benefits that come from generational wealth while giving them the chance to build their own wealth.
- Ensure all children have access to valuable and varied work experience opportunities.
- Offer all American children the opportunity to earn vouchers that will cover their college tuition or professional qualification costs.

The American Prescription

1. Preschool

High-quality preschool programs prepare children for the start of their formal education, ensuring that they enter kindergarten with all the cognitive tools to take advantage of the educational opportunities that are offered. A good preschool education provides significant and lasting benefits to children that they will carry with them for the rest of their lives. Research on the effectiveness of preschools has found that early childhood education correlates with improved health and a reduction in depression.[122,123] In terms of educational outcomes, preschool is associated with increased high-school graduation rates and a nearly 20 percent increase in the likelihood of college attendance. Preschool programs can have a particularly high impact on children from low-income families, closing the attainment gap with their wealthier peers and improving conditions at home by freeing up parents during the workday. One recent study found that expanding preschool provision could reduce child poverty by as much as 12 percent simply by providing parents with more flexibility regarding their working hours.[124]

This American prescription advocates the provision of free preschool for all children from the age of three months through to kindergarten entry at age five. This will be achieved through granting Head Start providers an annual allowance of $15,000 per child for each year of preschool age.

2. Elementary and Middle School

At present, one in five children across the United States spends time alone after the end of the school day.[125] This is particularly common for children in low-income families with a single parent or two working parents, as after school supervision is not compatible with the normal working hours of most jobs. In order to fully participate in the workforce, parents are frequently forced to compromise when it comes to child care, leading to additional disadvantages for children who may already face other issues that impede educational outcomes. Decades of research are consistent in showing a broad range of positive outcomes for children who attend high-quality after-school programs instead of being left unsupervised. In particular, a large study following 3000 elementary- and middle-school children from low-income families found very significant improvements in math test results, improved work habits, improved social skills, and significant reductions in school misconduct, aggressive behavior with peers, and drug and alcohol use.[126,127,128]

The American prescription recommends the provision of free before- and after-school programs for all elementary and middle school children across the nation to ensure that the resources spent on educating our youth deliver the greatest possible impact.

3. High School

The preschool and elementary/middle school elements of this American prescription focus on providing children with the tools they will need to maximize their educational outcomes. The high-school component of the prescription adds a unique and innovative four-year program that has three core goals:

1. Prepare young people to be functional, contributing members of society with an understanding of American civic values and a positive attitude toward their national and local communities.

2. Provide young people with the opportunity to save up to $25,000 through a summer work program, enabling them to enter the adult world with the kind of resources normally reserved for those who are fortunate enough to be born into a wealthy family.

3. Provide young people with the opportunity to earn free college tuition to ensure that no American child sees college as an unaffordable dream.

The importance of *earning* the way to these latter two outcomes is essential. This program is not designed to offer handouts. Its goal is to instill a sense of purpose and an understanding that there is something more important than the individual while offering an opportunity to build up a nest egg by carrying out paid work that is compensated fairly. In return for voluntarily completing the full, four-year program, the young person earns vouchers to cover four years of college tuition or other professional training. The embedding of values, a work ethic, and an aspirational attitude combine with access to college and a solid financial start in life to ensure that the American dream is attainable by everyone who is willing to grasp it.

3.1. The American Experience Summer Camp

In the summer before high school, all rising freshmen will be encouraged to attend an eight-week sleep-away summer camp. Camps will be based in mothballed former military and governmental facilities and will provide America's children with a common point of reference: a shared American experience. The educational program will follow in the great American summer-camp tradition of encouraging independence and physical activity, while introducing teens to peers from many different backgrounds and parts of the country. The camp ethos will be centered on the key values of self-reliance, self-respect, and civic and social responsibility. Practical classes will teach skills such as identifying and cooking healthy foods, financial planning, and media analysis and criticism, while students will also learn about the benefits of healthy eating, cardiovascular exercise, and mental relaxation. The program each day will include physical exercise and stretching for all students at a level appropriate to their individual fitness. Interactive sessions and seminars will focus on topics such as mutual respect, listening to understand, conflict resolution, and the importance of diversity, while civics classes will teach the history of America's great institutions, how business works in a free-market society, and what responsibilities we each have to our ourselves and our nation. Team-building exercises and tough physical and mental challenges will help build self-respect and respect for others, as well as providing opportunities to develop leadership skills. The program will also have the additional advantage of taking all American youth out of their immediate neighborhoods at the time they are most vulnerable to being drawn into antisocial or gang-related behavior, disrupting potentially dangerous patterns.

All attending students will receive the recommended minimum wage of $15 an hour for their participation in socially constructive educational courses, to the value of $600 per week for eight weeks (total compensation of $4,800 per student). This money will be paid into a special class of government- and bank-sponsored bank accounts (see 3.3, below), with students and their parents permitted to select their preferred financial institution.

3.2. The American Experience Summer Work Program

Each summer thereafter, preceding the start of their sophomore, junior and senior years, students will be supported in finding a paid eight-week work placement in the public, private, or volunteer sector. Options will include community service programs, courses organized by The Junior Reserve Officers' Training Corps (JROTC) or other youth organizations, and work in the government or commercial sectors. At least one placement in a business environment across the three years will be required. Students will have the option of finding a position for themselves or securing one through a government agency or charity. These work placements will give students an opportunity to build their resume, gain insight into careers that interest them, and gain invaluable experience for later life. All participating students will again receive the minimum wage for this program, paid into their American Experience bank account.

3.3. The American Experience Bank Account

All earnings from each year's summer program will be shielded from deductions in the same way as 401k contributions and will be paid into a special bank account sponsored jointly by the government and participating FDIC-insured banks. Students will have the option to withdraw up to 20 percent of their earnings from each year while retaining the tax and interest benefits of the account. The remaining 80 percent will remain inaccessible until graduation from high school. American Experience bank accounts will offer generous interest rates for accumulated savings to encourage students to leave the largest amount possible in the account until graduation. This will both maximize the value of the nest egg available on entering adulthood and encourage a healthy understanding of the value of budgeting and saving.

3.4. The American Dream College Fund

In order to ensure that no young American should be deterred from college by the expense involved or by concerns over future debt, every student who graduates from high school and completes the entire four-year American Experience program will have access to the American Experience college/professional education fund. This will come in the form of vouchers to cover up to four years of college tuition or professional training costing up to $15,000 per year. The student will be required to draw the full amount for educational purposes prior to reaching age twenty-five.

Conclusion

The economic costs and benefits of this wide-ranging program are detailed in the grid in appendix A, along with an analysis of costs and benefits for the other recommendations discussed in part 2 of this book. The dollar figures are significant. However, much of this investment will recycle through the economy and come back into our national coffers through taxation, increased employment, and spending across many sectors. Some benefits are impossible to calculate, but increased educational attainment and more college graduates will provide important resources for the further development of our technology sector. The social benefits, such as reductions in unemployment, substance abuse, youth crime, and teen pregnancies, meanwhile, will be priceless.

The immediate payoff will be a generation of Americans who are better educated, have more hope, are more engaged with their communities, more committed to our national values and more enthusiastic about all the positive features of life in this great country. In the longer term, those who pass through this program will carry what they have learned with them, reshaping attitudes in the workforce more broadly and passing their own values down to their children. The result will be a broad increase in the number of Americans who are able to live out the American dream, pursuing happiness for themselves and their families as part of a reunited national community.

APPENDIX A

The Benefits and Costs of Implementing the American Prescription

Improved Education at No Cost to the Parents

RECOMMENDATION	COST IMPACT
The American prescription recommends free education starting with preschool, which will significantly reduce costs for education and payments to daycare services. The massive job creation from this program will help offset a significant portion of the costs. All students will also be offered free supervised before- and after-school sessions to ensure that no child need to spend time without adult supervision at home due to the parents' work schedule	Ten states currently offer some form of free preschool but many of these programs are part-time and therefore have low adoption rates. Current projected costs for full-time day care across America are estimated at $15,000 per child per year x approximately 3 million preschoolers in each annual cohort (number of children not already covered by their own state). The projected cost to federal or state budgets is $45 billion for each annual cohort, which will amount to $225 billion per year when covering all 5 years of preschool.

BENEFIT IMPACT	NOTES
The positive impact of this program through job creation will be highly significant, with a projected 3.75 million new preschool worker jobs being created at an average recommended minimum wage of $45,000 per year. This will circulate $168.75 billion through the economy in additional wages, providing an important stimulus to GDP.	Approximately 20% of wages for these millions of new jobs will return to the treasury through taxation, producing more than $33 billion per year in incremental federal income tax and approximately $10 billion in incremental state income tax each year.

The American Experience Camp Program

RECOMMENDATION	COST IMPACT
Before their freshman year in high school, every rising ninth grader will be encouraged to attend an 8-week sleep-away American Experience civics camp.	The projected running costs per student for an 8-week camp experience are $1,500, giving a projected annual running cost of $1.5 million for each camp housing 1000 students. In the first year of the program, with one pilot camp per state and a total capacity nationwide of 50,000 students, the projected cost would be $75 million for 50 camps. After a five-year ramp-up period bringing the program to full capacity, 4000 camps nationwide would aim to serve the approx. 4 million students in each age group, at a cost of $6 billion per year. Participants will be compensated for their time at the rate of $600 per week, amounting to $4800 for the length of the camp. At full capacity, the cost to the federal budget for these participation payments will be $19.2 billion. The total cost of the program at full capacity will thus be $25.2 billion per year.
BENEFIT IMPACT	**NOTES**
Students will be selected from different school districts within the state, to reflect all ethnic and income backgrounds at each camp, ideally without extensive bussing needed within that state. Being away from home for 8 weeks will help all students gain a sense of independence and will also remove many children from their neighborhoods at a time when they are particularly vulnerable to involvement in crime and other anti-social behavior. An expected ancillary benefit of the camp program will be a significant reduction in crime, drug addiction, recruitment into gangs, and teenage pregnancies	The curriculum (sketched in chapter 21) is expected to yield tangible but hard-to-measure long-term economic benefits from increased health and nutritional awareness, improved financial responsibility, and increased entrepreneurial acumen. Students will be required to keep at least 80% of their annual earnings in an American Experience bank account, with the balance invested with no tax or benefit cost deductions. American Experience bank accounts will be offered with a high interest rate to incentivize financial responsibility.

Work Experience

RECOMMENDATION	COST IMPACT
To complete the American Experience program, each participant will undertake work experience during the summer prior to their sophomore, junior, and senior year. Ideally, each student will spend one summer at a private business, one summer at a government agency, and one summer working for a charitable organization.	The organization employing the student will be responsible for paying the student their $4,800 stipend per summer of work.
BENEFIT IMPACT	**NOTES**
Students will expand their resume and exposure to the world of work while building savings.	

The American Dream College Program

RECOMMENDATION	COST IMPACT
All students who successfully complete the 4-year American Experience program will be eligible for a voucher covering up to $15,000 per year for four years of further education costs (either at a university or for professional certification).	We project that approximately 50% of the 4 million eligible participants will take advantage of this program, at a cost of $30 billion dollars for each annual cohort. Once the first four cohorts have entered college, the ongoing cost of this program will be $120 billion per year.
BENEFIT IMPACT	**NOTES**
This program will virtually eliminate student debt going forward, removing an enormous anchor on career development and entrepreneurial activity. It will also make college/professional certification accessible for many young Americans who would otherwise have considered the costs to be beyond their reach. This will create a direct impact on economic activity through both higher wages and a more skilled population.	

Endnotes

1. Taylor Orth, "Two in Five Americans Say a Civil War Is at Least Somewhat Likely in the Next Decade." YouGov, August 26, 2022, https://today.yougov.com/politics/articles/43553-two-in-five-americans-civil-war-somewhat-likely.
2. Kaleigh Rogers, and Zohar Qamar, "What Americans Think about Political Violence." FiveThirtyEight, November 4, 2022, https://fivethirtyeight.com/features/what-americans-think-about-political-violence/.
3. Adam Barnes, "Shocking Poll Finds Many Americans Now Want to Secede from the United States," *The Hill*, July 15, 2021, https://thehill.com/changing-america/enrichment/arts-culture/563221-shocking-poll-finds-many-americans-now-want-to/.
4. Jennifer Agiesta, "CNN Poll: Americans' Confidence in Elections Has Faded since January 6." CNN, July 21, 2022, https://edition.cnn.com/2022/07/21/politics/cnn-poll-elections/index.html.
5. Jennifer Agiesta, and Ariel Edwards-Levy, "CNN Poll: Most Americans Feel Democracy Is under Attack in the US," CNN, September 15, 2021, https://edition.cnn.com/2021/09/15/politics/cnn-poll-most-americans-democracy-under-attack/index.html.
6. "2020 Census Urban Areas Facts," About Geographic Areas, United States Census Bureau, https://www.census.gov/programs-surveys/geography/guidance/geo-areas/urban-rural/2020-ua-facts.html.
7. "Mobile Fact Sheet," Pew Research Center, January 31, 2024, https://www.pewresearch.org/internet/fact-sheet/mobile/#:~:text=The%20vast%20majority%20of%20Americans,smartphone%20ownership%20conducted%20in%202011.
8. "Satisfaction with the United States," Gallup, https://news.gallup.com/poll/1669/general-mood-country.aspx.
9. "Congress and the Public," Gallup, https://news.gallup.com/poll/1600/congress-public.aspx.
10. Lydia Saad, "U.S. Political Ideology Steady; Conservatives, Moderates Tie," Gallup, January 17, 2022, https://news.gallup.com/poll/388988/political-ideology-steady-conservatives-moderates-tie.aspx.
11. Anthony Fowler, Seth J. Hill, Jeffrey B. Lewis, Chris Tausanovitch, Lynn Vavreck, and Christopher Warshaw, "Moderates," *American Political Science Review* 117, no. 2: 643–660.
12. Anthony Fowler, "America's Silent Majority Is Alive and Well—and More Moderate Than Either Party," *Newsweek*, October 14, 2022, https://www.newsweek.com/americas-silent-majority-alive-well-more-moderate-either-party-opinion-1751891.

13. Peter Apps, "Commentary: Is Vladimir Putin Deliberately Destabilizing U.S. Politics?" Reuters, July 28, 2016, https://www.reuters.com/article/us-putin-politics-commentary-idINKCN1072WE/.

14. Tom McCarthy, T. "How Russia Used Social Media to Divide Americans," *The Guardian*, October 14, 2017, https://www.theguardian.com/us-news/2017/oct/14/russia-us-politics-social-media-facebook.

15. Dror Walter, Yotam Ophir, and Kathleen Hall Jamieson, "Russian Twitter Accounts and the Partisan Polarization of Vaccine Discourse, 2015–2017," *American Journal of Public Health* 110, no. 5: 718–724.

16. As one of the founders of the discipline, I was able to insist that the discipline be called sport business in the singular rather than the plural sports business. My argument was that the world of sport business is a single industry in which the same lessons can be applied to all individual sports. The fact that we almost always talk of sport singular rather than sports back in England was entirely coincidental—honest!

17. For a wonderful insight into Dan's philosophy and approach to life, see his 2005 interview with Tamara Chapman, "Dan Ritchie Unscripted," in *The University of Denver Magazine*. https://magazine-archive.du.edu/current-issue/dan-ritchie-unscripted/

18. "Atlanta-Sandy Springs-Alpharetta, GA Metro Area," Census Reporter, https://censusreporter.org/profiles/31000US12060-atlanta-sandy-springs-alpharetta-ga-metro-area/.

19. Moshe Haspel, "Mapping Poverty over Time, 2005 to 2020," 33°n, https://33n.atlantaregional.com/monday-mapday/mapping-poverty-over-time-2005-to-2020.

20. "Children In Poverty in Georgia," The Annie E. Casey Foundation, By Location, https://datacenter.aecf.org/data/tables/43-children-in-poverty?loc=12&loct=3#detailed/3/108/true/2048,1729,37,871,573,36,867,38,18,16/any/322.

21. Marcus Lu, "Is the American Dream Over? Here's What the Data Says," Agenda Articles, World Economic Forum, September 2, 2020, https://www.weforum.org/agenda/2020/09/social-mobility-upwards-decline-usa-us-america-economics/.

22. Aaron D. Baugh, Allison A. Vanderbilt, and Reginald F. Baugh, "The Dynamics of Poverty, Educational Attainment, and the Children of the Disadvantaged Entering Medical School," *Advances in Medical Education and Practice* 2019, no. 10: 667–676.

23. Debra Cassens Weiss, "Study Finds 'Lopsided' Concentration of Socioeconomic Elites at Law Schools," *ABAJournal*, October 5, 2011, https://www.abajournal.com/news/article/study_finds_lopsided_concentration_of_socioeconomic_elites_at_law_schools.

24. "Colonial and Pre-federal Statistics," in *Historical Statistics of the United States: Colonial Times to 1957*, US Census Bureau, updated September 1975, https://www2.census.gov/prod2/statcomp/documents/CT1970p2-13.pdf.

25. "1900," Decennial Census Official Publications, Decennial Census of Population and Housing, US Census Bureau. https://www.census.gov/programs-surveys/decennial-census/decade/decennial-publications.1900.html.

26. Paul Kennedy, *The Rise and Fall of the Great Powers* (London: Fontana Press, 1989), 190.

27. "Decades of Manufacturing Decline and Outsourcing Left U.S. Supply Chains Vulnerable to Disruption," Joint Economic Committee Democrats, US Congress, February 1, 2022, https://www.jec.senate.gov/public/_cache/files/94bf8985-1e87-438b-9a3a-c3334489dd30/background-on-issues-in-us-manufacturing-and-supply-chains-final.pdf.

28. Rakesh Kochhar, and Stella Sechopoulos, "How the American Middle Class Has Changed in the Past Five Decades," Pew Research Center, April 20, 2022, https://www.pewresearch.org/short-reads/2022/04/20/how-the-american-middle-class-has-changed-in-the-past-five-decades/.

29. Ibid.

30. "The Productivity-Pay Gap," Economic Policy Institute, updated October 2022, https://www.epi.org/productivity-pay-gap/.

31. Abigail Johnson Hess, "College Costs Have Increased by 169% since 1980—But Pay for Young Workers Is Up by just 19%.: Georgetown Report," CNBC, November 2, 2021, https://www.cnbc.com/2021/11/02/the-gap-in-college-costs-and-earnings-for-young-workers-since-1980.html.

32. Marcus Lu, "Is the American Dream Over? Here's What the Data Says," World Economic Forum, Agenda Article, September 2, 2020, https://www.weforum.org/agenda/2020/09/social-mobility-upwards-decline-usa-us-america-economics/.

33. Ana Hernandez Kent, and Lowell R. Ricketts, "The State of U.S. Wealth Inequality." Federal Reserve Bank of St. Louis, February 5, 2025, https://www.stlouisfed.org/institute-for-economic-equity/the-state-of-us-wealth-inequality.

34. Ibid.

35. Ibid.

36. Juliana Menasce Horowitz, Ruth Igielnik, and Rakesh Kochhar, "Trends in Income and Wealth Inequality," Pew Research Center, January 2020, https://www.pewresearch.org/social-trends/2020/01/09/trends-in-income-and-wealth-inequality/#fnref-27661-13.

37. "All Nobel Prizes," The Nobel Prize, Nobel Foundation, https://www.nobelprize.org/prizes/lists/all-nobel-prizes/.

38. Adam Tyner, "Think Again: Is Education Funding in America Still Unequal?" Thomas B. Fordham Institute, July 11, 2023, https://fordhaminstitute.org/national/research/think-again-education-funding-america-still-unequal.

39. Stephen J. Wermiel, "Inequitable and Inadequate School Funding," *Human Rights Magazine* 48, no. 2 (*Wealth Disparities in Civil Rights*), American Bar Association, January 6, 2023, https://www.americanbar.org/groups/crsj/publications/human_rights_magazine_home/wealth-disparities-in-civil-rights/inequitable-and-inadequate-school-funding.

40. Brian A. Jacob, "The Challenges of Staffing Urban Schools with Effective Teachers," *The Future of Children* 17, no. 1 (Spring 2007)129–153, https://www.jstor.org/stable/i388444.

41. Catherine Brown, Scott Sargrad, and Meg Benner, "Hidden Money: The Outsized Role of Parental Contributions in School Finance," Center for American Progress, April 8, 2017, https://www.americanprogress.org/article/hidden-money/.

42. Anthony P. Carnevale, Ban Cheah, and Emma Wenzinger, *The College Payoff: More Education Doesn't Always Mean More Earnings*, report, McCourt School of Public Policy, Center on Education and the Workforce, Georgetown University, 2021, https://cew.georgetown.edu/wp-content/uploads/cew-college_payoff_2021-fr.pdf.

43. "Research, Statistics & Policy Analysis: Education and Lifetime Earnings," Social Security Research, Statistics & Policy Analysis, Social Security Administration, November 2015, https://www.ssa.gov/policy/docs/research-summaries/education-earnings.html.

44. Ana Hernandez Kent, and Lowell R. Ricketts, "The State of U.S. Wealth Inequality." Federal Reserve Bank of St. Louis, February 5, 2024, https://www.stlouisfed.org/institute-for-economic-equity/the-state-of-us-wealth-inequality.

45. US Census Bureau, "Census Bureau Releases New Educational Attainment Data," news release no. CB22-TPS.02, February 24, 2022, https://www.census.gov/newsroom/press-releases/2022/educational-attainment.html.

46. Laura Pappano, "First-Generation Students Unite," *The New York Times*, April 8, 2015, https://www.nytimes.com/2015/04/12/education/edlife/first-generation-students-unite.html.

47. Anne Case, and Angus Deaton, "Without a College Degree, Life in America Is Staggeringly Shorter." *The New York Times,* October 3, 2023, https://www.nytimes.com/2023/10/03/opinion/life-expectancy-college-degree.html.

48. "Fast Facts," National Center for Education Statistics, https://nces.ed.gov/fastfacts/display.asp?id=372#PK12-teachers.

49. US Census Bureau, "Public School Spending per Pupil Experiences Largest Year-to-Year Increase in More Than a Decade," press release no.CB23-TPS.61, May 18, 2023, https://www.census.gov/newsroom/press-releases/2023/public-school-spending.html.

50. "National Health Expenditure Data: Historical," Centers for Medicare and Medicaid Services, updated December 13, 2023, https://www.cms.gov/data-research/statistics-trends-and-reports/national-health-expenditure-data/historical.

51. "World Military Expenditure Reaches New Record High as European Spending Surges," Stockholm International Peace Research Institute, press release, April 24, 2023, https://www.sipri.org/media/press-release/2023/world-military-expenditure-reaches-new-record-high-european-spending-surges.

52. "What Is the National Debt?" Fiscal Data, US Treasury, https://fiscaldata.treasury.gov/americas-finance-guide/national-debt/.

53. *World Economic Outlook Database: October 2023*, International Monetary Fund, https://www.imf.org/en/Publications/WEO/weo-database/2023/October/weo-report.

54. Matthew McGough, Aubrey Winger, Shameek Rakshit, and Krutika Amin, "How Has U.S. Spending on Healthcare Changed over Time?" Peterson-KFF Health System Tracker, December 15, 2023, https://www.healthsystemtracker.org/chart-collection/u-s-spending-healthcare-changed-time/.

55. "How Much Is Health Spending Expected to Grow?" KFF, October 11, 2023, https://www.kff.org/slideshow/how-much-is-health-spending-expected-to-grow/.

56. Addie Fleron, and Shubham Singhal, "The Gathering Storm: The Uncertain Future of US Healthcare," Healthcare, McKinsey & Company, September 16, 2022, https://www.mckinsey.com/industries/healthcare/our-insights/the-gathering-storm-the-uncertain-future-of-us-healthcare.

57. *National Health Expenditure Data: Historical*, Centers for Medicare and Medicaid Services, updated December 13, 2023, https://www.cms.gov/data-research/statistics-trends-and-reports/national-health-expenditure-data/historical.

58. Eric C. Schneider, Arnav Shah, Michelle M. Doty, Roosa Tikkanen, Katherine Fields, Reginald D. Williams II, *Mirror, Mirror 2021: Reflecting Poorly: Health Care in the U.S. Compared to Other High-Income Countries*, Fund Reports, The Commonwealth Fund, August 4, 2021, https://www.commonwealthfund.org/publications/fund-reports/2021/aug/mirror-mirror-2021-reflecting-poorly.

59. David U. Himmelstein, Robert M. Lawless, Deborah Thorne, Pamela Foohey, and Steffie Woolhandler, "Medical Bankruptcy: Still Common Despite the Affordable Care Act," *American Journal of Public Health* 109, no. 3: 431–433, published online February 2019, https://ajph.aphapublications.org/doi/10.2105/AJPH.2018.304901?url_ver=Z39.88-2003&rfr_id=ori%3Arid%3Acrossref.org&rfr_dat=cr_pub++0pubmed.

60. Noam N. Levey, "100 Million People in America Are Saddled with Health Care Debt." KFF Health News, June 16, 2022, https://kffhealthnews.org/news/article/diagnosis-debt-investigation-100-million-americans-hidden-medical-debt/

61. Katharina Buchholz, "Savings: Quarter of Americans Have Few, One in 10 Have None," Forbes. June 20, 2023, https://www.forbes.com/sites/katharinabuchholz/2023/06/30/savings-quarter-of-americans-have-few-one-in-10-have-none-infographic/.

62. "Employer Health Benefits 2023: Summary of Findings," KFF, https://files.kff.org/attachment/Employer-Health-Benefits-Survey-2023-Annual-Survey-Summary-of-Findings.pdf.

63. Bernard Tierlinck, and Dani Stoilova, "Portable Benefits: Unlocking Innovation and Job Mobility," NYC/EDC, https://edc.nyc/insights/portable-benefits-unlocking-innovation-and-job-mobility

64. Rhett Buttle, Katie Vlietstra Wonnenberg, Angela Simaan, "Small-Business Owners' Views on Health Coverage and Costs," The Commonwealth Fund, September 9, 2019, https://www.commonwealthfund.org/publications/issue-briefs/2019/sep/small-business-owners-views-health-coverage-costs.

65. David M. Cutler, Raj Chetty, Michael Stepner, Sarah Abraham, Shelby Lin, Benjamin Scuderi, Nicholas Turner, and Augustin Bergeron, "The Association between Income and Life Expectancy in the United States, 2001–2014," *Journal of the American Medical Association* 315, no. 16: 1750–1766.

66. Hannes Schwandt, Janet Currie, Till von Wachter, Jonathan Kowarski, Derek Chapman, and Steven H. Woolf, "Changes in the Relationship between Income and Life Expectancy Before and During the COVID-19 Pandemic, California, 2015–2021," *Journal of the American Medical Association* 328, no. 4: 360–366, doi:10.1001/jama.2022.10952.

67. Yousra A. Mohamoud, Russell S. Kirby, and Deborah B. Ehrenthal, "Poverty, Urban-Rural Classification and Term Infant Mortality: A Population-Based Multilevel Analysis," *BMC Pregnancy and Childbirth* 19 (January 2019): 1–11, https://doi.org/10.1186/s12884-019-2190-1.

68. Stanislav Seydou Traore, Yacong Bo, Guangning Kou, and Quanjun Lyu, "Socioeconomic Inequality in Overweight/Obesity among US Children: NHANES 2001 to 2018," *Frontiers in Pediatrics* 11 (February 2023): https://doi.org/10.3389/fped.2023.1082558.

69. Rebecca L. Siegel, Kimberly D. Miller, and Ahmedin Jemal, "Cancer statistics, 2019," *CA: A Cancer Journal for Clinicians* 69, no. 1: 7–34, https://acsjournals.onlinelibrary.wiley.com/toc/15424863/2019/69/1.

70. Kate M. Shaw, Kristina A. Theis, Shannon Self-Brown, Douglas W. Roblin, and Lawrence Barker, "Chronic Disease Disparities by County Economic Status and Metropolitan Classification, Behavioral Risk Factor Surveillance System, 2013," *Preventing Chronic Disease* 13 (September 2016).

71. Megan Brenan, "Majority in U.S. Still Say Gov't Should Ensure Healthcare," Gallup, January 23, 2023, https://news.gallup.com/poll/468401/majority-say-gov-ensure-healthcare.aspx.

72. Jenny Blair, "Study: More Than 335,000 Lives Could Have Been Saved during Pandemic if U.S. Had Universal Health Care," Yale School of Public Health, June 20, 2022, https://ysph.yale.edu/news-article/yale-study-more-than-335000-lives-could-have-been-saved-during-pandemic-if-us-had-universal-health-care.

73. Ashley Kirzinger, Alex Montero, Grace Sparks, Isabelle Valdes, and Liz Hamel, "Public Opinion on Prescription Drugs and Their Prices," KFF, August 21, 2023, https://www.kff.org/health-costs/poll-finding/public-opinion-on-prescription-drugs-and-their-prices/.

74. Jonathan Easley, "Poll: Americans Overwhelmingly Oppose Sanctuary Cities," *The Hill*, February 21, 2017, https://thehill.com/homenews/administration/320487-poll-americans-overwhelmingly-oppose-sanctuary-cities/.

75. Jens Manuel Krogstad, Amina Dunn, and Jeffrey S. Passel, "Most Americans Say the Declining Share of White People in the U.S. Is Neither Good nor Bad for Society," Pew Research Center, August 23, 2021, https://www.pewresearch.org/short-reads/2021/08/23/most-americans-say-the-declining-share-of-white-people-in-the-u-s-is-neither-good-nor-bad-for-society/.

76. Jeffrey M. Jones, "More Americans See U.S. Crime Problem as Serious," Gallup, November 16, 2023, https://news.gallup.com/poll/544442/americans-crime-problem-serious.aspx.

77. Ken Dilanian, "Most People Think the U.S. Crime Rate Is Rising. They're Wrong," NBC News, December 16, 2023, https://www.nbcnews.com/news/us-news/people-think-crime-rate-up-actually-down-rcna129585.

78. Jeff Asher, "Crime in 2023: Murder Plummeted, Violent and Property Crime Likely Fell Nationally," Jeff-alytics, Substack, December 11, 2023, https://jasher.substack.com/p/crime-in-2023-murder-plummeted-violent.

79. "Historical Trends: Crime," Gallup, poll, 2023, https://news.gallup.com/poll/1603/crime.aspx.

80. John Gramlich, "Violent Crime Is a Key Midterm Voting Issue, but What Does the Data Say?" Pew Research Center, October 31, 2022, https://www.pewresearch.org/short-reads/2022/10/31/violent-crime-is-a-key-midterm-voting-issue-but-what-does-the-data-say/.

81. "Crime Data Explorer: National, Year 2022," Federal Bureau of Investigation, https://cde.ucr.cjis.gov/LATEST/webapp/#/pages/explorer/crime/crime-trend.

82. James R. Jones, "Media and Social Media's Impact on Citizens' Perception of the Frequency of Crime Occurrence in the United States," *American International Journal of Social Science* 6, no. 3 (September 2017): 97–102, https://www.aijssnet.com/journal/index/514

83. Erin Grinshteyn, and David Hemenway, "Violent Death Rates in the US Compared to Those of the other High-Income Countries, 2015," *Preventive Medicine* 123 (June 2019): 20–26, https://doi.org/10.1016/j.ypmed.2019.02.026.

84. "Historical Trends: Crime," Gallup, poll, 2023, https://news.gallup.com/poll/1603/crime.aspx.

85. Lydia Saad, "Fear of Conventional Crime at Record Lows: Downward Trend Tracks Drop in Nation's Crime Rate," Gallup, media release, October 22, 2001, https://news.gallup.com/poll/5002/fear-conventional-crime-record-lows.aspx.

86. Gary Langer, "Confidence in Police Practices Drops to a New Low: POLL," ABC News, February 3, 2023, https://abcnews.go.com/Politics/confidence-police-practices-drops-new-low-poll/story?id=96858308

87. Ryan Gabrielson, Eric Sagara, and Ryan Grochowski Jones, "Deadly Force, in Black and White," ProPublica, October 10, 2014, https://www.propublica.org/article/deadly-force-in-black-and-white.

88. John Gramlich, "Black Imprisonment Rate in the U.S. Has Fallen by a Third since 2006," Pew Research Center, May 6, 2020, https://www.pewresearch.org/short-reads/2020/05/06/share-of-black-white-hispanic-americans-in-prison-2018-vs-2006/.

89. "Demographic Differences in Federal Sentencing," United States Sentencing Commission, November 14, 2023, https://www.ussc.gov/sites/default/files/pdf/research-and-publications/research-publications/2023/20231114_Demographic-Differences.pdf.

90. Tom LoBianco, "Report: Aide Says Nixon's War on Drugs Targeted Blacks, Hippies," CNN Politics, updated March 24, 2016, https://edition.cnn.com/2016/03/23/politics/john-ehrlichman-richard-nixon-drug-war-blacks-hippie/index.html.

91. *Department of Justice Report Regarding the Criminal Investigation into the Shooting Death of Michael Brown by Ferguson, Missouri Police Officer Darren Wilson*, Department of Justice, report, March 4, 2015, https://www.justice.gov/sites/default/files/opa/press-releases/attachments/2015/03/04/doj_report_on_shooting_of_michael_brown_1.pdf.

92. Seth W. Stoughton, "Law Enforcement's 'Warrior' Problem," *Harvard Law Review Forum* 128, no. 6 (April 2015): 128: 225.

93. "Historical Trends: Guns," Gallup, 2023, https://news.gallup.com/poll/1645/guns.aspx.

94. Steven Shepard, "Gun Control Support Surges in Polls." Politico, February 28, 2018, https://www.politico.com/story/2018/02/28/gun-control-polling-parkland-430099.

95. Donie O'Sullivan, "Her Son Was Killed—Then Came the Russian Trolls," CNN, updated June 29, 2018, https://edition.cnn.com/2018/06/26/us/russian-trolls-exploit-philando-castiles-death/index.html.

96. Teo Armus, "Texas Secession Was a Key Theme in Russian Disinformation Campaign During 2016 Elections, Report Says," *The Texas Tribune*, December 17, 2018, https://www.texastribune.org/2018/12/17/texas-secession-russia-disinformation-2016-social-media-new-knowledge/

97. *The Global Risks Report 2024*." World Economic Forum, https://www3.weforum.org/docs/WEF_The_Global_Risks_Report_2024.pdf.

98. Mustafa Suleyman, *The Coming Wave* (London: Bodley Head, 2023.)

99. "Decennial Census of Population and Housing by Decades," US Census Bureau, https://www.census.gov/programs-surveys/decennial-census/decade.html.

100. "Long-Term Implications of the 2024 Future Years Defense Program," Congressional Budget Office, October 25, 2023, https://www.cbo.gov/publication/59511.

101. David Brennan, "How Americans Really Feel about NATO," *Newsweek*, April 12, 2023, https://www.newsweek.com/us-nato-public-opinion-spending-1793956.

102. Bryant Harris, "Poll Finds Strong Support for Arming Ukraine, Israel and Taiwan," Defense News, November 30, 2023, https://www.defensenews.com/congress/2023/11/30/poll-finds-strong-support-for-arming-ukraine-israel-and-taiwan/.

103. Andy Cerda, "About Half of Republicans Now Say the U.S. Is Providing Too Much Aid to Ukraine," Pew Research Center, December 8, 2023, https://www.pewresearch.org/short-reads/2023/12/08/about-half-of-republicans-now-say-the-us-is-providing-too-much-aid-to-ukraine/.

104. "U.S. Exports—Statistics & Facts," Statista, Statista Research Department, February 16, 2024, https://www.statista.com/topics/1715/us-export/#topicOverview

105. Arnaud Costinot, and Andres Rodríguez-Clare, "The US Gains from Trade: Valuation Using the Demand for Foreign Factor Services," *Journal of Economic Perspectives* 32, no. 2 (Spring 2018): 3–24 https://www.aeaweb.org/articles?id=10.1257/jep.32.2.3.

106. Jeffrey M. Jones, "Belief in God in U.S. Dips to 81%, a New Low," Gallup, June 17, 2022, https://news.gallup.com/poll/393737/belief-god-dips-new-low.aspx.

107. Gregory A. Smith, "About Three-in-Ten U.S. Adults Are Now Religiously Unaffiliated," Pew Research Center, December 14, 2021, https://www.pewresearch.org/religion/2021/12/14/about-three-in-ten-u-s-adults-are-now-religiously-unaffiliated/.

108. Jeffrey M. Jones, "U.S. Church Membership Falls below Majority for First Time," Gallup News, March 29, 2021, https://news.gallup.com/poll/341963/church-membership-falls-below-majority-first-time.aspx.

109. "Belief in God," Religious Landscape Study, 2007–2014, Pew Research Center, https://www.pewresearch.org/religion/religious-landscape-study/belief-in-god/.

110. Douglas S. Massey, and Monica Espinoza Higgins, "The Effect of Immigration on Religious Belief and Practice: A Theologizing or Alienating Experience?", *Social Science Research* 40, no. 5 (September 2011): 1371–1389, https://www.sciencedirect.com/science/article/abs/pii/S0049089X10000839.

111. "Belief in God by Immigrant Status," Religious Landscape Study, 2007–2014, Pew Research Center, https://www.pewresearch.org/religion/religious-landscape-study/compare/belief-in-god/by/immigrant-status/

112. Nichole Argo, and Hammad Sheikh, "The Belonging Barometer: The State of Belonging in America," American Immigration Council, March 7, 2023, https://www.americanimmigrationcouncil.org/research/the-belonging-barometer.

113. Dan Witters, "Loneliness in U.S. Subsides from Pandemic High," Gallup, April 4, 2023, https://news.gallup.com/poll/473057/loneliness-subsides-pandemic-high.aspx.

114. Trevor Haynes, "Dopamine, Smartphones & You: A Battle for Your Time," *Science in the News* (blog), Harvard Graduate School of Arts and Sciences, May 1, 2018, https://sitn.hms.harvard.edu/flash/2018/dopamine-smartphones-battle-time/.

115. Robert D. Putnam, *Bowling Alone: The Collapse and Revival of American Community* (New York: Simon and Schuster, 2000).

116. Joseph Brean, "Canadians' faith in God Is 'Decoupling' from Their Attachment to Religion," *National Post*, April 6, 2023, https://nationalpost.com/news/canada/canadians-faith-in-god-religion-poll.

117. "Being Christian in Western Europe: Beliefs about God," Being Christian in Western Europe, Pew Research Center, May 29, 2018, https://www.pewresearch.org/religion/2018/05/29/beliefs-about-god/

118. Megan Brenan, "Views of State of Moral Values in U.S. at New Low," Gallup, June 9, 2023, https://news.gallup.com/poll/506960/views-state-moral-values-new-low.aspx.

119. "Moral Issues," Gallup, 2023, https://news.gallup.com/poll/1681/moral-issues.aspx.

120. Aaron Zitner, "America Pulls Back from Values That Once Defined It, WSJ-NORC Poll Finds," *The Wall Street Journal*, March 27, 2023, https://www.wsj.com/articles/americans-pull-back-from-values-that-once-defined-u-s-wsj-norc-poll-finds-df8534cd.

121. 68 Stat. 249—"Joint Resolution to Amend the Pledge of Allegiance to the Flag of the United States of America," https://www.govinfo.gov/app/details/STATUTE-68/STATUTE-68-Pg249-3/summary.

122. Valerie Strauss, "New Look at Benefits of Quality Preschool Education," *The Washington Post*, May 8, 2023, https://www.washingtonpost.com/education/2023/05/08/new-look-benefits-quality-preschool-education/.

123. Robert A. Hahn, and W. Steven Barnett, "Early Childhood Education: Health, Equity, and Economics," *Annual Review of Public Health* 44 (April 2023): 75–92,

124. Caroline Danielson, and Tess Thorman, *The Impact of Expanding Public Preschool on Child Poverty in California*, report, Public Policy Institute of California, June 2019, https://www.ppic.org/wp-content/uploads/the-impact-of-expanding-public-preschool-on-child-poverty-in-california.pdf.

125. "Afterschool Programs: Benefits for Youth, Families, and Communities," Youth.Gov., https://youth.gov/youth-topics/afterschool-programs/benefits-youth-families-and-communities.

126. Deborah Lowe Vandell, Elizabeth R. Reisner, and Kim M. Pierce, "Outcomes Linked to High-Quality Afterschool Programs: Longitudinal Findings from the Study of Promising Afterschool Programs," Policy Studies Associates, Inc., October 2007.

127. Claudia Martínez, and Marcela Perticará, "Home Alone Versus After-School Programs: The Effects of Adult Supervision on Child Academic Outcomes," *International Journal of Educational Research* 104 (article 101601), https://doi.org/10.1016/j.ijer.2020.101601.

128. Anna Aizer, "Home Alone: Supervision after School and Child Behavior," *Journal of Public Economics* 88, nos. 9–10 (August 2004): 1835–1848, https://doi.org/10.1016/S0047-2727(03)00022-7.

About the Author

Bernie J. Mullin has lived the American dream for more than fifty years. An academic thought leader and the first ever immigrant to serve as CEO of a major league sports franchise, Bernie has devoted his life to building winning cultures and sustainable communities. In *Reimagining America's Dream*, he uses his hard-won expertise to tackle the most important problem of our time.